Social Being and Time

Social Archaeology

General Editor
Ian Hodder, University of Cambridge

Advisory Editors
Margaret Conkey, University of California at Berkeley; Mark Leone,
University of Maryland; Alain Schnapp, U.E.R. d'Art et d'Archéologie, Paris;
Stephen Shennan, University of Southampton; Bruce Trigger, McGill University

Social Being and Time

Christopher Gosden

BLACKWELL
Oxford UK & Cambridge USA

First published 1994

Blackwell Publishers
108 Cowley Road, Oxford OX4 1JF, UK

238 Main Street
Cambridge, Massachusetts 02142, USA

British Library Cataloguing in Publication Data

A CIP catalogue record for this book is available from the British Library.

Library of Congress Cataloging-in-Publication Data

Library of Congress CIP Data has been applied for.

ISBN 0-631-185348   0-631-190236 (pbk)

Typeset in 11 on 13 pt Garamond
by Times Graphics, Singapore
Printed in Great Britain by
Page Bros. Ltd, Norwich

This book is printed on acid-free paper

To Jane

Contents

List of Figures

Acknowledgements

A major theme of this book is that a single linear notion of time is not at all useful in understanding the long-term human past. Instead, I argue that we should move towards a more complex view in which the present is seen as a point of oscillation between past styles of action and thought and the potentials held by the future.

In its own way the limited history represented by the writing of this book is an argument against a linear structure to human action. In the book I have circled around the subject of time and change, and it is impossible to sum up succinctly the paths I have taken and the people who have influenced me. However, various acknowledgements can and should be made. First of all, I have been lucky enough to work in an intellectual milieu, in the Department of Archaeology at La Trobe, where concerns of theory and data have been given equal weight. As a department we have argued about problems of time, change and the nature of archaeological evidence and have been asked to keep the noise down in Melbourne restaurants when the vehemence of our discussions unsettled other diners. Jim Allen, Brendan Marshall, Tim Murray, Nikki Stern, Glenn Summerhayes and Cathy Webb have all provided food for thought and discussion. Richard Cosgrove, Christina Pavlides and Anita Smith have read sections of this book and provided comments. Ron Southern introduced me to Heidegger, a fact I find difficult to forgive, and commented in detail on a number of chapters. Stella Bromilow and Ros Allen put in much hard work producing the final manuscript. Margaret Wade drew the illustrations. Matthew Phelan looked at the earlier chapters, assessing both style and content.

Elsewhere in Australia, Jack Golson read a large slab of the book and helped reorientate my approach in the early chapters. Robin Torrence and Peter White also provided insightful comments.

I started writing the book whilst a visiting lecturer in the Department of Archaeology at Southampton and benefited from discussions on time and the nature of the social process with Tim Champion, Clive Gamble, Elaine Morris, Steve Shennan and Peter Ucko. Much of the writing of the initial draft was carried out whilst on sabbatical in Cambridge. Here Mark Edmonds, J.D. Hill and Sander van der Leeuw all provided comment and criticism. I am particularly grateful to Ian Hodder for being encouraging throughout the writing and for providing detailed comments on the final draft of the manuscript. John Davey at Blackwell was a most insightful and efficient editor. I am most grateful to Sue Martin for numerous improvements to the text in style and substance.

Jane Kaye has played the greatest part in the book's production. I dedicate the book to her.

CG
April 1993

1

About Time

Once upon a time, time itself was the hidden thread of any story, so that people concentrated on the events which unfolded in sequence, rather than the sequence itself. Over the last two centuries, time has become not just a medium but a message, and is now a central concern in many disciplines from astrophysics to anthropology. Strangely, archaeology is not in the forefront of thought about time, although time has always been a central concern. Only in the last few years has there been any real debate about the gap between abstract calendars, constructed through radiometric dating methods, and the rhythms of social life, or concern with the existence of long-term social processes beyond the ken of other disciplines. The reasons why archaeologists have developed little in the way of theory about time are explored below, but have derived from the absence of a theory concerning the human creation of time.

This book is about time: in it I shall present a series of ideas useful for thinking about the long spans of time studied by archaeologists. However, one of my central contentions is that time is not an abstract entity, but a quality of human involvement with the world: we do not pass through time, time passes through us. This being so, we cannot understand time by looking at time alone, but rather through considering the nature of involvement people have with the world. A stress on involvement derives from strands of social thought developed over the last century which are a reaction against the traditional view that a detached view of the world is the only road to truth. One of the major aims of the book is to hunt out such strands within social thought which provide insight into our forms of being in the world and thus constitute a starting point for understanding temporal relations.

Puzzlement about time is ancient. Both Aristotle and Augustine were worried by problems of measured time, the human experience of time and the gap separating human life and the time of the cosmos. However, modern concerns with time are sharper and pervade many aspects of human life. We live in a world united in global time, but divided into many time zones. The form of unity imposed upon the world by the construction of global time at the beginning of this century has had the paradoxical effect of highlighting the very diversity of culturally based forms of time. The dissonance between an over-arching global time and local rhythms, plus the equation between time and money which makes both a scarce resource, is the cause of profound thought and anxiety. The academic reaction to this daily concern has led to a proliferating literature on time, some of which will be surveyed in the course of this book. First, however, let us consider both practical and intellectual influences on our views of time and the manner in which these have flowed through into archaeology.

Measured Time versus Experienced Time

A basic antinomy in views of time is that between measured time and time as experienced by individuals and groups. Measured time can be seen as a series of moments occurring in sequence and which can be counted: the ticking of a clock or the beat of a metronome give us this sense of measured sequence in everyday life. By contrast, the time of human experience is not purely successive and defies measurement. Past, present and future meet in complex forms, such that the present is only given meaning through retaining elements of the past and anticipating the future. Combinations of past, present and future occur in culturally determined ways, rather than deriving from pan-human characteristics. The distinction between measured and human time is important to archaeology as we attempt to understand the human creation of time within a chronological framework created by measured time.

The last 200 years have seen major changes to our thoughts on both measured and human time. The nineteenth century saw two major extensions of measured time, both of which are relevant to archaeology. Newton had seen measured time as 'Absolute, true, and mathematical time, of itself, and from its own nature, [which] flows equally without relation to anything external' (quoted in Kern 1983: 11). At the end of the last century a system of measured, external time was set up on a global scale for the first time. The general impetus behind the creation of a system of world time was provoked by the needs of international capitalism; the immediate spur was provided by the railways and the telegraph. In the 1870s there were over 200 local times between the east and west coasts of the USA, which made the running of a unified national rail system very difficult. In 1883 this confusion was resolved through the imposition of a series of time zones across the nation. In the following year time and space were linked in a global system when it was agreed that Greenwich should become the zero meridian and world time should be measured from there. The nascent international community was slow to adopt this system, however, and it was not until 1912 at the International Conference on Time in Paris that the telegraph became the agreed means for beaming time signals around the world. In the following year the first time signal was transmitted from the Eiffel Tower (Kern 1983: 11–14). Global time was created through the linking of time and space into a single system of calculation.

The second major extension of measured time had occurred earlier in the nineteenth century: the creation of a long time-scale within which geological and biological processes can operate. The large spans of time provided by the uniformitarian notions of geological processes of Charles Lyell and others were the necessary precondition for theories such as Darwinian evolution. Darwin's notion of descent with modification was based on continuous, but slight, variations from one generation to the next. Huge spans of time were needed for these small genetic changes to result in the biological diversity we see today. In both biological and geological theories, time is the abstract medium in which change takes place; time is not immanent in the processes of change (Fabian 1983: 13). The view of time as external to processes of change is relatively unproblematical when applied to natural processes, but it is much more dubious when applied to human history. Change which occurs in measured time is devoid of any human agency or social impetus; and it was exactly this view of time and change which early social evolutionists, in anthropology and archaeology, adopted.

To take just one example, although an influential one, L.H. Morgan ignored time in his most general work, *Ancient Society* (first published 1873; 1985), and presented an historical scheme for social change which ran from savagery to civilization. He saw the fact that all the peoples of the earth exemplify the stages of savagery, barbarism and civilization as demonstrating the unity of origins of humanity. Morgan combined information from ethnography and historical sources to come up with a global scheme of human change, based on the notion that so-called savage groups around the world preserved in their social forms previous stages in the progressive history of humanity. Present-day exemplars could therefore be used to give meaning to the past. For instance, Australian Aborigines and Athapascan tribes around Hudson's Bay formed examples of the savage stage of life. Through this manoeuvre time became spatialized: a matter of physical or metaphorical distance from the centres of the Anglo-Saxon world (Fabian 1983: 15).

Morgan's grand comparative scheme had features which derived from the intellectual milieu of the late nineteenth century, but is the sort of scheme which has recurred periodically in archaeology and anthropology ever since. The range of societies existing in the here and now provide the comparanda for most, if not all, societies which have ever existed. To understand the past we must first know the present. The gap which separates past and present is caused by an abstract continuum and flow of time; more of the same, rather than the creation and recreation of real difference. The revolution of the twentieth century was the development of radiometric techniques which allowed measured time to be extended.

However, the radiocarbon revolution in the middle of the twentieth century did not represent a revolution in *notions* of time, but made it possible to construct a scale of measurement for the portion of prehistory during which most change is seen to have taken place. Change was again conceived in terms of social forms known from the present world: the European Palaeolithic echoed Inuit ways of life, the Neolithic looked like Tonga and the Iron Age became an African lineage system. Again time was seen in terms of contemporary spatial differences, and the changes seen in Europe contained the implication that much of the rest of the world was without a prehistory. Although the neo-evolutionary model of band, tribe, chiefdom and state is in disrepute, the measured time implicit in the model still lives on, vitiating any real attempts to devise schemes of social change with other concepts of time built into them.

Change was much discussed in the 1970s and 1980s, but this discussion often took place in the terms supplied by other disciplines.

Debates over continuous or discontinuous change arose from the notion of punctuated equilibria within evolutionary thought or catastrophe theory and, more recently, non-linear forms of change have been canvassed, borrowing from chaos theory. Most recently, post-structuralism has seen change as a constant and endemic feature of all social forms, so that human life has come to be seen as a continual flickering of meaning. The chimeric nature of human meaning and forms of life has made it very difficult to develop ideas on time within post-structuralist approaches. For instance, a volume intending to introduce post-structuralist thought to archaeology has no reference to time, temporality or change in its index (Bapty and Yates 1990). Exceptions to this lack of thought on time are, however, contained in work on narrative structures, surveyed in more detail in chapter 5.

Outside archaeology there have been many challenges to the idea of a single measured time. Kant saw time (and space) not as an external medium within which people moved, but as an ordering device of the human mind. Time made it possible to order the fluxes of experience and derived from the way in which all human minds worked. Time was produced jointly but experienced individually, making it a 'collective singular' in Kant's view. A major change in the western world's view of time came with Einstein's theory of relativity, which subsumed Newtonian physics. Einstein showed how time in one reference system, moving away from an observer at a constant velocity, appears to slow down from the point of view of that observer. Time was linked to the nature of accelerated bodies. Every body in the universe generates a gravitational force and gravity is equivalent to acceleration. Every reference body thus has its own time. Einstein replaced the single Newtonian clock with as many clocks as we like; these clocks tell different times, but they are all correct (Kern 1983: 19). Fabian (1983: 16) has noted that it is curious that archaeology and anthropology should have built their temporal theories of human society around the notion of a single form of measured time just at the period when this idea was about to be discarded by physics. It is even more curious that the idea of a single form of time measurement should have persisted ever since.

This clinging to a single form of measured time is very strange in view of the degree of discussion on the human experience and social creation of time. Durkheim felt that time-scales derived from the rhythm of social life, even if he was inclined to see this rhythm as the repetition of rites, feasts and ceremonies (Durkheim 1965). If time is socially created and dependent upon the structure of the social formations which give rise to it, then there must be as many different forms of time as there are forms of society. Geertz (1975) has made the same point more recently, looking at how the changes in an individual's life are seen by the Balinese to contrast with an enduring social order. Both Durkheim and Geertz underplay the changeable nature of time by emphasizing the recurring or constant nature of non-European views. But from both the message is clear: all forms of time derive from social formations and that is true of our own constructions as much as any other.

Time has obsessed philosophers. Since Plato western thinkers have sought abstract essences lying within the realm of logic removed from the accidents of daily life. A knowledge of essences and their combinations was thought to be secure and unchallengeable, and it was believed that such forms of knowing could only be reached through personal detachment from the world, which allowed the essential to be winnowed from the accidental. Geometrical constructions were seen as the quintessence of logical, elegant and, above all, timeless knowledge. Over the last 200 years rational, detached forms of knowledge have come under increasing attack. Theoretical thought, which generalizes from particular instances, is extremely practical and effective, as the recent proliferation of technology shows. But it must not be forgotten that theoretical knowledge is a refined element of the on-going flow of life, much of which is unconscious.

Much recent thought in philosophy and elsewhere has returned to the body as the site of what makes us human and as the element which helps us immerse ourselves in the flow of life. Proust's life's work was to capture his life and the sense that memory was both contained in his body and triggered by material things. 'The past is hidden somewhere outside the realm, beyond the reach of intellect, in some material object (in the sensation which the material object will give us) which we do not suspect' (Proust 1966: 57–8). A return from the theoretical to daily life is a move from the timeless to the timed. Practical daily involvement with the world is temporal to its core. Reaction against the detached theoretical stance has brought with it a concern with time as a quality of involvement with the world, and forms of involvement are sought in theology, philosophy and much of social theory.

Heidegger is in the forefront of both criticisms of the detached theoretical stance and attempts to begin philosophy from within daily life. Heidegger follows Proust in seeing time as not deriving from our heads, but from our bodies. In Heidegger's view, time can be seen as part of the character of our physical involvement with the world. This notion of involvement is central to my own views on time, and will be discussed in more detail in chapters 5 and 6. Heidegger's views were partly developed to emphasize being, rather than knowing; practical action, rather than the philosophical tradition.

Although Heidegger is increasingly influential, much of the last thirty years in social thought has seen an emphasis on knowledge and meaning, rather than being. The capacity to make the world meaningful is seen by many as the central human characteristic. The construction and communication of meaning is also seen to have its own special temporal structures. Much recent work on narrative has been concerned with how notions of time both create and are altered by the way stories are told. An excellent exploration of the form of narratives in a number of disciplines is to be found in Bender and Wellbery (1991), which also looks at the problems of harmonizing measured and human time. Also within studies of narrative is a concern with how time has been used to distance the object of study. Both Fabian (1983) and N. Thomas (1989) have explored the manner in which the notion of the ethnographic present has been used to freeze the frame of action in non-western societies and contrast them with our own, in which progressive historical change is seen to be integral.

Archaeology and Time

Only recently has the problem of bringing together measured time and human time been discussed within archaeology (Shanks and Tilley 1987: ch. 5). Such discussion has raised the problem of how far the abstract measured sequences of radiometric time will allow us to understand the changing rhythms of social life and to investigate in the past the point Durkheim made in the present about the social creation of time. These problems have been raised, but no solution to them has been offered. Central to this book is an attempt to develop ideas on the human creation of time. Time is the crucial element in all human activities, and in order to understand it we do not need more refined means of measurement, but concepts which can catch temporality and change. Humans are characterized by particular ways of creating and binding time. Following Heidegger, time is not simply a mental ordering device, but an aspect of bodily involvement with the world.

People are locked together with the world; we create material settings for life and these help create us as social beings. There are considerable problems with Heidegger's approach, however, not the least of which is a lack of concern with the actual processes of history. Marx's thought provides a corrective here; a means to look at how human action has created the world in particular historical settings.

The structure of the present book follows the need to situate people in the world in order to understand time. Chapter 4 looks at the nature of human involvement in the world, which necessitates breaking away from a central concept of European thought, the distinction between subject and object. Instead we need to consider how people and the world shape each other. I begin this consideration through looking at the work of Hegel and Marx, focusing particularly on the human creation of space and using an archaeological example from Neolithic Britain to bring out the main points in an archaeological context. The examples in this and the following chapters do not provide a full exposition of how my position can be applied to archaeological data, but rather sketch out some of the possibilities of the approach: it would take another book to provide fully worked out case studies. Chapter 5 switches from space to time and looks first at what inspiration phenomenology, early hermeneutics and the work of Bourdieu can provide when considering how time is produced through the effects of people on the world. Chapter 6 considers the links between power and time as two key attributes of human action, while chapter 7 takes ideas developed in previous chapters and applies them to the very long-term sequences of the Palaeolithic.

Much constructive work has recently been done on the nature of long-term change in human societies. Long-term changes have been generally thought of as created by evolutionary or ethological processes, or brought about by the relationship of people to their environment. But in the last few years there has been a growing recognition that social processes may unfold over centuries and millennia. Such recognition challenges us to rethink both the nature of social processes and their connections with time. Hodder (1990) sees long-term change over tens of thousands of years as being due to the working out of structures of thought and culture, whereas Bradley (1990; 1991) views the long term as the working out of lasting ritual structures in a manner which parallels Durkheim's thoughts on the continuity of ritual life.

Interest in long-term structures has also manifested itself in a recent concentration on Braudel and the 'long duration'. Bintliff (1991) and

Knapp (1992) have discussed Braudel and the *Annales* school at some length, following on from Bailey's earlier discussions of history and evolutionary processes (1983; 1987). As will be explored in greater detail in chapter 6, Braudel is mainly of interest because of his idea that history takes place on a number of levels: the short-term history of events, the medium-term history of economic cycles and the long-term history of population and subsistence forms. Against the background of the above discussion, it can be seen that attempts to view long-term change as a human product, rather than as a result of natural forces operating in abstract time, represent a break with long traditions in archaeological thought. The fact that the long-term past can be human is something new, and provides a fulcrum for re-orientating archaeological ideas and concerns.

A few words are necessary on what the long term is not. There is a growing literature outside archaeology which decries the loss of natural rhythm in modern life. Rifkin (1989) charts the growth of modern forms of measured time and the increased stress this places on efficiency and getting the greatest result from the least possible time investment. He feels that clocks and computers, together with the 'nano-second culture' they have created, have distanced us from the biological rhythms to which we must return: 'With the introduction of each new device [clocks, computers etc.], the human species has detached itself further from the biological and physical rhythms of the planet. We have journeyed from close participation with the tempo of nature to near isolation from the earth's rhythms' (Rifkin 1989: 84). A much more subtle version of the same view is provided by Young (1988), who looks at the links between human habit and natural cycles and decries the modern 'hurry-sickness'. These views seem to me wrong-headed, for biological rhythms are not natural patterns of time to which we can return if we break our dependence on measured time. Biological rhythms are to human time what sex is to gender: a biological structure which is always worked on culturally. There has never been a period in the last 3.5 million years in which natural rhythms were human rhythms, and we have no evidence that Palaeolithic groups were in tune with, or at the mercy of, the environment. There is no natural temporal pattern to which we need to return. There is also no possibility of using evolutionary theory to look at either the rates, or the directions, of human change. Human beings have a peculiar temporal relation to the world, and this temporality must be the starting point for all exploration. An examination of the exact temporal peculiarity of people will be deferred until chapter 7: much theoretical and substantive discussion is needed before this point can be reached.

People and the World

At the centre of this book lies the relationship of people to the world and some initial definition of terms is needed. Throughout the book I shall refer to the 'world', and my stance towards the world, as material reality, is a realist stance. Realism can be seen as a middle road between two other 'isms': positivism and constructivism. Few these days would admit to being a positivist, but positivism is one of the most influential views of the world and was responsible for much of nineteenth-century science. Positivism is the study of definite observable phenomena and the relations connecting them. At the basis of the positivist stance is the idea that the world is composed of a single set of phenomena and relations, which can be apprehended and understood by correct observation. The world exists independently of the human observer and presents itself to perception. Positivism is a road to truth, for correct perception of the world can tell us how the world is and can explain the chains of cause and effect that bind phenomena. Science and positivist philosophy were concerned to uncover invariant laws of cause and effect, which when brought together would tell us how the world worked. For constructivists, by contrast, the independent world is in doubt, and all we can say is that the world is as we perceive it; the world exists as a series of meanings for us, and although we can look at the generation of meaning in the mind or in society, we cannot look at the relationship of meanings to the world. Structuralism, which is explored in chapter 3, is a perfect example of constructivist thought.

Realism has elements of both positivism and constructivism. For realists (e.g. Bhaskar 1989a; 1989b) the world exists independently of us and we can only attempt to understand the nature of the world's existence. However, we never apprehend the world as objective observers, as positivists claim that we can, but as beings involved both in the world and in social relations. Involvement sparks interest in some aspects of the world and not others; it also provides us with particular forms of knowledge and modes of talking about reality. Although the world exists, we can never know it objectively, as it is. We always work from positions of interest determined by social and historical relations. However, our positions of interest are not the sole determinant of knowledge, as in the constructivist view. Bhaskar (1989b: 13) has maintained that such approaches are flawed by what he calls the 'epistemic fallacy': the definition of being in terms of meaning. For realists, the structure of the world limits what we can say, but these limits are determined not just by reality itself but also by our forms of knowing and telling. Knowledge through involvement in a material reality is the key to realism, and to my personal stance. Like Bhaskar, I believe that knowledge is not developed in a disinterested pursuit of truth, but should help us emancipate ourselves from the unhealthy social and material structures of late capitalism. Realism is a vital element in any emancipative science (Bhaskar 1989b: vii).

Working from the realist stance, it is not possible to privilege mind as the source of meaning (a critique of views of mind is taken up in chapter 7). Knowledge arises from being, and is an element of our action in the world. Such a view necessitates a theory which links being and meaning. To make this link we have to be able to distinguish areas of life which are meaningless, because they are habitual, and areas which are thought out. Entry into habitual forms of life comes not through considering human action in isolation, but through thinking about how material culture and human action influence each other. Material things are at once the product of human action and productive of further action. We are socialized into various material settings. Buildings, rooms and furniture tell us how to behave towards each other and to them as material things. The clues we get from the material world are not so much something we know, as something we are. Interactions between our bodies and material culture form a substrate of habituality, which is beyond meaning, but forms the very stuff of life. The taken-for-granted nature of habit makes it much more difficult to study than conscious meaning. It is also difficult to put habit and its material settings into words (Miller 1987). Wittgenstein said that we could see beyond the limits of language, but we could not speak beyond them, and of that which we cannot speak we must pass over in silence. Habitual being is a difficult area to see into or discuss. However, it is not sealed totally from sight and words and the mutual creation of people and things forms the road to follow in attempting to understand habit.

The other important aspect of material culture is its enduring quality. Social landscapes, buildings and portable material culture last from one generation to the next, and this renders them the medium through which habits are inculcated. Without material culture it is impossible to imagine long-term trends in social forms. The long term can be seen as a series of layers of habitualities; these forms of habit are both material and temporal. These two elements, the material and the temporal, form a basic structure for this book. Chapters 2 to 4 look at human material involvements, whilst chapters 5 to 7 consider time directly. Each chapter has an extended theoretical discussion, which taken together cover many of the main issues confronting social theory today. These discussions of theory are both directed and partisan: they are aimed at a theory of time and concentrate on the way in which people and the world are interwoven. Chapter 2 begins with a concrete example of the approach I adopt, which will demonstrate the benefits of making being and time central to our attempts to understand the past.

2

Understanding Long-term Social Change

Fort Venus was constructed over two weeks in April 1769 in Matavai Bay in Tahiti, at the command of Captain James Cook. The fort was substantial: it had a bank and ditch at each end, the side facing the river had two heavy guns, and on the seaward side a palisade was set up with six smaller guns. Forty-five men could be accommodated inside, as well as the armourer's forge, the cook's oven and, at the centre of the fort, the observatory (Beaglehole 1974: 179). The fort was not a military installation in the ordinary sense, but built so as to protect an astronomical observatory. Its name did not derive from the libidinous reputation that Tahiti was coming to hold in the western mind, but from the astronomical body to be observed. The three Pacific voyages of Cook during the 1770s played a vital part in creating for European minds an accurate picture of the last major portion of the earth's surface to be explored by white people. A good part of Cook's achievement lay in mapping many of the island groups of the Pacific and in helping to solve that continuing puzzle of the eighteenth century: longitude.

For the European sailor, both mapping and moving around the world required a knowledge of latitude and longitude. Latitude is simply calculated in the northern hemisphere by measuring the altitude of the North Star above the horizon: the further north the observer goes, the higher the pole star. Once southern oceans were entered by European sailors, the declination of the sun could be used to work out latitude. Longitude requires more exacting calculation. Since the earth turns on its axis, the same astronomical bodies are visible along a given parallel of longitude; they are simply visible at different times. In the calculation of longitude time and space are intimately linked. In order to calculate longitude, 'all that is needed is (1) to compare the time of observation of a given celestial event (for example, an eclipse) at a place of known longitude with the observed time at the site; or (2) to keep constant track of the time at a place of known longitude and compare that with local time' (Landes 1983: 106). Both of these methods required extremely accurate timekeeping. In 1713–14, by Act of Parliament, the British government offered £20,000 – then an enormous sum – to the first person able to calculate longitude to within one degree; but it was not until 1764 that a considerable step forward was taken when the 'watch-machine' of John Harrison, a self-taught watchmaker, passed a stringent test of accuracy on a return journey to Barbados. Unfortunately for Harrison, it took many years of litigation to obtain just a part of the sum due to him from the government. The size of the sum offered shows just how important was the ability to map the globe and travel across it at will. Longitude was not just a conjunction of time and space, but an even more potent mixture of time, space, power and money.

Cook's observations of the transit of Venus were not a success, despite the elaborate preparations. The transit of Venus was so called because the planet passed across the face of the sun. The fact that this one event could be observed from many different parts of the globe helped establish the links between time and longitude. The sum of these observations also aimed towards an even grander purpose, which was to use Venus to help calculate the distance of the earth from the sun, and to use this distance in turn to calculate the size of the universe (Beaglehole 1974: 99–100). The observations of Cook's party, which featured a huge pendulum clock brought from Greenwich, were hampered by an unaccountable haze surrounding Venus, which made it very difficult to give an accurate time to the first point of contact between the planet and the outer rim of the sun.

Despite this disappointment, taken as a whole Cook's voyages represent a rounding out of western knowledge about the world and a major step in mapping the earth. These modern European maps were not based on the human or natural features of the world, as medieval maps had been, but were constructed through a system of abstract calculation, a neutral grid of coordinates in space. Within this grid natural or human features could be plotted and then used for a further form of calculation: that of profit and value. Cook is often seen as a discoverer and explorer. It makes more sense to see him as a creator, one who helped fashion a particular set of timed and measured relations. We of European descent take for granted the relations of time and space in which we live, forgetting that these were painfully created over a period of centuries during the genesis of the modern world. Although time and space may seem to us to form a neutral, objective framework, this framework was constructed with empires in mind, as an aid to both knowledge and control. Not for nothing is Cook known as 'Adam Smith's global agent', a herald of capitalism and free enterprise.

I propose to use evidence from the Pacific to explore quite a different construction from that of Cook, which sees time and space not as a neutral framework within which human action can be charted, but as deriving from human involvement with the world. In looking at prehistoric evidence from the Pacific we shall consider both time and space as elements of being and becoming, as these unfold over long periods of time. Time and space need to be rehumanized against the construction of abstract schemes over the last few centuries; these constructions need also to be judged against radiocarbon dating, our own archaeological means of abstract measurement. Radiometric dating is to the archaeologist an orientating device of equivalent importance to that of longitude to the sailor; but both have the same dangers. We should not mistake the one form of time measurement provided by radiometric means for all forms of time. Radiometric dating translates the passage of time into a form we can start to understand: however, grasping the different forms of human time is our real goal.

What is human time and how is it created? The initial sketch of the argument presented in this chapter will be amplified in the rest of the book. I hope that the Pacific prehistoric evidence adduced here will help to orientate the reader in the chapters which follow.

The Human Creation of Time and Space: A Structure of Reference

There is no such thing as an isolated act. Every action we perform is contained within a network of actions stretching across time and space. For instance, the act of flint knapping has implicit within it the purposes for which the finished tools will be used. These purposes exist in the future and may involve activities which will be carried out in another location. Flint tools may used for scraping skins or shaping wood; both skin and wood are destined for other purposes, part of further chains of action. Consequently, every act contains within it implicit links to other acts separated in time and space. These future acts orientate and shape the present one and it is the flow of life as a whole which gives each act point and purpose. These chains of action knit together to form a network. I call this network a system of reference, because every act implicity refers to many others. It is important to note that in using the word reference I am not implying that the connections between actions are always made consciously. In fact, the opposite is more probably the case – most of our chains of action and the connections forged between acts in time and space are habitual and unconscious. Reference between actions is an implicit condition of action, not something consciously thought out. A practised flint knapper can produce flakes of the right type whilst carrying on a conversation, reviewing the events of the day or keeping an eye on the children. Practice does not necessarily make perfect, but it does create habit. It is the mass of habitual actions and the referential structure they form which carries the main burden of our lives, giving them shape and direction.

The space of human action is not a geometrical entity to be represented easily on a piece of paper, but rather room-for-manoeuvre, a space in which skills can be deployed. Our skills are created to fit the spaces in which they are used and the spaces of human life are the result of past skilled action. It is through human action that landscapes are ordered, dwellings maintained and mobile forms of material culture are created which are suitable for patterns of movement. The material world is not a passive medium for social action, but a set of material forces which play a role in human action in a variety of ways. First of all, the world is not set apart from us, as a series of objects confronting a knowing subject because it is the world into which we are socialized. Notions of time, space and human relations are inculcated into our bodily being as we grow up. These notions, which form the basis of all action, are not something which we are necessarily conscious of, they are not something we know, but something we are. Material settings are thus internal to our social being, not external. A room can make us feel at ease because it conveys a sense of rightness we find hard to put into words. Because it is so much a part of us, there is a level of engagement with the world which is always ineffable.

The referential system of action does not just unfold in space, but also in time. Our actions can flow in known material settings because of a series of anticipations of the future derived from retention of the past. Material things, especially things that we are used to, promote anticipation. Practised cyclists do not have to consciously adjust their weight when turning a corner, and indeed too much thought about the process of riding can impede action. A training in carpentry allows anticipation of the best tools for a particular set of materials. Although there is conscious learning involved in such training, to do with the calculation of angles necessary to make a mortise-and-tenon joint, for example, there is also bodily inculcation of a series of routines, a series of steps in time. There are some things we can only learn through action. These are retained in our bodies and form the bedrock of our lives. Practical action does not involve the unvarying playing out of unconscious routines, but a constant interaction between person and material. The wood a carpenter uses may have unexpected properties, enabling more to be done with it than anticipated, or constraining the planned set of actions. Again, material thngs are not simply passive brute objects, but create a complex interaction between skilled work and the varying materials. On the part of the human actor, this interaction will require both the exercise of habit and the exercise of thought. Thought is necessary when the material being worked unexpectedly enables or prevents sets of actions. When everything is going smoothly, habit is enough; when anticipation breaks down, thought is needed. A major theme of this book is that thought arises from within the flow of life, helping us to cope with problems encountered by habitual action.

All action is timed action, which uses the imprint of the past to create an anticipation of the future. Together the body and material things form the flow of the past into the future. Human time flows on a number of levels. Each level represents a different aspect of the framework of reference. Longer-term frames of reference are those within which we are socialized, made up of a particular shape of the landscape, historically special sets of relations between people and definite forms of interaction between people and the world. These longer-term frameworks are those of which we are least conscious, out of which our basic sense of rightness derives. From the point of view of archaeological technique, background forms of reference can be picked up through off-site methods. Long-term systems of reference are contained within the shape of the cultural landscape, the processes of erosion and deposition and the nature of humanly induced patterns of vegetation. They are also evidenced by the distribution of artefacts within the landscape. Densities of stone tools, pottery and so on can show us centres of social gravity, areas in which people were intimately involved with the world and areas which were relatively unused. The movement of materials can also demonstrate connections within space. Within this larger structure of landscape and artefacts are contained the more point-specific sorts of evidence deriving from short-term and individual acts. The emplacement of a burial or a hearth, or a single knapping episode, bring us closer to conscious acts in which the unthought habit meets thought-out symbolic forms. The landscape and its artefacts form a complex intermingling of conscious and unconscious acts, the former more related to short-term changeable elements of life, the latter to do with the long term. Conscious and symbolic actions are most likely to arise where problems are encountered. Habit and thought are not separated by an impenetrable barrier, but are different elements of a single structure of action. The main thing dividing habit and the symbolic is time-scale. Habit weaves the basic fabric of life, symbolic acts represent a quicker stitch which forms not ornamentation, but a means of strengthening the weak points in the overall cloth.

Let us consider a brief example of a structure of reference. In the Arawe Islands off the south coast of West New Britain Province, Papua New Guinea much of people's time and effort is taken up in gardening. Laying out a new garden requires a set of skills, conscious and unconscious, which are most obvious to an outsider, possessing none of them. The area of new garden land to be cleared and planted is not the decision of an individual or a family, but of the clan, as the clan as a whole cooperates to clear the area of rainforest. There are a host of considerations to be taken into account when thinking of future levels of food production, which include the exchange obligations of the group, the necessity to fund feasts for marriage and circumcision, the willingness of people to be away from the village to work in their gardens, the ambitions of individuals involved and so on. There are also practical considerations, such as the level of planting stocks of taro, sweet potato, yam and banana, or the need to put certain parcels of land aside for cash crops. Some of these decisions are calculated, but all are predicated upon implicit levels of knowledge about the amounts of work needed to make and maintain a certain area of garden, the likely willingness and capabilities of others in the group to carry out the work involved and the sorts of yields which will realistically accrue. Also, certain crops can only be grown if the magic ensuring their growth is owned by the group, and there are difficult estimates to be made of the spiritual standing of the clan and the implications this will have for the likely fertility of the crops. Much rests on people's feel for the human, spiritual and practical situation, and this will determine how ambitious the clan will be. Once the work starts much unconscious knowledge is brought to play in the use of axes, fire and digging sticks, but also in the sorts of combinations of men, women and children possible or desirable to carry out a set of tasks.

To an outsider, there appears to be a dizzying array of elements to be taken into account and an infinitely dense set of connections and implications arising form each action. Although the complexity of decision-making is considerable, the whole process is made possible because of the amount that does *not* have to be thought out. Many of the actions concerning both things and people in setting up a garden are 'second nature' and derive from basic feelings of rightness and wrongness. Each clan has a sense of itself and its place in the wider social matrix. This translates into a feel for the sorts of projects it should take on and can expect to execute with the human, physical and spiritual resources at its disposal. The process of gardening has undergone immense transformations in the course of this century with the introduction of metal tools, new food crops and the profit motive. However, despite the many innovations, people still draw on long traditions to do with clearing, planting, social cooperation and the demands of the social system. These traditions form a background frame of reference which make actions flow through and within material and social settings.

The above example shows that no action exists on its own – clearing implies planting, planting leads to harvesting and the harvest can be used for consumption and exchange. Each set of actions is carried out through individuals and the group, forming a changing set of social and material combinations. Action creates space, in this case the area to be covered by a new garden, and space enables the deployment of skilled action. Time is also involved, not just in terms of the weeks that it will take to prepare a garden, but in the anticipations of the future harvest and the chains of action the garden's produce can promote.

One immediate implication of the idea of a system of reference is that there are no such things as social relations. Most models of social action separate material and social relations, often seeing the social as based upon or deriving from the material. Such a view arises out of the division between subject and object running through much of western thought. Social relations occur between knowing subjects, whereas material relations are those between subjects and objects. Material relations are thought to be less volatile as there is only one active partner, the subject; they thus form a stable, predictable basis from which social relations derive. However, in the view developed here people and the world are inseparable, each affecting the other as the system of reference creates the spaces and times in which skilled action can be deployed.

Having briefly sketched out some of the main characteristics of a system of reference it is now possible to apply these to the archaeological data from the Pacific. Much of this data has been collected with other schemes of thought in mind, and we need to consider the theoretical background to Pacific prehistory before we can look at the evidence directly. The most important model used in Pacific archaeology is based around a split between social and material relations, such as that criticized above. The linking of the productive capacities of social groups to the degree of inequality found within them has provided the basis of social evolutionary schemes which took much inspiration from the Pacific, but were then applied throughout the world.

Captain Cook was not only a navigator: he and his crew made the first detailed accounts of people in many areas of the Pacific. Cook's voyages provided the basis for ethnography within the Pacific. Much of this ethnographic work has been carried out since the mid-twentieth century, and has been influenced by a resurgence of evolutionary thought within anthropology: these neo-evolutionists are responsible for the construction of world history in terms of the movement from band to tribe to chiefdom to state. This movement was thought to be powered by changes in subsistence, with farming seen as the major reason for the movement from social forms with few inequalities to those with an increasing number of social ranks. One of the main influences in the construction of this scheme has been Sahlins, whose Ph.D. thesis *Social Stratification in Polynesia*, published in 1958, contained a comparative survey of Polynesian forms of life, concentrating on the links between social hierarchy and subsistence. For Sahlins in this period of his thought the Polynesians represented a group of 'genetically related cultures' (Sahlins 1958: ix) and variations in their ways of life in the present were not due to differences in origin, but were directly related to the technology used and the structure of the environment of each island group. The degree of social stratification, measured by the number of social ranks, varied in direct proportion to the productivity of the local environment. Generosity was the basis for chiefly power, and a productive subsistence system could fund chiefly largesse, allowing for large and regular redistributions of craft items and food. The main constraint on production was the nature of the island environment. Atoll environments severely constrained food production and atoll societies had little social differentiation. By contrast, the large islands, such as Tonga, Tahiti and Hawai'i, had the most productive and varied set of environmental zones and the most complex social forms. Adaptation to the environment was seen as the place to start in building generalizations about social forms.

This model makes a definite separation between economic and social relations, separating them so that they can be recombined. The economic world is to do with objects and forms the cutting edge of the social process, the area in which energy is harnessed from the environment and circulated through the social structure. The ability of a social form to harness energy had direct implications for the social process and particularly the social structure, the latter being a result of the amount of energy flowing through the system. The band-to-state model came to dominate social archaeology in the late 1960s and still has particular influence today in both Europe and North America. Pacific examples have been exported, partly through the influence of Sahlins's writings, with Papua New Guinea representing tribal societies, whereas Hawai'i is seen to straddle the boundary between chiefdom and state. We shall encounter the social categories devised within the neo-evolutionary model later in this book, together with reactions against them. Here we need to consider how these social forms have been applied to the Pacific itself and the sorts of prehistories which have been the result.

Much of the archaeological fieldwork and synthesis carried out in the Pacific has happened since the publication of *Social Stratification in Polynesia*. Not all the work undertaken has been influenced by the neo-evolutionary synthesis, but much of it has, especially in Polynesia. Kirch (1984) provides an excellent statement of the evolutionary position, in which he charts the growth of social complexity in a number of island groups from a putative Ancestral Polynesian Society. This ancestral social form is seen already to exhibit some aspects of hierarchy when it first entered the Pacific in the shape of the Lapita cultural complex (Kirch 1984: ch. 3). Hierarchy bloomed or was curtailed depending upon the possibilities for subsistence intensification in different island groups. Hawai'i became the most clearly differentiated society because 'Hawai'i clearly offered the greatest range of environmental opportunities' (Kirch 1984: 279). In the understanding of Polynesian prehistory the present plays a double role. First, evidence from comparative ethnography and historical linguistics allows the reconstruction of Ancestral Polynesian Society, following the logic that the traits which all societies exhibit in the present must be derived from the common ancestor. Second, the present (or the situation at European contact) provides the endpoint for the prehistoric trajectory. In the middle, between ancestor and present outcome, the environment is crucial, and although cultural choice is allowed a role there is no theory which specifies how this operated. We are left with a peculiarly timeless form of movement and no sense that any period of the past was radically different from the present.

In the present brief exploration of Pacific prehistory I start from the premise that past forms of society have been definitely different from that seen in the present. Forms of human life derive from people's involvement with the world, together with the spatial and temporal aspects of human action, so that as involvement and action alter so too will social forms. Pacific prehistory is firstly a process of colonization, which is in itself a form of altering space and time as settlement spreads and changes shape. Secondly, people have not passively adapted to the environments of the Pacific, but have shaped them for their own ends.

The Prehistoric Evidence

33,000–3500 years ago

Deep continuities can be discerned in Pacific life which create the social structuring of time and space. These go back to the first occupation of the Pacific by human beings. The evidence from the period spanning the late Holocene to the late Pleistocene is still sparse, but it is possible to discern long-term trends influencing all later periods.

The first movement onto Pacific islands occurred 33,000 years ago (Allen et al. 1989), as shown by the sites on New Ireland (figure 2.1). Such a phase of primary colonization represents a true creation of time and space as people are able to order themselves on the landscape anew. Spatial and social forms are mutually constitutive. All social relations have a spatial aspect to them and the relative positions of individuals

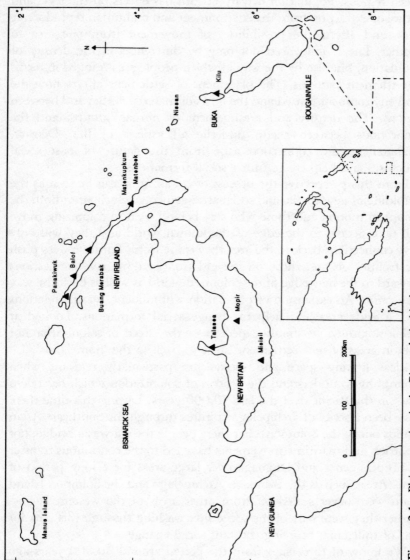

Figure 2.1 Pleistocene sites in the Bismarck Archipelago.

and groups help to determine the form and nature of the relationships between them. Spatial formations are made up of demographic structures representing differences in the density of populations between regions. Population density in turn has effects on the level and nature of extraction from the environment and on human reproductive rates, and affects the possibilities of movement from one area to another. Life is influenced not only by differences in the density of population, but also by the way in which people are arranged in terms of settlement patterns. The placement of settlement affects how the local environment is used and the flows of material within and between regions. The density and arrangement of human groups, and the connections between them, underlie all aspects of life. Density, arrangement and connection arise from the nature of past social structures and help create future social formations.

From this perspective the process of colonization can be seen as the unfolding of new spatial and social arrangements, which affect both the groups in motion and those who stay behind. A new colonizing move will take people to the edge of the known world and they will only have connections back to the area they came from. Future moves push the frontier on and those on the old frontier now have connections forward to the new edge of the colonized world as well as back the way they came. An expansion of population will influence spatial relations over a wide area and help to change social formations. Looked at archaeologically, we should expect to see the effects of colonization not only in areas of new settlement but also back in the 'homelands'.

Ideas linking space and society are particularly relevant when attempting to understand the process of colonization which has taken place in the Pacific over the last 30,000 years. During this time there have been a series of archipelago cultures through the Southeast Asian islands out to the Solomons. For these people the sea was a bridge, not a barrier, and maritime movements have led to the continuous transfer of people, genes and language over large areas for a long period of time. Areas such as the Bismarck Archipelago and the Solomon Island chain were never sealed off from other areas of the western Pacific. Rather they were part of the social flux washing through this area for tens of millennia, bringing constant social change.

We know of three sites from the period around 30,000 years ago (figure 2.1), two on New Ireland and one in the North Solomons on Buka; this last site necessitates an open sea crossing of up to 150 km (Allen 1991). In their earliest deposits these caves have low levels of material compared to later evidence and there are many indications of use of the sea. Moving from a continental landmass to comparatively small islands might pose problems of scale for people with spatially extensive ways of life; also the tropical rainforests of the area have dispersed resources and most food sources are plants, with little in the way of animal food. A tentative explanation for the archaeological evidence from this period is that we are looking at small groups of people who used their competence at sailing to move regularly between dispersed resources, and concentrated their efforts on the coast rather than inland. High levels of mobility using the sea seem to be the key, and we might term these people 'maritime hunter-gatherers'.

From 20,000 BP onwards a somewhat different strategy can be discerned. Rather than moving themselves between dispersed resources, people start to move useful items to them. Obsidian, a volcanic glass which originates on neighbouring New Britain, has been found in New Ireland caves some 350 kilometres away (figure 2.1).

Contemporary with the first finds of obsidian is the appearance of the small marsupial, cuscus (*Phalanger orientalis*), in the sites, and the possibility is that this was introduced by people, along with a wallaby which was found in later deposits (Allen et al. 1989). Although not involved in the domestication of animals, people were extending their natural ranges (Flannery and White 1991) and altering the structure of the environment, thus breaking down the dividing line we draw between hunter-gatherers and farmers. From 15,000 BP onwards there is evidence of people living in the inland areas of New Ireland (although none of these are very far from the sea), and around the mid-Holocene the cave sites are abandoned. There is then little evidence until the appearance of Lapita sites at 3500 BP (as discussed in the next section).

From this early evidence, we can start to see something of the long tradition of life in the Pacific on which groups of the late Holocene could draw. When discussing the islands of the remote Pacific a term that is often used is 'transported landscape', which refers to the fact that most of the useful plants and animals found on smaller Pacific islands were taken there by people (Kirch 1984: 135–9). Not only were the plants and animals transported, but also a body of knowledge on how to combine them. This knowledge was implicit as well as explicit, part of people's bodily and social being in the Pacific. The movement of useful resources started well before the mode of subsistence we would call gardening came into existence and dates back to the late

Pleistocene. The ability of people to position and reposition themselves in time and space during the process of colonization and later depended upon an interaction between them and the world.

In particular, this takes the form of a special directedness towards the world, encouraging people to change it. Part of the very long-term history of the Pacific lies in the growth in people's ability to take poor island environments and change the temporal and spatial distribution of resources to make them more suitable for human settlement, as well as using patterns of mobility at sea to change their own distribution relative to resources. The late Pleistocene evidence provides the long view of the creation of transported landscapes which could be put together in the late Holocene to allow the settlement of the Pacific.

The last 3500 years

The closer we get to the present, the greater is the temptation to shape the evidence into forms of life with which we are familiar today. The neo-evolutionary model set up a dichotomy between forms of life based on farming and those which were not. Within this model all forms of social hierarchy are thought to be based upon the surplus supplied by farming. The late Holocene period in lowland Melanesia is seen to provide evidence for farming systems, which may be due to immigration from the west (Spriggs 1989) or due to indigenous development. Farming systems are linked to the sets of archaeological evidence known as the Lapita cultural complex, which Kirch further interprets as Ancestral Polynesian society. The Lapita period is seen to represent a break with what went before, both in terms of the growth of social inequality and the ability to colonize. In this view the Lapita period represents a great leap forward from types of life quite unlike the present to a recognizable social structure with a well-understood subsistence base.

However, the notion that Lapita assemblages represent the first point at which the prehistoric past suddenly comes to resemble the present should be questioned. There are a number of grounds for believing that the style of life between 3500 and 2000 BP is quite different from any that we recognize in the present. For this period the evidence can be shaped in summary form, and this summary starts from the considerable uniformity in the archaeological evidence throughout the western Pacific. The assemblages of this period go by the name of 'Lapita' and are found from Manus Island, north of New Guinea, to Tonga and Samoa (figure 2.2). The evidence derives mainly from coastal sites

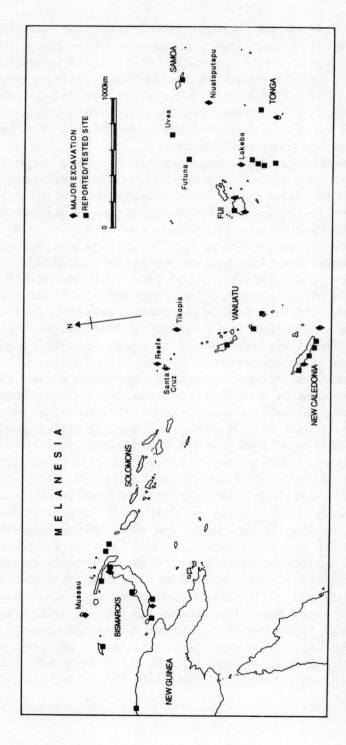

Figure 2.2 The south-west Pacific showing all known Lapita sites. (From Kirch and Hunt 1988, *Archaeology of the Lapita Cultural Complex: A critical review*, fig. 2.1. Courtesy of the Thomas Burke Memorial Washington State Museum.)

which have pottery with toothed stamped decoration and incised lines, sophisticated shell assemblages, chipped stone which often includes obsidian which has moved some distance from its source, ground stone axes and a suite of plant remains similar to those used in the present (Gosden et al. 1989; Green 1979; Kirch and Hunt 1988). Here, I want to focus on whether these assemblages represent any social unity and what sort of long-term trends are displayed by the social forces underlying the use of material culture.

The mid-Holocene period immediately prior to the Lapita phase is one of enormous environmental change, especially in coastal regions. Rising sea levels after the last glacial severed many land connections and created new coastal environments higher than the old ones. The period 3500 BP to the present represents a period of relative stability in coastal environments, contrasting with that in the previous millennia. It was within this relatively stable setting that considerable social changes took place. The Lapita period is one of colonization, with the first movements of people into Fiji, Tonga and Samoa. These early settlers took with them suites of plants and animals on which Pacific life is based, such as taro, yam, breadfruit, *canarium*, the pig, dog and chicken. These population movements set in train the complete colonization of the Pacific over the last thousand years.

The Lapita assemblages are widespread geographically and long-lived chronologically. In discussions of Lapita many of us have fixed on the striking similiarity of material culture throughout the western Pacific at this time, and it is certainly true that such items as pottery, axes and shell assemblages do not vary all that much from Manus to Tonga. However, homogeneity goes deeper than that. It has recently become evident that all the major domesticated plants and animals in use today were available at the beginning of the Lapita period (Gosden 1992; Kirch 1989). The use of these species entailed landscape practices resulting in the erosion and deposition of considerable quantities of soil. For instance, on New Caledonia the plain of Moindou is covered by at least 9 metres of alluvium. Paddle-impressed pottery found 6.5 metres down dates to at least 2000 years ago (Spriggs 1984a: 193). This indicates that erosion may well have started within the Lapita period. Less dramatic but better-dated instances of erosion occur further west in the Bismarck Archipelago. In the Arawe Islands off the south coast of West New Britain we have found evidence for the erosion of clays from the higher slopes of the islands and subsequent deposition on beach flats. Erosion had started by

3000 BP at the latest and finished around 1000 years ago (Gosden 1989a). Similarly timed erosional phases have been found elsewhere in the Bismarck Archipelago (Gosden et al. 1989: 573). The appearance of Lapita assemblages seems to be correlated with a greater intensity, or at least destructiveness, in the use of the landscape.

Human action from the Lapita period onwards transformed the shape of the coastal landscape, creating a new world for people to live in. In some areas the erosion of soil in Lapita and later periods from high to low areas allowed the extension of gardening systems. On the small island of Tikopia, Kirch and Yen estimate that a million cubic metres of soil was eroded from the volcanic core of the mountains onto the lowlands, a process caused by the firing of vegetation on the upper slopes (Kirch and Yen 1982: 329). This created the major areas of garden land in use today. The Lapita period not only changed the configuration of settlement in the western Pacific through colonization, but also reshaped many of the landscapes of the region.

Embedded within the changing landscape is the first real domestic evidence from the Pacific. Many archaeologists have been convinced that the evidence from sites represents big, long-lasting and stable settlements, which because of their size and duration must have had a stable agricultural base (Gosden et al. 1989). On reviewing the evidence, I am no longer certain of this. Lapita sites are big and contain large amounts of artefactual evidence, but this may be partly because they were used over long periods of time and, in the case of the richest sites, are in water-logged environments where there is excellent preservation. When we consider the density of artefacts against the length of time over which the sites built up, discard rates are low and there may not have been that many pots or stone tools in use at any one time (Gosden 1991). Low levels of material culture in use at any period may indicate that these places were not settlements identical to coastal villages today, but spots on the landscape to which people returned on regular basis. Furthermore, although all the tree crops and animals used in Melanesia today are found in waterlogged Lapita sites, which preserve plant remains (Gosden and Webb in press), we should not leap to the conclusion that stable farming systems identical to those found today were in existence. Indeed, the high levels of soil erosion from the start of the Lapita period onwards indicate forms of land use unlike the swidden gardening of the present, which does not cause massive erosion.

A further insight into the types of site use during the Lapita period comes not from the sites themselves but from the general social situation surrounding them. During the Lapita period, as noted above, material culture is similar over a huge area and the most striking aspect of this similarity is pottery. From the Bismarck Archipelago to Tonga and Samoa there was 3500 years ago a design suite with marked regularity both in the elements of decoration and in their means of layout on the pot; this was combined with a limited set of forms. The most striking aspect of the pottery assemblages, however, is not simply their widespread nature, but the fact that similarities are maintained through time by contemporary changes in widely spread regions. The initially complex forms of dentate stamping found over 3000 years ago become simpler with the passage of time, and eventually give way to incised and applied decorations (see Kirch 1990: 121–3) and this happens not at single sites but throughout the area from the Bismarck Archipelago to Vanuatu. The locus of larger cause within the area resides at the level of the Lapita phenomenon as a whole, with some mechanisms leading to coordinated changes.

Some have remarked that these similarities are maintained by trade. Kirch (1988; 1990) notes that obsidian, chert, metavolcanic rocks, pottery and oven stones moved throughout the area covered by Lapita. He divides these areas of movement into two: a western zone stretching from the Bismarck Archipelago to Vanuatu, and an eastern one from Fiji to Tonga and Samoa (Kirch 1988: 106). The movement of these materials he sees as taking place through exchange, and he makes explicit parallels with the exchange system known as the kula ring, whilst at the same time viewing Lapita exchange as an ancestral system providing the point of origin for more recent forms. Present-day trading systems are characterized by local variability of material culture, as we shall see below, and seem to operate to create and maintain regional differences in forms of life. In the period 3500 to 2000 BP material culture is similar over a wide area, and changes which do occur are contemporary throughout the western Pacific. This fact alone indicates that the nature of life at this time was quite different from any that we see at the present. The different nature of the overall structure leads us to question the form of the building blocks upon which society was based: the individual sites. Rather than seeing individual sites as stable villages and the similarities of material culture over huge areas as being held together by widespread trading, we must embrace the possibility that Lapita forms represent a mobile way of life, which in some ways continues long-lasting traditions deriving from

Pleistocene forms of movement. An emphasis on mobility would recast Lapita sites as spots on the landscape to which people returned regularly, which perhaps had stands of nut-bearing trees and areas of cleared land for garden plots nearby.

An emphasis on mobility and change places the similarities of material culture in a new light. To try to understand the nature of the Lapita material culture, I want to use the phrase 'dynamic traditionalism'. On the one hand, there is evidence of huge changes: the colonizing moves, the alteration of the landscape and the introduction of new elements of material culture such as pottery represent a basic re-ordering of the world. On the other hand are the widespread similarities in material forms which are maintained for over 1500 years. It might be tempting to try to interpret the decorations of Lapita pots in terms of the meanings they held for people at the time, but within the framework being constructed here it is of more interest to see them as a lasting network of connections which extended in space beyond the movements of any individuals and beyond their lifespan. Pottery designs and their geographical distributions created a system of presences and absences, a vast thread of connections over a huge area. Such system of presences and absences structures time and space, giving shape and bounds to the social world. In particular, the stability of material culture provides a thread of continuity through all the many changes of life. Lapita decorations represent a means of shaping time, a note of repetition found throughout a large area, binding an otherwise unstable way of life. The notion of 'dynamic traditionalism' can be used to explore how material culture creates traditions within an otherwise dynamic framework. This particular form of material culture and symbolism can only be understood from within the flow of life, as it is used to bind otherwise disparate elements and to help people cope with a unique set of spatial and temporal problems.

The last 500 years

Little is known of the situation between 2000 and 800 years ago. However, around this latter date, the trading systems and forms of life which we can observe in the present appear to have come into existence. The kula ring is the best known of the coastal exchange systems of Melanesia (Leach and Leach 1983). It is part of a network of exchange systems which ultimately encompasses the whole of coastal Papua New Guinea and beyond. The possibility that these individual exchange systems may be joined into some larger whole is indicated by the fact that all the systems studied archaeologically have a similar antiquity.

Archaeological work has taken place in areas covered by present-day trading systems on both the north and south coasts of Papua New Guinea and in the kula area. The trading groups of the south Papuan coast have been the best studied (Allen 1984, Irwin 1983 and 1985 provide summaries). The area today and in the recent past has a number of groups specializing in trade and often engaging in trade for subsistence items. A major trade item is pottery, which is important to prehistorians as it is preserved archaeologically and can be sourced to provide evidence of trading patterns. Styles of pottery directly ancestral to that in use today appeared throughout the area some 800 years ago. By 500 years ago specialist producing and trading centres had emerged, many of which continue to be active in the present. Such emergence is paralleled by a shift from low volumes of pottery production, produced in a non-specialized fashion and exchanged locally, to centralized high-volume production of specialized wares (Allen 1984; Irwin 1985). It cannot be coincidence that similar changes take place at the same time not just on the south coast but also on the New Guinea side of the island. Here Lilley (1986; 1988) has investigated through archaeological means the trading system documented ethnographically by T.G. Harding (1967). In the recent past the Siassi traders moved between the north coast of New Guinea and West New Britain carrying a large range of food and craft items. The main pots which moved through this system were made on the north New Guinea coast, and production of these started just before 500 BP. The Siassi traders seem to have started their operations by some 350 years ago, as evidenced by the distribution of obsidian from West New Britain and pottery from the north coast. Coincidentally or not, this was much the same time as the first Europeans were exploring the area. In the kula region data is more sketchy, but there are indications that these systems too are very recent (Irwin 1983).

Malinowski felt that the kula was a timeless system and gave no thought to its history, as by implication it had none. Archaeological work has proved this not to be true. The kula is, in fact, part of a network of systems, each of which come into existence during the last 500 years. The complexity of connections between trading systems and their joint genesis indicates that their rise and subsequent operations were linked. Furthermore, we are not just dealing with systems of trade. Contemporary with the rise of trade is a general move to defended hilltop settlements, and it is likely that the endemic warfare which Europeans noted at contact also arose at this time. Also, trade itself is not a series of commercial transactions, but is shot through with issues of ritual and personal well-being. The rise of trade systems did not represent an alteration of one aspect of people's lives, but in fact signalled a new manner of life. This new form of social being was not a planned creation, and its genesis and growth was beyond the conscious experience of any individual.

The broader system of trade, coming into existence 500 years ago, created an overall social geography within which people's decisions are not just predicated on local circumstances but are tuned in to a broader set of horizons. The larger system composed of all the trading groups is itself built of a number of geographical and temporal levels. Nested within the larger system is a series of smaller groupings which can be defined in different ways. At an intermediate level are individual trading networks like the kula or the hiri on the south Papuan coast. These are not discretely bounded but can be distinguished from the whole through an intensity of interaction and by a localized set of dispositions: for instance, the kula ring is marked out by the opposite flow rule, where armbands move against necklaces, which is not found in other neighbouring patterns of trade.

We can say something more about the nature of this system by looking at what has happened in the period since European colonization. Colonization represents a severe shock to existing forms of life and it helps to highlight elements of life which are central to people's existence and those which are somewhat less important. Here we find evidence which again runs counter to the neo-evolutionary view. Following the argument that adaptation to the environment is basic to all aspects of life, we would expect people's relationship to the environment to change least, with ritual, social hierarchy and exchange changing more readily in the face of colonization. In fact, in the Arawes the opposite seems to be the case. The subsistence sphere changed most rapidly, with the introduction of new food crops, new breeds of pig and chicken and steel axes. These factors together meant that more land could be cleared and that higher yields were obtained. It is only with these post-contact changes in the subsistence system that large permanent villages were set up in the Arawe area for the first time; the defended hamlets of the late prehistoric period moved often and were probably only associated with small garden plots (Gosden 1989a). On the other hand, although there has been considerable expansion in the rates of trade and inflation in customary payments, due to larger amounts of food and the entry of money into the area, the structure of ritual and ceremonial life and the social contacts which sustain it are much less changed.

These findings seem to reverse those of the neo-evolutionary model, with social relations being more resistant to change than the subsistence sphere. This might make ritual, exchange and so on appear to be the most vital strand in people's lives. However, an argument for social determinism as a counter-balance to adaptationist views runs against the grain of the argument proposed here. Neither the sphere normally seen as the social, nor subsistence, can be separated one from the other. Each is involved in mutual production of the other. People's relations with the world are not divided into social and economic, but form webs of interconnections between people and things. As neither social nor economic relations exist in isolation, it makes no sense to say that one is more basic than the other. The flow of our actions derives from our feel for both people and things and it is the very continuity of reference that allows us to understand change. Altered circumstances in one area of life – for instance, the post-contact changes to gardening in Papua New Guinea – change the overall warp and weft of life in complex ways; and although the relations of ritual and exchange have undergone less change over the last hundred years than has gardening, the new material circumstances have given people a different relationship to the world and to each other. For instance, many of the restrictions on production have been lost: a hundred years ago, only people with certain social and ritual standing could plant and grow particular crops. These restrictions still exist, but by all accounts are breaking down fast; and these changes channel through into human relations, as the people whose production was earlier restricted through ritual are freed from dependence on those who could grow what they wanted.

A Summary of the Argument

People create time and space through their actions. Time and space, in turn, become part of the structure of habitual action, shaping the nature of reference between actions. Time and space are created on a number of different levels through social action. The long-term trajectory of people in the Pacific has been based around a willingness to change the landscape to further enable action, or to create flexible patterns of action through mobility. These two themes provide a basic form of directedness for all the structures of reference which have been created over shorter spans of time.

Within any one period, such as that between 3500 and 2000 BP when Lapita assemblages are found, structures of reference bring about patterns of action which create pattern in the archaeological evidence. Action has a regional structure to it: there are points in the landscape where people are intimately involved with the world and points where little activity is carried out. The spots on the landscape that we call sites are result from the repetition of action in the same locality. But action is not just on a regional level during this period: it is structured across the whole of the western Pacific, as is shown by the contemporaneous changes in material culture. Consequently, habitual action must also have to do with huge dimensions of time and space which are very difficult to comprehend.

Much action is unthought, but problems which arise in the structure of habit are brought to consciousness. The existence of widespread identical pottery decorations shows that people were attempting to link up disparate points in space. The repeated actions which may have been carried out with the standardized forms of material culture helped to deal with the dynamism of a situation in which colonization changed the human world rapidly and human action was reshaping the physical world. Pottery forms and decoration were actually consciously developed and thought out. However, over time these became part of people's network of habit. Conscious thought and its products are constantly becoming part of the group's unconscious social being. Life is an intermingling of habitual and conscious elements, as well as the unfolding of human action on different times-scales. Long-term frameworks of reference lie behind action over the shorter term. History can be seen to operate on a series of different levels. However, these levels are not discrete and easily separated, but are intermingled with longer-term forms of practice, creating a set of resources which can be drawn on as the need arises. The areas of life which we might see as symbolic, such as Lapita pottery decoration, cannot be understood apart from the overall flow of life, but are instead part of the response to particular problems of reference, a conscious gloss on unconscious forms of life.

Life itself, in the short or the long term, is not primarily to do with consciousness and structures of meaning, but rather to do with a set of habits created in the body. However, much thought in recent archaeology would question this view, seeing symbolic forms as central to human life and human history. In the next chapter my argument will be developed through a critique of these views, before we return to the search for an understanding of life as a series of forms of being in the world.

3

Meaning, Mind and Matter

What does it mean to be human?

Today this question has an old-fashioned ring to it. Repeated answers revolving around tool use, intelligence and language, have been given over the last 150 years. The innovation of this century is to frame an answer around the idea that it is the creation and communication of meaning which is at the heart of what it means to be human. This answer echoes through many areas of the social sciences and is now dominant in some strands of archaeology. The aim of this chapter is to put forward a critique of the notion that our humanity is bound up with our meanings, to explain why in my view hermeneutic or post-structuralist approaches to the human past are unsatisfying, and to seek a more complex mingling of meaning and unthought action.

The question of humanness is double-edged, however, and leads us to consider the cultural circumstances under which such a question arises. Questioning about global human characteristics is not a natural human activity found in all cultures. Rather it is a response to the setting up of a world system through industrial capitalism which has brought Europeans in touch with a range of cultural forms quite unlike their own. Questions of the diversity and unity of human life have sprung from this contact. Archaeology is now practised in many countries of the world and can provide information on both ultimate human origins and the development of local cultural forms. Archaeology, both historically and in the present, is intimately involved in definitions of humanness.

My aim here is to develop a view of humanness centred around people's involvement with the world and to probe the temporal structures of that involvement. A stress on physical involvement runs counter to views which highlight the meaningful qualities of human life. A view centred around meaning derives from structuralism, hermeneutics and post-structuralist thought. Archaeology's tracks away from new archaeology led first into structuralist (Hodder 1982) and then post-structuralist and hermeneutic thought (Bapty and Yates 1990) in a manner which mirrored closely the moves of other disciplines. Despite a counter-balance from those emphasizing Marxism (Spriggs 1984b) and theories of practice (Barrett 1987), much of social archaeology has come to be centred around the understanding of symbolic systems in the past and the metaphors of language and text. My main point in critiquing these views is not that a stress on meaning is wrong, but that it is too limited to provide a full sense of human action in the world and its temporal structures. What is needed is a model of how meaning derives from human action and the temporal nature of both meaningful and habitual, unthought action.

The move towards seeing meaning as central to life cannot be seen as straightforward, even in a simplified account such as this. Instead we can see that over the last two centuries there has been a slow decay in people's feel for the world and a consequent move towards words and meanings. In the early days of capitalism the startling new physical circumstances in which people lived focused attention on relations with the material world, and rapid change brought a consideration of history to the fore. In the twentieth century it was easier to take mass urban living and the enormous productivity of industrialism for granted. What has become more noticeable is the vast proliferation of symbolic forms, whether these be to do with advertising, fashion or the opera. Through the nineteenth and early twentieth centuries various theorists tried to come to terms with modernity through developing a unified model of life, stressing both practical action and forms of meaning and symbolism. In the twentieth century, meaning and symbolic forms have supplanted attempts to create a balanced model of life and thought. Intellectual currents have also played their part and, through areas of thought such as structuralism, language has come to be seen as the quintessential symbolic form, providing the model for understanding all forms of meaning. In the most recent period, the notion of text has come to dominate, deriving inspiration from this more general stress on language. The moves towards language and then text

represent a progressive loss of subtlety in handling people's relationship
with the world, moving from attempts to understand both meaning
and action in a balanced manner, to a single stress on meaning, using
text as a central metaphor. Given archaeology's stress on material
culture, it is ironic that notions of meaning and text have come to
dominate areas of the discipline, reducing our feel for the very
materiality of our evidence and the insights this can give us into human
involvement in the world.

The World and the Word Combined

The rapid process of industrialization throughout the nineteenth century
created a new material world for all sections of European society. It is
no surprise that this process caused an enormous amount of thought
about human relations to the material world. As science and technology came to dominate intellectual, social and economic life there was
increasing concern that human life was being channelled in directions
which were industrially efficient, but which did not provide the basis
for a full and rounded life.

Goethe, for instance, stressed the intuition of life as a living whole
and objected to the separation of science from the rest of experience. In
demanding a science based on 'wonder as a permanent state of mind'
and stating that 'one only understands what one loves', Goethe was
reacting to the separation of the emotional and the intellectual sides of
human life. Similarly, he pondered the problem of rendering experience into words, maintaining that words could only express some of the
range of human emotional and intuitive experience. Here Goethe was
part of a German *Sprachskepsis* also to be found in Nietzsche, famous
for his saying that language was the first lie. In the face of the
breakdown of traditional communities and the increasing fragmentation of human experience with the onset of the Industrial Revolution,
Goethe tried to develop a picture of the total range of human
responses, some of which lay beyond the ken of science or current forms
of language. New human and material relations could not easily be put
into words. Blame was laid both on those relations and on the words
at people's disposal. At the heart of responses to modernity have been
problems of action and meaning. In the course of this book we shall
consider a number of attempts to unify action and meaning, such as
those by Hegel, Marx and Heidegger, but here I am concerned with a

loss of the sense of this problem and the move towards a concentration on meaning alone.

Initial attempts to grasp in thought people's new orientations to the world were through notions of unity. Hegel, a younger contemporary of Goethe, tried to understand the movement of life and thought as a whole and to replace a fragmented social reality with some sense of totality: 'Hegel's thought supplied a demand for unification that was doubtless an intense emotional craving. . . . Hegel's synthesis of subject and object, matter and spirit, the divine and the human was no mere intellectual formula; it operated as an immense release, a liberation' (Dewey 1960: 10). Although the actual nature of his thought is quite different, a similar striving for wholeness is well represented in the thought of Dilthey. Dilthey is a crucial figure in that he represents a major inspiration for hermeneutics, the study of meaning.

Dilthey attempted to bridge a series of opposites (experience and thought, practice and theory, reality and ideas) and in so doing move towards a sense of the fullness of life that Goethe and others had felt was missing from modern life: 'The basic conception of my philosophy is that up to now no one has put *whole, full and unmutilated experience* at the basis of philosophizing, that is to say, the whole and full reality' (quoted in Ermath 1978: 24). The movement of Dilthey's thought was towards some form of totality, and central to this was the concept of understanding (*Verstehen*). Dilthey was one of the first to insist upon the distinction between explanation and understanding as providing the borderline between the natural and the human science. In Dilthey's eyes *Verstehen* started with the immediate, intuitive understanding of life, which was then formalized through systematic reflection. For life to be understood in all its variety, ordinary daily activities must be the starting point for reflection. The everyday is so well-known and familiar that it is difficult to bring to consciousness; the ordinary is silently at work in every human situation.

Dilthey identified two means for getting to know life. First, there is immersion in a form of life: getting to know it on its own terms, through cultivating an insider's perspective. Such an immanent critique should then be subjected to extensive comparison, to bring out the elements of a form of life found elsewhere in the world. Through his career Dilthey shifted from a stress on the insider's perspective, a solitary re-living of others' experience centring round the idea of *Erlebnis* (= lived experience), to a greater sense of community and shared forms of life. Thus Habermas's criticism that Dilthey tended to emphasize the interpreter's need for '*empathy*, of basically solitary reproduction and re-experiencing' rather than '*participation in communication learned in interaction*' (Habermas 1972: 180, original emphasis) was most relevant to the early part of his career. In his later work, Dilthey moved away from a stress on the individual and towards the idea of 'objective mind'. The objective mind was a communal phenomenon, described by Dilthey as 'the atmosphere of all the meanings in which we live'.

Changes in Dilthey's view of language are central to this shift. Dilthey moved from a scepticism about language as a means of shaping and expressing human experience to a more nuanced view. With the growth of the idea of objective mind Dilthey came to see language as a crucial element in the creation of shared meanings. Lived experience was made available to communication and interpretation. However, there were also limits to languge. Sometimes Dilthey saw the experience of life and conceptual, linguistic thought as antinomies and sometimes as cooperating to provide the full richness of experience (Ermath 1978: 349). As we shall see, this ambivalence to language is in contrast to the later hermeneutic movement where language is seen as the one and only central metaphor for human life. Whatever his attitude to language, Dilthey was important because he extended hermeneutics from simply textual analysis to include all forms of signification. Also central to his view was the importance of history. Although influenced at some points by Nietzsche's *Sprachskepsis* (= scepticism over the power of language to capture experience), Dilthey always reacted strongly against Nietzsche's view of history, described as cud-chewing and the dead burying the living. For Dilthey, lived experience arose out of participation in historical forms of life. This stress on the importance of history and the idea that thought was an historical product rather than a search for eternal truth runs through all later manifestations of hermeneutics.

For Dilthey, as we have seen, language and experience were related in problematical ways. This problem was taken up early this century by Heidegger, who probed modern forms of life and the relationship that language has to unthought practical action. Like Goethe before him, Heidegger cultivated a sense of childlike wonder; the main cause for wonder deriving from the very fact of existence – that there is something rather than nothing. Heidegger was sceptical about knowledge. Following Nietzsche, he saw knowing as an expression of the will-to-power; with western forms of knowing, all species of

instrumental reason turning the world into a series of objects for the
subject. With age, Heidegger became particularly sceptical about
attempts to ground philosophy in ultimate truths, seeing the search for
unshakeable philosophical foundations as the final expression of
European attempts to dominate the world through thought. Sceptical
about claims to knowledge and reason, Heidegger became an unusual
sort of philosopher (indeed he eschewed the label, preferring to call
himself a thinker), concentrating on the brute fact of existence rather
than on thought. Heidegger attempted to return to forms of primordial
existence beyond the will-to-power and to regain what he saw as
people's proper place within the universe. Much of his attempt to
understand forms of being is itself hard to understand, as he avoided
all rigorous method or systematic attempt to explain himself. The one
characteristic of his thought found throughout his long life is an
obsession with language and its relationship to life.

We shall look at Heidegger's work in greater detail in chapter 5.
Here I want to look at his general attempts to find a proper human
relationship with the world. This view stressed the mutual involvement
of things and people, moving away from a set of images which helped
create a sense of human distance from the material world. Heidegger
tackled these problems at the level of thought. In particular, he
attacked western metaphysics – that is, the system of imagery which he
thought underlay not just philosophy but also everyday turns of
thought. These images centred around the idea that we as human
subjects have an internal life of the mind and that we look out upon the
physical world, which exists external to us, out there. This picture of
people and the world lies behind the definitions of subject and object,
the former conscious and knowing, the latter passive and the object of
knowledge. The division between knowing subject and perceived object
leads to what Heidegger called 'representational thought': thought as
a series of depictions of external reality, which could be said to be true
if the depiction accorded with the nature of external reality. The main
problem with such patterns of thought is that they distance people
from the world and tend to make the 'inner' life of the mind more real
than 'external' reality. In Heidegger's view the tendency to see ideas as
more real than things has been extant in western thought since Plato
and tends to privilege knowing rather than being, epistemology rather
than ontology.

Heidegger's thought is an attempt to reassess human beings place in
the world, focusing on everyday action amongst mundane things,

rather than abstracted forms of knowledge. His attempt to reformulate people's place in the world came in a period of vast change, fundamental to which was industrial capitalism, a system of life dedicated to a set of relationships with the world centred round the profit motive. Heidegger's thought can be seen as part of a long debate on how industrialism affected the German *Geist*, which had been under way at least since Goethe wrote *Faust*. Industralization occurred in Germany extremely rapidly in the last four decades of the nineteenth century, so that by 1907 it is calculated that only half of the 60 million Germans still lived in the place where they were born (Zimmerman 1990: 7). Rapid urbanization and the growth of factory production broke up both traditional communities and old values. Political forms were also re-ordered through German national unification, and Germany's place in Europe changed with a successful war in the 1870s and an unsuccessful one between 1914–18.

Heidegger was part of a search for stability within this flux, although he was not advocating a return to the old order, but looking for a new one. This search led him to join the National Socialists, the most obvious symptom of Germany's moral plight, an affiliation he never repudiated (Farias 1989). The quest for new values also led him to reject much of the tradition of philosophy, which he felt to be immersed in distancing practices. The distancing practices of the inner mental life versus external reality were also those lying at the heart of capitalism, which practised forms of instrumental logic to manipulate the world and through which the world was seen as raw material, something to be taken advantage of and used. Capitalism's practice was based on a view of the life of the mind: the engineer constructed his or her actions theoretically, laying out a sequence of cause and effect before putting them into practice. Reality had to represented correctly, through the operation of the mind, before it could be manipulated profitably. Representational thought, which privileged mental constructions of physical reality, was to be found in both industry and philosophy and in both areas they were used for the purposes of controlling the world.

Heidegger's criticisms of representational thought, and the subject/object dichotomy around which it was based, necessitated not only a new model of meaning but a new model of being. Meaning could not be seen to belong to an abstract sphere of symbols which stood for the world. Meanings are not a series of messages we receive from the world, in the same way as a television receives broadcasts. The reason for this is that people, unlike television sets, are not passive receivers, but actors in and on the world. Furthermore, we are not in the world in a purely spatial sense, like a television in a room. Rather we are in the world in the same way that people are in love, or in the theatre: we have immediate and active involvement in our material surroundings. This view of our being does not centre on meaning, or ideas, or truth as the correct perception of reality. Rather it looks at how we and the things that surround us are interwoven, they in us and us in them. The interior versus exterior metaphor loses its power when Heidegger's view is followed, as do the conventional definitions of subject and object.

However, although we are intimately involved in the world we have come to forget this fact. Plato, the arch-villain in Heidegger's thought, saw the world as Idea, something to be represented in thought, and this view of the world was taken up and developed by Enlightenment rationalists. The logical, representable properties of the world became more present and important than immediate sensuous reality. Together with the growth of instrumental logic, which sees the world primarily as raw material and other human beings as labour power, these notions and patterns of action have led to a separation of people from the world. This is the process Weber called *Entzauberung*, the loss of magic; and both he and Heidegger saw that boredom, blandness and alienation had permeated people's relationships with each other and with material things.

Heidegger's critique of representational thought and the forms of meaning it privileged strove to change people's views of themselves and material things. Heidegger saw the proper relationship of people to the world as a unity of difference (Hiedegger 1977) in which people and things are joined into a unity where each keep their speical properties. People are the knowing element of the physical world, tuned into change and decay by knowledge of their own death.The unity of difference between people and things is fundamentally temporal, based on change rather than any essential relationships of one to the other. Thought, language and action are all part of our relationship to the world, which when properly employed bring out the special qualities of people and things. Things as well as people have causative powers channelling, constraining and enabling human action; but these causative powers are not knowable (Heidegger 1971). The physical causative powers of things are revealed to people through poetical forms of action, language and thought, which help people attend to the special qualities of things. With meaning comes a diverse unity and the temporal flow of life, which is far removed from representational forms of thought and the instrumental logic which attends them. Heidegger, ever a paradoxical thinker, is a major inspiration of hermeneutic forms of thought in the twentieth century, but also a major critic of the idea that meanings can be found in an abstracted realm at a distance from everyday life.

There are considerable problems, as well as potentials, with Heidegger's thought, not least of which is his steadfast refusal to deal with human relations. However, his importance here lies in the thoroughgoing criticisms he made of the idea that meaning arises in a simple relation between an inner, knowing subject and an outer, known object. But he is just as important for continuing to stress that it is people's relationship to the world which is crucial, even though current views of this relationship may be dangerous. Heidegger wanted to plunge thought back into the stream of life and action, not seeing a great antinomy between being and knowing.

Other reactions to representational thought have taken the opposite direction and attempted to abstract people and their mental life from the physical world altogether. This extreme form of distancing people from the world has come to dominate social theory at the end of the twentieth century. The ultimate inspiration for these distancing forms of thought is as old as the century itself and goes under the name of structuralism. Let us turn next to structuralism, a consideration of which provides the starting point for a critique of thought which ignores the relationship of people to the world. It is also a form of thought which has been influential in archaeology, importing its faults with it.

The World and the Word Divided: Structuralism

Structuralism has been one of the most powerful intellectual movements of the twentieth century, and although its time is well past its influence still lives on in post-structuralism. Structuralism is important in its own right, but also for its historical legacy which still has considerable influence today; I shall argue here that this influence is largely deleterious. There are two main lasting influences deriving from structuralism. The first of these is what might be called an internal view of meaning: meaning derives from the relationship between words and concepts rather than the links between people and the world. Secondly, following the early inspiration of Saussure, language has become the main paradigm for understanding all forms of meaning. The influence of structuralism has allowed social science to consider the internal logics of social forms as a real power for change, rather than seeing change as deriving from the environment, but this has taken place through dismissing all theories about people's relationship to the world.

The ultimate inspiration for structuralism is the linguistic theory of Saussure (1959), who divided language into words and the concepts they referred to. Central to his view is the distinction between the signifier (a word) and the concept referred to (the signified). One of the crucial things to note about this distinction is that the objects, emotions or mental states referred to by words are ignored (Sturrock 1979: 6). The use of language is the manipulation of relationships between a series of words and the mental concepts they designate. The objects referred to through language are known as referents, and there is only an arbitrary and conventional relationship between language and the world. Historical conventions govern which words are applied to which referents.

Linguistic structures are arbitrary in relation to the natural world, but they are governed by their own internal logics of difference and similarity. Hence language is viewed as a structured set of differences: words gain their meanings from all the meanings that they exclude, all the words that they are not. The stress on meaning deriving from internal logic rather than external relationships gives structuralism a strongly relativist bent. Languages are local, culturally bounded phenomena dividing the world up in their own ways. So, for instance, ways of designating colours vary considerably throughout the world depending upon cultural forms, rather than on any natural way of dividing up the series of wavelengths which make up the spectrum of colours.

Saussure's ideas came to be applied more widely in anthropology and thence in other social sciences through the thought of Lévi-Strauss. Lévi-Strauss took the basic idea that language is a structured set of differences and applied it to all areas of human culture. His approach to anthropology may be seen as an extended linguistic analogy, referring back to Saussure's view of language. However, he curbed the form of relativism implicit in the view of language as a conventional structure by searching for a common basis for all structuring of human experience. He found this common structure in the nature of the human mind. Lévi-Strauss saw the human mind as operating through a series of oppositions, and Leach has pointed out that these oppositions may derive from the basic symmetry of the human body, where the left side is 'opposed' by an identical, but different, right side. Human life is therefore seen as a series of simple oppositions between terms (left/right, black/white, day/night), and the variety of cultural forms can be referred back to this simple oppositional structure. Related myths, for instance, are seen as transformations of each other, transformations which can be understood by referring them back to the cultural oppositions underlying them. These oppositions are always seen as conceptual rather than real: they are not, for instance, oppositions of class and interest, or forms of domination and resistance.

One of the strengths of structuralism was that it looked beneath the surface, below the appearances of things to their roots. In a well-known quote from *Tristes tropiques* (1955), Lévi-Strauss says that his three main sources of inspiration are geology, Marxism and psychoanalysis, as all three derived surface appearances from deeper underlying realities. Especially in cultural studies, this sense that superficial variety depends on and derives from a simpler underlying structure is crucial. For a thinker such as Lévi-Strauss, the purpose in studying human societies is to dive beneath the surface and perceive the basal structures of human life and thought.

Structuralism also reassessed the relation of the individual to the social whole. Societies are seen as complexes of symbolic and conceptual codes. Each individual partakes of these codes and is shaped by them, but does not have full control of any of them. Creation is as much a social force, deriving from the broad changes in symbolic forms, as an individual act. Cultures are thus social products rather than deriving solely or mainly from the genius of individuals abundantly imbued with the spirit of their time. As cultural forms derive from common conceptual schemes it is difficult to maintain the distinction between 'high' and 'low' culture, where high culture is the product of genius and low culture derives from the masses. All patterns of culture derive from joint ordering principles and all elements of culture are comparable. Such a view is exemplified by the work of Barthes. In his best known book, *Mythologies* (1957), he attempts to understand a whole range of cultural phenomena ranging from soap powders to wrestling matches. Here structuralism blends into semiology, the general study of signs and symbols, which not only took over some structuralist principles of analysis, but also the eclectic nature of social study it inspired.

For Lévi-Strauss, the world is a conceptual construct first and foremost, and if he has a concern for material things it is as reflections of immaterial concepts. He emphasizes the constructed nature of social reality and attempts to probe the subterranean roots of that reality, trying to uncover a series of basic and simple structures. The world is essentially a social order, rather than the reflection of any form of natural order. The strength of a view which emphasizes the constructed nature of social reality is that it opens up the possibility of change. If the world can be constructed, it can be reconstructed, at least to the limits provided by the basic structure of the human mind. It is this broadening of the possibility of change which made structuralism controversial in its early days and which still gives it a whiff of subversion today.

Paradoxically, this source of strength was also a cause of weakness. By concentrating so hard on internal relationships, structuralists lost any sense of the broader connectedness of human life. From Saussure's model of linguistics came the central focus on the relationship between signifier and signified, both of which, as word and concept, were purely human products. The relationship was between one aspect of cultural forms (words) and another (concepts), and there was no sense of people's relationship to the outside world. As the relationship of cultural structures to the natural world was considered to be arbitrary, it was in fact impossible and useless to study this relationship, as it was deemed to have no structure of its own. The ultimate goal of Lévi-Strauss's analysis was the human mind itself and the manner in which the working of the human mind created structured cultural forms. This analysis could move seamlessly from myth to myth or from myth to generative process without external referent. Meaning begat meaning in forms of the mind's making. There was no need to include any other elements in the analysis. As Sperber (1979: 33) has pointed out, for Lévi-Strauss the world is of interest because it provides food for thought, rather than because it provides food. Structuralism had very little sense of being in the world; people are thinking animals and it is the processes of their thought that need to be studied, rather than the sphere of practical action.

Also of crucial importance was the centrality of language to this process. Although structuralism came to embrace all forms of signification, language was seen as the prototypical sign structure: an understanding of the structure of language would allow the under-standing of all sign structures. This implicit assumption was relatively unproblematical (although not unchallengeable) as long as abstract, non-material forms of signification were the subjects of study; however, as soon as structuralist forms of analysis were enlarged to embrace material symbols, then the assumption that the structuralist view of language held the key to all forms of signification became doubtful. First and most important, the relation between material symbols and their meanings is not necessarily arbitrary. The colour of blood may symbolize danger, as the spilling of blood is often a dangerous act. Material symbols do not form a closed structure of their own, insulated from the world, but have threads of connection to the world. Their structures are transformed not just through the properties of the human mind, but also because there are limits to the symbolic connotations that symbols can be given. Once symbolic forms are embodied in things they open up new areas of cause and effect from which it is impossible to exclude the external world and concentrate solely on the human mind.

Saussure's linguistics was a reaction against the historical linguistics practised for much of the nineteenth century, which was designed to throw light on topics such as the origins of the Indo-European languages. By excluding history and historical change Saussure wanted to explore the insights which could be gained from viewing language as a frozen system, with its own structures and properties. A lack of interest in history was an implicit, rather than explicit, quality of structuralism as applied to cultural forms. When structuralism came to be used outside the linguistic sphere, more basic than a lack of concern for history was the impossibility of a theory which linked people to the world. Indeed, any real theory of human action was made impossible by structuralism's concentration on meaning. It was only in odd hybrids, such as structural Marxism, that the notion of life as a structured set of differences could be used to throw light on the history of the relationship between people and the world. A concentration on meaning rather than practice, and indeed the exaggeration of the differences between meaning and practice, is to be found in structuralism's late entry into archaeology.

Archaeology and Structuralism

Despite some French archaeologists' moves towards structuralism (Leroi-Gourhan 1965) and a determined push within historical archaeology in this direction (Deetz 1977; Glassie 1975), structuralism had very little impact on archaeology until it was out of fashion as a style of thought in other disciplines. In Symbolic and Structural Archaeology, Hodder (1982) put forward a carefully modulated view, taking some inspiration from structuralism but by no means attempting to discern binary oppositions underlying all areas of human life. According to Hodder's view, cultural forms were not simply machines for survival but were organized around sets of rules concerned with such categories as purity and boundedness. The job of the archaeologist, he declared, is to perceive structures underlying a particular culture's variability: 'the codes and rules according to which observed systems of interrelations are produced' (Hodder 1982: 7). Following from this, 'Material culture can then be viewed as a structured set of differences' (ibid.). Lévi-Strauss is criticized by Hodder for lacking a theory of practice and for not relating mental structures to their context of use, thus highlighting context as a theme that has continued through Hodder's work. The importance of a structuralist attempt to delve beneath the superficial variety of culture to its underlying codes is that the archaeological record need not and cannot be seen as a reflection of society. 'Burial pattern, then, is not a direct behavioural reflection of social pattern. It is structured through symbolically meaningful codes which can be manipulated in social strategies' (ibid.: 10). Social differences and tensions can be hidden or exaggerated through material forms, and these forms may not relate straightforwardly to issues that archaeologists have been interested in such as subsistence and social structure, but rather derive from underlying attitudes to death, dirt and food.

The contributors to *Symbolic and Structural Archaeology* varied considerably in their attitudes to symbols and structures. Conkey, in her examination of Palaeolithic French art, uses a more directly structuralist approach. Conkey stresses that she is looking at the first art productions of *Homo sapiens* and that the structural attributes of this art may tell us about the fundamental sources of meaning within the art (Conkey 1982: 116). She holds that all human behavioural systems have an underlying semantic structure which exists as a series of relationships, and that these cultural and cognitive structures 'set the matrix for the enactment of daily life' (ibid.: 117). Paradoxically, the key feature of Palaeolithic art that Conkey picks out is its lack of structure. The images on cave walls are unbounded and they float in space in an uncertain temporal and spatial relationship to each other.

The lack of images explicitly linked into temporal sequences suggests timelessness and the use of natural features of cave walls to create the shapes of animals suggests some continuity between art and reality. There is a lack of structure within the art and no explicit division between culture and nature. The lack of bounding and structure limits the way in which the art can function as a referential system. The cave art, in particular, may have been a static phenomenon both in its construction and its placing on cave walls, and what created temporal and spatial rhythms was visits to the art, the viewers – not the images viewed – adding timing (ibid.: 124).

In that volume both Hodder and Conkey saw human societies as a matter of semantics and symbols. The overall meaning of symbolic schemes was maintained by differences between individual symbols, the relations of each to the whole. A broader survey of structuralist approaches within archaeology is contained in Hodder (1986: ch. 3), and he raises some of the same criticisms as I have done here, while stressing the usefulness of structuralism in understanding transformations in cultural forms. This relational view of difference and meaning lies at the heart of structuralism and is the element which has been most deliberately carried over into post-structuralist thought. Although Hodder in particular emphasizes practice and context, practical action is seen to derive from schemes of meaning, rather than from any dialectical relationship between meaning and the world. Material culture is reduced to structured sets of differences and any full sense of the materiality of the world is lost. The disembodiment of the world is also a key feature of both hermeneutics and post-structuralist thought; I shall go on to examine this, first in general and then in terms of how it has been applied in archaeology.

All the World's a Text: Hermeneutics and Post-structuralism

Hermeneutics, the study of meaning, has made the problem of meaning central to much of social science in the post-war period. Much of the need to study meaning has come from a critique of positivism. Positivism held that an objective view of the world was possible; that there was a single best point of view from which the truth of the world could be apprehended. The business of science was to develop methods to apprehend the world aright, through techniques which could be regularly repeated to test whether the same result was always obtained. Hermeneutics led the way towards post-positivist philosophy by questioning the notion that there is a single best view of reality. A central tenet of much hermeneutic thought is that views of the world are culturally bound, and while western science may be a very technically effective view of the world, it is only one way of seeing things. Starting from the assumption of a plurality of views, hermeneutics seeks to understand the historical conditions which give rise to particular traditions of seeing the world, how these traditions influence perception and the structure of accounts used to talk about the world.

For Gadamer and Ricoeur, the leading German and French exponent of hermeneutics respectively, language is central to human experience and there is no such thing as pre- or non-linguistic human experience. All attempts to understand meaning must start with language. Gadamer's view of the object world is largely determined by his attitude to science (Warnke 1987: 2–3). He sees hermeneutics as a branch of practical philosophy which needs to defend our political and ethical sense of the world against technology based on science (see Bernstein 1986: ch. 3 on this point). For Gadamer (1975), the central feature of science is the method which it uses to amass 'ratified knowledge'. In contrast, hermeneutics is aimed at increasing forms of understanding which stress *phronesis* (ethical know-how). Language is the medium of all meaning and structures ethical know-how.

Such a structuring process takes place within historical traditions. History operates in us to create 'prejudices'. Prejudice can be enabling and can help us to deal with the world, as well as blinkering and narrowing our views (blind prejudices have this latter effect). Here Gadamer uses the term 'prejudice' to convey the forms of sedimentation of past experience which then help create future experience. Gadamer's main concern is with how forms of interpretation take place within traditions. Traditions help form prejudices, but they also represent the ground on which prejudices are risked. Any form of life is created by a dialogical encounter between past and present, as meanings derived from past experience are tested against the exigencies of the present. History forces ever new encounters between past and present to which there can be no end. There is thus no ground for absolute truth, no vantage point outside of history from which meaning can be judged. All claims to truth are assessed by relative standards; those hammered out by particular communities in the course of their history. The central themes of dialogue and conversation have been taken up by recent American philosophers such as Bernstein (1983; 1986) and Rorty (1980; 1989), to be viewed not only as the central philosophical activity but the crucial feature of an ethical life. Of recent years the dominance of language in all areas of the social sciences has reached a peak, and in no area more so than in the thought of Ricoeur.

Ricoeur's central question is the one which started this chapter: 'what makes us human?' His essential answer to this question is that people are language and that laying out the principles of textual meaning can help us to understand humanity. The crucial word in the previous sentence is 'textual', which is at the heart of Ricoeur's view of language. The human subject is seen as being placed in language before it is placed in consciousness. There is no pure phenomenological consciousness; people are created through various processes of signification and meaning. Some forms of meaning are created in face-to-face situations, for example in conversation, whilst others derive from meanings created and sustained over the longer term. Longer-term meanings are maintained through concrete intermediaries, which Ricoeur calls 'texts'. The notion of text obviously derives from books, which solidify meaning into more or less lasting forms. The concept of text, however, is used much more broadly by Ricoeur to refer to any type of signification lasting longer than a face-to-face encounter. Hence, material objects, institutions or the layout of the landscape can all be considered texts to be read in differing ways. Our world is composed of a sum total of symbolic references and the intersecting points of a myriad of texts.

As with Gadamer, texts have an historical dimension deriving from past traditions. The present is then a meeting point between past and present texts which brings about a series of rereadings, as old texts are subjected to new interpretations. Re-interpretation means that the originator of a text (usually known as the author) has his or her original intentions in writing the text transcended. Likewise the reader of a new text has his or her self-understanding challenged as he or she is brought into contact with new sets of meanings. For instance, the British reader of a nineteenth-century Russian novel imputes meanings to the text undreamt of by the author. On the other hand, a reader initially unfamiliar with Russian life in the last century is brought up against habits of thought, speech and action foreign to their own and consequently find views of the world that they have taken for granted challenged. This process comes very close to what Gadamer refers to as the fusing of horizons.

Life for Ricoeur is a series of texts, material and immaterial, and change is brought about by new texts entering the sum total of symbolic frames of reference and altering them. In his later work Ricoeur has become interested in the manner in which this process operates, particularly from the point of view of how time structures this process. (These ideas will be considered in more detail in chapter 6.) In Ricoeur's later work (1984; 1985; 1988) life is not seen as composed of static texts, but a flow of meaning: narrative. Narratives are structured in time and impose forms of order on disordered reality. Narrative is a simplification of life through the imposition of forms of time. Ricoeur distinguishes three kinds of time. First, there is private mortal time, in which each of us lives our own private set of meanings, knowing that they will come to an end with our death. Public time, on the other hand, is that of language which makes a portion of our private experience more generally accessible. Language exists within communities which have a longer lifespan than individuals. The public time of language is a slower, broader time in which individuals participate during their lifetimes. At the juncture of these two lies human time, which is lived between private, personal experience and the public time of language. Human time is the line at which social and private horizons meet and fuse. The proper role of hermeneutics is not passively to understand meaning, but to strip away the masks of culture and look at the construction of meaning. Such a stripping down of culture forces us to look at the communities within which meaning is forged and at whether these bring about a healthy blend of public and private life.

From this brief account it is easy to see why Gadamer and Ricoeur have been extremely influential in recent social theory. However, the main point to highlight here is the total dominance of language in their attempts to understand the human world. This dominance takes a number of forms. Language is first of all seen as the centre of human existence. Our core social being consists of meanings which are created through language. Language pre-exists the individual and speaks human existence rather than people speaking it. The world exists for us as a totality of symbolic forms, with each type of symbol working in the same manner as language. The world only exists as meaning, and these meanings are a series of languages, or texts, which meet and mutually influence each other. Hermeneutics, which in Heidegger's usage was a startling attempt to force thought to the core of human existence, has come to see the world as a series of languages, a Babel of competing tongues.

What is lost by this is any sense of the efficacity of the object world itself. The world as symbol can never escape from the human realm, can never stand out recalcitrant to human purposes. Any sense of mutual creativity and shaping is lost. And while Gadamer and Ricoeur are extremely interesting when writing on how people create a world for themselves in public and private terms, and provide salutary warnings about science's technological warping of our views, theirs is not a fully inclusive theory of people in the world. This criticism can also be raised against post-structuralism, which is an eclectic blend of structuralist and hermeneutic thought.

Post-structuralism is not one thing, but many. We shall look at other thinkers often given this label, such as Foucault, in later chapters, but here I shall concentrate on the work of Derrida (1978; 1981; 1988). Derrida has been the main influence in writing about language to emerge from post-structuralist thought and he is the key to understanding the post-structuralist position on language and the world.

Derrida takes from structuralism the division between a phonic signifier and a mental signified, a division which constructs language as a system of differences rather than seeing it as a series of independently meaningful units. Like the structuralists, Derrida is concerned with the internal structure of language and not with its reference to the world. By excluding its referential function, language can be seen as a thing apart, a self-contained entity whose relationship to the world is unproblematical because it is unknowable. Language does not make the world present to us, but conjures up meaning through the play of differences. Language, like music, operates through movement. A single note means nothing, it can only excite a response as part of the overall flow of the piece, and even if we do pick out individual notes they are gone by the time we have registered them. Musical notes do not mean anything in terms of the world; they exist within the self-referential world of music. So it is with language and texts. Movement is all, and we cannot isolate and stabilize individual meanings, nor can we pin words to solid material objects. In Derrida's world to mean is not to be.

According to Derrida, western thought has been obsessed with *presence*, expecting words to attach themselves to concrete things and situations, evoking them for us. Furthermore, we in the West structure our thought around a series of polarities – being *vs* nothing, man *vs* woman, speech *vs* writing – in which the second term is seen to be a negative, corrupt version of the first. This evaluation privileges unity, identity, immediacy and presentness, for instance when speech, as the face-to-face meeting of speaker and listener, facilitates the immediate, unmediated transmission of meaning. The idea of self-present meaning is seen to be the unspoken ideal of western metaphysics, which Derrida terms logocentrism.

The ideal of self-present meaning can only be maintained through the repression of the fact that meaning is created through difference and not presence. It is the differential structure of language, as a structured set of differences, that Derrida wants to probe. Like Freud and Lévi-Strauss, he wants to probe beneath surface appearances to what lies beneath, but in his probing Derrida more closely resembles Freud looking for the unconscious than Lévi-Strauss searching for solid structures beneath surface variety. Derrida feels that every text contains not only the message which the author wanted to convey, but also an anti-text which systematically inscribes other messages through and behind the overt one. Derrida calls his search deconstruction, which attempts not a destruction of meaning, but a teasing out of the warring forces of signification within the text (Johnson 1981: xviii). No final meanings are possible on the part of either the author or the interpreter, but rather deconstruction opens the way for continual reinterpretation and conflict between meanings. The openness of meaning is increased by the fact that, just as words take on meaning from other words around them, so do texts. Texts and their meanings do not exist in isolation, but are created through traditions and styles which bind works together. The fact of intertextuality opens out the play of meaning infinitely: texts cannot just be deconstructed in isolation but in terms of all the texts around them which reinforce or refract their voice. The idea of intertextuality is especially important to Derrida as he aims his deconstructive sights at the particular tradition of philosophy, and the motives lying behind what is often called the Plato-Kant canon.

The question of motive is crucial. Philosophical texts within the Plato-Kant canon are written to be clear, rational and convincing, providing a methodical movement towards truth. But behind the rational façade Derrida espies libidinal and playful urges writing their anti-texts. Play, emotion and eroticism are often openly acknowledged in literature, but not in philosophy, limiting the manner in which philosophers can view the world. As one attacking the cool, calculating rationality of much of analytical philosophy, Derrida can be seen to be very much a part of the attack on positivism and thus situated within a tradition stretching back to Nietzsche and Heidegger (Rapaport

1989). Derrida wants barriers between different forms of expression, as these are codified into disciplines, broken down, and looks forward to an open plane of textuality stretching from what we would now call philosophy all the way to poetry in which disruptive, playful, punning forms of language hold sway. An influential, if rather domesticated, version of the need to break down barriers is Rorty's (1989; 1991) attempt to shift philosophy away from being a solid foundation for all knowledge towards being a part of a general therapeutic conversation, although Rorty's added rider that philosophy should often be private, the process of self-invention, has all the resonance of one hand clapping.

For Derrida, language chases its own tale. Never coming to the point, language is an endless chain of creation and immediate re-creation. Such a view has immediate consequences for history. We cannot seek the essential meaning of events or single origins or delimited periods. For Derrida, history is like Nietzsche's, a genealogy: a tangled web of family connections constructed by each family member from their own point of view and sometimes given mythical beginnings to round out the plot. For instance, the story of philosophy that is often told is a linear one beginning with Socrates/Plato, who let the powers of reason loose in the world only for them to be submerged, re-emerging during the Enlightenment to become the spirit of the modern age. But contrary stories are possible, such as that told by Heidegger, for whom the emergence of reason dulled our feeling for the world and led us to be forgetful of Being.

Post-structuralism took from structuralism the view that meaning is internal to language and other symbolic forms. Meaning does not arise from contact with the world. A similar view is found within hermeneutics' concentration on tradition and forms of narrative. Both these sets of views have the advantage over structuralism in that they acknowledge change and history. They have the continuing disadvantage that forms of meaning are hermetically sealed from the world. The strength of post-structuralism is that it opens up possibilities, acknowledging the many elements to the human personality and the countless form of expression possible, which have been channelled and narrowed into modern disciplinary forms, using the term discipline in both its senses. The breaking down of categories has allowed for much exploration, albeit only in terms of meaning and signification. Before looking further at the problems of these forms of the thought, let us consider one example of the entry of post-structuralism into archaeology and the views which it engenders.

Post-structuralism, Hermeneutics and Archaeology

Post-structuralist and hermeneutic approaches have recently entered archaeology at a rush. A number of volumes have recently appeared which introduce post-structuralist and hermeneutic thinkers into the archaeological context (Bapty and Yates 1990; Shanks 1992; Tilley 1990; 1991). However, many of the contributions do not stress applications to archaeological evidence. I will concentrate here on one writer who does apply his broader ideas to archaeology. Yates (1990), in a book designed to introduce post-structuralist thought to archaeology, concentrates on Derrida and Lacan and how their thought can encourage different readings of archaeological evidence, in this case some Bronze Age Swedish rock art. Yates starts by noting that the use of the idea of text in archaeology emphasizes the networking of differences. Artefacts are not bits of the past present in the present, but are joined in chains of signifiers which gain meaning from other sets of signifiers with which they are articulated, forming as a whole an ever-shifting frame of references (Yates 1990: 154–5). He sees both Hodder and Barrett as trying to limit this play of signifiers: Hodder through the definitions of context, which define the terms in which signifiers can be viewed (ibid.: 159); Barrett through recourse to the material nature of the world which is seen to exist as a stability outside the endless play of meanings (ibid.: 156). Rather than resort to any form of limitation on meaning, Yates feels that we should see the past in terms of metonymy and metaphor, sets of relations of signifiers, for 'the past is structured like a language' (ibid.: 169). Age is a matter of lateral distance along the chain of signifiers and the past is a rhetorical space, allowing us to say things in the present which we otherwise could not. The things which would remain otherwise unspoken can be used to deconstruct the present, while still maintaining the integrity and difference of the past. Our knowledge of the past can be used to explicate 'the relationship of the work to itself' (ibid.: 171), displaying again the self-referential nature of all forms of signification. The past is another way in which society speaks to itself.

Using this framework Yates explores rock art as signification, looking not at how these images fitted into Bronze Age society in northern Bohuslän, thus side-stepping Hodder's problem of context, but focusing on what the art can mean to us – or rather, what the images mean to Yates.

Where you may see men and animals, ships and circles, I see only the
free production of signs, in which man as we know him would
disappear, since there would be nothing left against which he could
validate his identity, and something new emerge. I see man-becoming-
beast, becoming-mineral (becoming-ship, becoming-wood), man-
becoming-abstract (becoming-disk), animal-becoming-ship, and so on.
I see the rupture of exclusivity and the opening up of new possibilities,
the liberation of self, the historicisation of man predicated upon his
deconstruction. (Yates 1990: 196)

Here Yates approaches Rorty's view of philosophy as personal quest
and an individual set of meanings. In Yates's approach we can see both
the good and the bad elements of the post-structuralist stance. On the
one hand he opens up the range of interpretations that can be given to the
Bohuslän images, which had previusly emphasized sexual differences between men and women and the coupling of these pairs in terms of mar-
riages, categories all solidly rooted in the present. Yates thinks around
these categories and, as we have seen, not only broadens the nature of the
couplings that may be taking place but introduces the notion of shape-
shifting, blurring the divisions between individuals and people and
things.

What is important here is an attitude to the material world. In his
opening remarks Yates demonstrates the fear of the material world that
runs through much of post-structuralist thought: a fear that meaning
will become grounded in the concrete in the same sense that a ship becomes grounded on a sandbank, that the rolling swell of signification will
cease. This fear is tied to an assumption that the material realm escapes
signification and is therefore beyond history and change. Positivism gave
the empirical world a bad name through attempting to ground its
thought on material facts. The hermeneutic and post-structuralist moves
away from positivism have also taken them away from the empirical,
and reference to the material world is now seen to represent a failure of
nerve, an attempt to reintroduce stable, ahistorical categories.

In contrast to these views I want to stress that although the
objectivist view of the world is objectionable, this should not lead us to
ignore the world totally. Post-structuralism and hermeneutics represent
a joint attempt to move from an objective view of the world towards
the idea that all truth is contingent, being culturally and historically
based. Given such contingency, it is necessary to look at how views
arise out of the cultural matrix and how these views are used.

Hermeneutics and post-structuralism represent a continuing attempt to put science in its place, as one approach to the world among many, attempts which are as old as science itself.

Post-structuralism, in particular, sees meaning as insubstantial and ever-changing. The role of the cultural critic, such as Derrida, is not just to understand cultural forms, but to stir the pot of meaning and to tend the fires beneath to create a bubbling stew of signification. The emphasis on movement and instability comes not just from within academic thought: there are also good social and economic reasons for these trains of thought. In by far the best of recent commentaries on post-modernism, Harvey (1989) has sought the material basis of patterns of thought in new forms of capitalism. In contrast to older forms of mass production, recent forms of capitalism have emphasized the flexibility of production, with short production runs producing a great variety of goods. Others have taken a slightly different tack and emphasized the power of knowledge rather than machinery, where theoretical research is as important as the ability to produce large quantities of goods at a low cost (Bell 1978). Different forms of the manipulation of knowledge have also been highlighted as peculiarities of recent capitalism, such as Baudrillard's (1981) emphasis on the deliberate creation of needs through the manipulation of symbols. The concerted effects of these factors has been to emphasize rapid change and instability in the material conditions of our lives, with new goods appearing to meet needs we never knew we had. The massive and apparently permanent nature of fordist mass production has been replaced by more nuanced and short-lived ranges of goods. Rapidly changing forms of production and consumption are likely to make us in the west see life as an endless play of signifiers, devoid of sound and fury.

There are also reasons internal to academic life which stress the ineffability of meaning. Since the Second World War there has been a vast proliferation of academic activity, such that the academic realm has become far larger than any individual can grasp in their lifetime; thus, for all practical purposes, academia has become an infinite semantic universe. Growth has altered the people within this universe: whereas Wittgenstein never read other philosophers as they said nothing to him, Derrida writes only in commentary on other people's writings. Derrida works in a textual arena composed of philosophy, literature and the arts, and is not often called upon to think about how words and things relate. For those of us writing about material culture, however, such relationships are vital.

Early in the twentieth century Heidegger sought an escape from positivism and a rampant technology through a new relation of people to the world. Central to this was his criticism of representational thought, with its central divide between subject and object. He sought to overcome the subject-object division through the immersion of life and thought within the world. Symbolism, thought and meaning did not form a rarified realm within which we could escape from instrumental logic and its exploitative approach to the world. However, post-war philosophies have sought such an escape, by concentrating on meaning, using language as the measure of all systems of meaning. These later views see any attempt to think about people's place in the world as a resurgence of the positivist urge to control the world through knowledge. Language and meaning do not form a neatly bounded domain. Wittgenstein said that we could see beyond the limits of language, but we could not speak beyond them, and that of which we cannot speak we must pass over in silence. I challenge the view that language or meaning have easily discernible limits. Language and being should not be seen as two contrasting elements of life to be related, but not joined. They have instead an infinitely permeable area between them. Being and knowing have different purposes; the latter can direct our attentions, the former directs our actions.

In this book I am attempting to return to the world we have lost and to examine the links between habit and thought. This means something of a return to the problems of the relationship of people to the world which preoccupied a number of thinkers earlier in the twentieth century. The archaeological example in the last chapter showed that the decorations on Lapita pottery are not evidence of a symbolic sphere detached from the rest of life, but are a form of material culture embedded within the flow of life in the western Pacific and an attempt to cope with some of the problems raised by life. The structure of decorations on Lapita pottery were long-lasting and may have acted to stabilize meaning, helping to provide a thread of continuity in a shifting social situation. To provide an initial answer to what makes us human, we can say that humanity is created through action in the world, that structures of meaning are predicated on those actions and that different forms of time are created through conscious and unconscious action. In the next chapter we shall move towards a model of people's being in the world, first focusing on the intellectual resources of the western tradition on which we can draw to create such a model, and then applying the ideas discussed above to archaeological evidence.

4

Towards a Social Ontology

In chapter 3 I put forward my reasons for being dissatisfied with a stance which concentrates on knowing as the key to understanding human history. Running counter to an emphasis on knowing are those strands of thought focused on being, which examine the flesh-and-blood existence of people in their material surroundings. A focus on being inclines people to say 'I am, therefore I think', reversing the Cartesian epigram, and to concentrate on the things that we are as a starting point for understanding the things that we know. In this chapter I shall explore the notion of social ontology, a structure of being springing from social and material relations in which material existence and thought are intermixed. My starting points are Hegel and Marx, because both thinkers tried to make sense of the modern world as it emerged at the end of the eighteenth century. Both looked at the world not as a static phenomenon, but as a process of becoming. In this process people were a particularly active element. Social groups working on the world produced the material things needed to sustain life, but in the process created knowledge about the world and ultimately shaped the social persona of all those involved. The production of things, knowledge and people immediately invokes discussion of the distinction between subjects and objects. Hegel and Marx wrestled with the subject-object distinction in different ways and tried to show the historical conditions under which such a split came to dominate our thought. Latter-day thinkers within the same tradition, such as Lukács, have also had pertinent things to say on the problems of subjectification and objectification. These discussions will be critically reviewed. Whilst Hegelian and Marxist thought have much to offer, they contain little explicit consideration of the creation of time and space (Harvey 1982), nor do they give the object world an active enough role in the social process. The present chapter forms a pair with chapter 5, as both together consider time and space. Although realizing that it is impossible to split these two terms, for convenience of discussion I shall concentrate on the creation of space in this chapter, leaving thought about time to the next. In both cases, these two dimensions of life are considered in the context of the other two main dimensions of social life: mutuality and materiality.

Materialism in Hegel and Marx

Hegel (1770–1831) created an enormous system of thought within which he tried to solve many philosophical and historical problems. Hegel's life spans the initial period of industrialization in Europe, as well as the changes brought about by the French Revolution. His thought can be seen as a longing for unity in rapidly fragmenting and changing social worlds. He occupied a similar cultural milieu to that of Goethe and had a similar reaction against positivism and mechanistic forms of thought. However, whereas Goethe stressed empathy and an intuition for life as a whole, Hegel sought to develop a rational form of thought which would provide a true means for understanding reality (Marcuse 1973).

Hegel attempted to comprehend in thought the whole of the physical universe and the social world (Berlin 1963). The method he used was dialectical thought. The roots of dialectical thought go back to the Ancient world (Kolakowski 1978), run through early Christian theology and came together as part of Romantic thought in the latter part of the eighteenth century (Habermas 1972; Singer 1983). In this later manifestation there was a tendency to see societies in history as organic wholes which embraced both nature and the spirit and which were moved by the latter. The initial key to Hegel's approach is the idea of movement. Hegel saw the universe not as a static phenomenon, but as a process of becoming. Sometimes he discussed the unfolding of the universe in an abstract manner, considering logical time rather than real time (in *The Science of Logic*); at other points he came closer to real historical time (in *The Philosophy of History*). In all cases he is difficult to understand. Not only is his language impenetrable, but it is also very difficult to gain an understanding of a part of Hegel's thought without having some feeling for the whole. I propose to start with his most abstract expositions and move towards the more concrete, as being the best way of achieving an understanding of his attempt to understand people in the world.

In Hegel's view all things are defined not only by what they are, but also by what they are not. Any particular thing only has separate identity because it is bounded by a whole series of things which are different from it. A meadow with no limits or a sea with no shore would be neither meadow nor sea. Identity is twofold, compounded both of positive and negative characteristics. Such a view is taken to the limit in *The Science of Logic* where Hegel considers being. Being, as such, can only be defined by its opposite, nothingness. Nothingness gives being shape and bounds. It is also something to be overcome. All being is therefore movement, an attempt to overcome nothingness, and is therefore, strictly speaking, not being but becoming. The movement of opposites against each other is at the root of all being. This movement is a dialectical one.

The world, which is apparently stable, is in fact an interplay of movements, a series of positive and negative charges in perpetual motion. Following this conception, Hegel makes the odd-sounding statement that negativity drives movement. All things are constantly ranged against, and attempt to overcome, their opposites. The universe is composed of sets of oppositions which are locked together in a huge system of 'universal contradiction', an interplay of identity and non-identity. Each thing has its own characteristics but is also articulated into an overall system which defines all the things which it is not. Identity and otherness work together to change each other. The most dynamic element in the whole structure is mind.

Mind is the universe come to self-consciousness. Through its power of reflection mind can start to comprehend the process of being and work on it. Mind has the power to shape itself and the universe. Self-consciousness brings freedom. Freedom depends in turn on understanding and for the mind to understand itself it must grasp all the things which it is not. The mind must grasp in thought the series of negativities of which the universe is composed and which help define mind. Thought is an active element in reality and by changing the nature of itself it changes the system of relations constituting itself which together make up the physical universe. As mind's comprehension increases it brings about new sets of relationships, new valences of positivity and negativity. Thought gradually overcomes contradictions and unifies reality, by processes which we cannot go into here. Hegel sees the end of this process as absolute thought; pure thought which has no object, no unmastered external reality. This staggering conception unites thought and physical reality into a single changing system. The prime force for change in this system is mind and its conceptions. Due to the primacy given to mind, Hegel's philosophy has been justly called an idealist one.

We now have some of the main elements of Hegel's dialectical thought before us. Central to his conception is the idea of negativity and contradiction; it is this that makes his thought dialectical. Reality is seen as a process of becoming, in which each element in the whole attempts to overcome its negativities. Reality as motion is part of Hegel's reactions against positivism, which tended to see the world as a fixed set of relations to be observed and understood. This separation between observer and observed finds no place in Hegel's thought. Mind is the most dynamic element in the universe, able to conceive of the relations making up reality and through this evolving conception to change these relations. Thought thus partakes of the dialectical nature of reality and is part of the system of opposing elements. A slightly more concrete example drawn from Hegel will clarify how these abstract notions led him to see the world.

In *The Phenomenology of the Spirit* Hegel lays out the process by which thought and the thinking subject come to self-consciousness. The most famous example given in the explication of this process is the relationship between master and slave (this example is partly famous because of the influence it had on Marx's development of the notion of alienated labour, as we will see below). Here, Hegel is discussing coming to self-consciousness through an idealized example and was not referring to real historical individuals, although the example was given fuller historical content elsewhere in his work. We pick up the story of the growth of self-consciousness at the point where two consciousnesses oppose each other. Following the principle of negation, each needs the other in order to establish a sense of self. Each needs the other to define themselves and, through each looking at what they are not, they can learn more about what they are. An analogous situation in the real world would be the fact that an encounter with an alien culture tells us more about our own social world through the contrasts it supplies, highlighting the things we take for granted. The opposition of the two individuals is not a peaceful one. Each represents for the other an aspect of negativity and Otherness. In Hegel's account the attempt to overcome this opposition leads to an unequal relationship, which he terms as master and slave.

The master forces the slave to work and provide the things they need to live. The relationship thus frees the master from the need to labour. On the face of it the master is in a far more enviable position than the slave. However, as always in Hegel, things are not what they seem. The existential result of the relationship is that the slave is in much fuller contact with the world and the oppositions it offers than the master. First of all, the master comes to see the slave as a thing rather than a human being. As it is the slave who helps the master define his or her own personality, the lack of recognition of the human, conscious status of the slave diminishes the master's ability to understand her- or himself. The slave, by contrast, is all too aware of the human qualities of the master and grows in self-knowledge as a result. Furthermore, the slave is in daily and intimate contact with the material world, altering it through work. The objects that the slave produces objectifies his or her consciousness, transforming the slave's capabilities and energies into objects. These objects stand out against the slave as another form of otherness and increase the process of self-recognition. The master's contact with otherness shrinks and with it goes the ability to act within the series of negative and positive relations which make up the world. By contrast, the slave is a knowing subject in the world defining his or her own personality through contrasts with other human beings and the material world. With the growth of self-definition comes an increased control over human and material relations. Increased control eventually allows the slave to gain freedom through a sudden, revolutionary movement which overcomes the negative, constraining elements in the master-slave relationship.

In this manner freedom is increased in the world and new sets of relations are set up which contain new sets of contradictions. Such sudden change is sometimes known as the 'negation of the negation', through which negative qualities of a particular situation are themselves negated and a new process of becoming is instituted. Hegel referred to this process through the term *Aufhebung*. As Hegel himself said '*Aufhebung* has in the German language a double meaning in that it signifies conserving, *preserving* and at the same time making cease, *making an end*' (quoted in McLellan 1969: 52; Hegel's original emphasis). History thus retains some elements from previous phases of existence but puts an end to the relationships within which they were contained. These new relationships are the mark of change.

Hegel's central focus in the *Phenomenology* was on the subject-object relation, seeing the two as locked in a mutually creative relationship. His logical scheme had much in common with German idealists such as Schiller, who saw history as representing an original unified state between people and the world, splitting into a form of alienation before recombining into a later differentiated unity. Thus for Hegel people come to know themselves through knowledge that the external world is different from themselves. They learn the meaning of human characteristics by comparing them with things that they are not. The object world is the negation of subjectivity and the recognition of this negation brings knowledge, showing negation in its positive aspect. However, the knowledge of objects is not gained passively. People attempt to appropriate the world as an object of desire. Appropriation is in the form of work on the world. Working in the world leads to an active knowledge of how different the world is to people. Such difference is initially overpowering; people are overpowered by the things that they have made and this leads to an estrangement of consciousness. With the growth of self-knowledge this estrangement is overcome by reason and objects are re-incorporated into the subject. The self thus actualizes itself in alienated form and restores self-unity by recognizing that this alienation is the result of self-expression. Historical development is a process of differentiation. An originally generalized humanity comes to concrete particular forms by discovering and incorporating increasingly more aspects of the world into itself and by eventually recognizing itself as the moving spirit in the world.

Although trying to avoid the extremes of idealism and empiricism, Hegel saw the spirit as the moving force of world history. Therefore, although he incorporated the world into his scheme in an active manner, the overall effect was an idealist one. This scheme is crucial to Marx's own, both in the elements he retained from it and the aspects he rejected. It is the elements which Marx rejected from Hegel which are emphasized and the difference between the two stressed by commentators. In contrast, I shall argue that there are rather more fundamental elements of Hegel's scheme in Marx than is often recognized. The nub of the usual difference between Hegel and Marx is seen in the fact that Marx attempted to understand world history in terms of real people and not as the movement of the world spirit, thus rejecting the abstract and often mystical elements in Hegel. Although Marx gave his history a more realistic shape, it is possible to discern underneath a logical structure inherited from Hegel and a teleological movement to history. Powering this movement is the pendulum swing of the subject-object dialectic, the resolution of which ends in an eventual stilling of history, glossed as Absolute Knowledge in Hegel, and Communism in Marx.

Marx: Making Subjects and Objects

Marx was both appalled and fascinated by the unfolding of capitalism during the nineteenth century. He shared this reaction with many of his contemporaries, who revelled in the new opportunities that industrial production offered, but were also astounded by the moral and physical impoverishment factory work brought to many people. The new world was liberating and bewildering by turns: 'All fixed, fast-frozen relations, with their train of ancient and venerable prejudices and opinions, are swept away, all new-formed ones become antiquated before they can ossify. All that is solid melts into air, all that is holy is profaned . . .' (quoted in Berman 1988: 21, who takes the phrase 'All that is solid melts into air' as the theme of his account of modernity). Marx turned to the dialectical method to grasp the nature of pervasive contradictions, both taking inspiration from, and reacting against, Hegel.

Dialectics, as Hegel developed them, are sometimes termed an attempt to overcome 'one-sidedness'. An idea cannot be understood in the absence of its contrary. Marx, in picking up Hegel's method, reacted against what he saw as the one-sided nature of Hegel's thought. This derived from the abstract and idealized nature of Hegel's schemes. Hegel stressed reason and the spirit, such that reality was a process whereby the spirit realized itself. Marcuse pointed out that this stress on reason brought pure philosophy to its own negation, which is to be found in social theory: theory aimed towards the understanding of real social relations. In Marcuse's view (1973: pt II) Hegel was partly responsible for the rise of social theory in that he removed the stress on individuals following their own ends and replaced it with an holistic concept embracing the contradictory sets of relations people have with the material world.

In this regard Marx's work can be seen as an *Aufhebung* of Hegel's. Marx's conception of society and history brought elements of Hegel's thought to an end; they were overcome. Marx did, however, retain many of the elements of the older writer's work. Prominent amongst these is the notion of the totality of relations as a set of pervasive contradictions, the parts of which can only be understood within the relation of the greater whole. The relationship between Hegel and

Marx is controversial. The most famous quote from Marx about this relationship is that he found Hegel standing on his head and set him on his feet. Whereas for Hegel change mainly took place in logical time, for Marx change could not be located in real human history. Thus while he followed the Hegelian method, especially in his early work, he gave it quite a different form: 'Hegel's dialectic is the basic form of all dialectics, but only *after* it has been stripped of its mystical form, and it is precisely this which distinguishes my method' (Marx to Kugelmann, 1868, quoted in McLellan 1977: 524; original emphasis). Rather than attempting to understand the self-realization of the spirit, Marx starts from the 'real man of flesh and blood, standing on the solid round earth and breathing in and out all the powers of nature' (Marx, Frühe Schriften I: 639, quoted in McLellan 1969).

For Marx, nature alone is not a starting point from which to understand society. Instead he follows Hegel and says that it is the two-sided relationship between people and the physical world which is important. Labour is the means by which people alter the world and in a two-way process are altered by it. The world thus provides raw materials to ensure physical survival and safety. Interaction with the world is also a process of self-creation for individuals and society as a whole. Creative activity in the world alters the shape of the physical environment, but humans acting on the world are altered by their encounter with it. Labour is a process of self-creation as a well as of physical creation. Labour and production are for Marx a crucial material starting point when attempting to understand human society. Labour is not primarily an economic category, however, but rather an existential one. Human self-creation in particular historical and social settings is the real subject of Marx's work. Categories of political economic thought are utilized in order to understand this process of self-creation (Marx 1954).

People create their being through labour, but in Marx's view, in all human societies which have existed so far the process of self-creation has been fettered. People are forced into relations with the world and with others which are not of their own choosing and this hampers personal and social growth. Relationships of class and kinship shape human relations and the process of labour and these invariably deform social experience in unhealthy ways. We can easily see here echoes of Hegel's view of the master and slave relationship, with the deleterious consequences it had for both parties. Human history is moved by the need to overcome these unhealthy relationships; moved by contradictions between objective conditions of life and human desires. Human desires attempt to transcend social constraints and, in Marx's view, this can only come about successfully through revolutionary change blowing apart the social fetters. To put the same thought in Hegelian terms, society is striving to overcome its negative elements. In recent social forms labour and production are modulated through relations of class, which forms a dialectical and contradictory structure. The major negative element in capitalist society is seen to be the working class, which concentrates into itself the total negativity of society. This negativity is composed of 'universal suffering and universal injustice', which must be overcome for society to be healthy and free. Working-class labour is most alienated and is the form of activity where free self-creation is least possible.

The crux of the differences between Marx and Hegel, as these are explored in Marx's own writings and in later works, lies in a number of key words: alienation and objectification in the early literature are joined by reification after Lukács. Marx's first and most thorough criticisms of Hegel are contained in the *Economic and Philosophical Manuscripts* of 1844 (Marx 1963). Here he concentrated on the subject-object relation in Hegel, which is part of Marx's coming to terms with his philosophical heritage and putting philosophical ideas in a form which could be worked out through categories abstracted from political economy.

As we have seen in Hegel's logical history, in coming to know objects as other than themselves, people come to know appropriated objects: objects which have been worked on by people. These objects initially appear as alien and remain alien until reappropriated by reason, which recognizes them as products of the human spirit. In reviewing this scheme Marx felt that Hegel had confused other and alien; things are different from people but they are not *necessarily* alien. Human products are the result of objectification. In them, human powers and energy are given concrete form. This objectification of human powers is not always an alienation of them. Under the right conditions, such as communism where private property no longer exists, material production could be the means by which unity can be established between people and nature (Arthur 1982: 15). Under capitalism, by contrast, workers labour on products not of their choosing, under conditions in which they cannot develop their own capabilities, and they must surrender their product to the owners of industry. Here alienation overwhelms objectification, people become estranged from the material world they and others have made, which is in fact an estrangement from human powers and capabilities. As Berger and Pullberg (1966: 61) pointed out, objectification is a necessary part of any society; people must create a world for themselves through the expenditure of their capabilities. Alienation, where products stand opposed to people as alien powers, is only found in some social forms and finds its most developed expression in capitalism.

Hegel, in this view, confused alienation and objectification through not being sufficiently concerned with the historical conditions in which production takes place. Indeed, Marx sees a crucial expression of Hegel's idealism in the fact that Hegel primarily views labour as mental activity, not as physical work (Marx 1963: 174–5). And it is work, in all its manifestations, that Marx sees as crucial to human existence. Not only must people work to survive, but also human powers are personified in production and material things are subjectified in persons. Hegel's dialectical link between people and the world is retained in Marx, who stresses the possible positive effects of labour. The free expenditure of human powers will lead to the open and healthy development of those powers. Marx's final aim is to conceive of and realize social forms in which people's capabilities can be worked out to the full. A healthy society rests on a healthy relationship with nature and all human impediments to such a relationship should be done away with.

Marx's view of the subject-object relationship is at base not an economic one, although it is worked out most fully in the categories of political economy found in *Capital* (Marx 1954). Subject and object are locked in an existential dialectic. The nature of the existential development is given more concrete form than in Hegel, but it still has the same structure and it is possible to see communism as a homologue of Absolute Knowledge. Although nature and humanity are intimately related there is a split between them, where nature is an external force standing out against humanity's inner life. Although Marx attempted to develop the idea of people's sensuous activity, he was never entirely successful due to the retention of so much of Hegel's view of people in the world and the scheme of history attached to it. Not only was history drawn by dialectical logic towards its end, but also the full implications of human beings' relationship to the world were not worked out. Implicit in Marx's view was the idea that although human society had a history the external world did not. He never explored in any detail the ways in which people had changed the world, or how these changes set up new conditions for social action. The full implications of the dialectic between people and nature were never followed through.

In Marx, as in Hegel, there is a unity between the dialectical form of analysis and the dialectical movements of the social world. In both schemes there is an attempt to break down the divide between subject and object. While people may be considered separate from external reality for certain purposes of thought, ultimately they are locked together in a structure of mutual causation. Indeed, Marx stressed that it was a peculiarity of thought in western Europe in recent centuries to make a separation between people and the physical world in which they live, this separation arising from the heightened conditions of alienation found in capitalist societies, where people feel distanced from the world and each other. Changes in external reality were mirrored in the thought of the analyst and both dance to the same two-step rhythm of the dialectic.

The overall logical form of Marx's analysis consisted of the thesis of the objective conditions of human life which meets the antithesis of human desires and requires a synthesis in new social forms with different and often greater forms of alienation. The human dialectic's upward motion reaches a pitch with the capitalist alienation of the working class, and this tension is resolved in a final and real synthesis of the classless society. Because reality has a dialectical form, thought can only comprehend it dialectically through a series of contradictory concepts bound into a unity of contradiction. In Marx's thought, as in Hegel's subject and object are locked into a mutually defining pair, just as subjective and objective forces are. Subjective and objective forces meet in labour, the process of human creation, and it is here that the analysis of history must begin. Although Marx saw clearly the historical conditions under which the subject-object distinction arose, and saw it as an element of the history of thought to be overcome, the fact that he attributed fully active powers to people and saw the material world as raw material to be worked on made it difficult to overcome the distinction. One of the major elements of the scheme I suggest here is to see both material culture and human beings as active forces in the creation of social life, although each has its own special forms of cause. This theme will be taken up below.

The oneness of thought and reality mean that as one changes the other changes, so that both are changing all the time. Constant change has two consequences. First of all, it means that there is no objective point form which to view the world: we cannot step outside the antagonisms and attractions that the world and people in it hold for us. There is no dispassionate point of view; no point of non-involvement. Only scholars who attempt to withdraw from the world could cultivate such a distanced viewpoint of it. Second, there is no unchanging human essence to contemplate. Human beings are the products of history and all elements of the human personality are socially created. Human beings change through the process of interacting with the world in socially sanctioned ways, the process of interaction creating both a view of the world and a view of the self. Marx felt that a further failure of thought in modern western Europe was to mistake present conditions of life for eternal and natural ones. The elevation of present social and psychological conditions to the realm of unchanging norms of life in all times and places had the obvious effect of holding back change. If life in the present was based on the naturally given elements of the human personality it would be useless, not to say foolish, to attempt social change. Marx stressed both the continual change of the human personality under varying social conditions and hence also the possibility for further change. Here we arrive at the practical nub of Marx's work and the point at which he differed most from Hegel. The older thinker was satisfied with the Prussian state as a regulator of human life and saw change occurring in a much more abstract sphere. For Marx the struggle was in the here and now and he attempted to highlight both the alienated, unhealthy patterns of life in the present and the possibilities for change.

Lukács: Hegelian Marxism

It is an understatement of considerable magnitude to say that Marx has evoked controversy about the nature and purpose of thought about society. Lukács' first major Marxist work, *History and Class Consciousness* (1971), represents a continuation of the controversial nature of this thought and has been termed the 'character document of Hegelian Marxism' (Jay 1984: 84). Here Lukács took the stance that to know is to do, using this as a principle to unify all elements of human life. Lukács participated in the early twentieth-century attempts to bring together thought and life into a unity. This concern was also central to the thought of such seemingly disparate figures as Heidegger and Wittgenstein. Goldmann (1977: 1–4) has pointed out that in the period around the First World War, Heidegger helped create existentialism and Lukács developed western Marxism, both of which are central to all later thought. An attack on the separation of subject and object was at the heart of both these intellectual movements, giving them more in common than would at first appear. Lukács based his views around the notion of totality, whilst Heidegger developed a notion of Being, as we shall see in chapter 5.

Just as the founding document of Marxist social theory can be seen to be *Capital* and Engels' *Anti-Dühring* the start of dialectical materialism, then the starting point of western Marxism is Lukács' (1971) *History and Class Consciousness* (Bhaskar 1989b: 115). Lukács work was not so much written in agreement with Marx, but in disagreement with Engels, particularly the latter's application of dialectics to the study of nature. In developing his argument Lukács went back not only to Hegel, but to Vico (Parkinson 1977: 40). Engels saw the same dialectical processes at work in society and nature; hence both can be studied in the same manner. History was almost a part of the processes of nature and human concepts were a conscious reflex of the dialectical motion of the natural world (McLellan 1979: 13). In contrast Lukács took from Vico the principle that we only know what we have made, and the reflex of this principle, which Lukács added for himself: to know is to do. Knowledge differentiated human action from the workings of nature, in Lukács view. For Lukács knowledge came through practice and not contemplation. Lukács saw praxis as the objectification of subjectivity and not the mutual interaction of subject and object (Jay 1984: 114).

For Lukács the crucial feature of Marxism was that it was a method. In particular it was a method for grasping totality, for placing the individual parts of human history together in a whole. Such a totality was a convergence of practical action and knowing. People can understand human history because they have had a part in its creation. Nature is a different matter and Lukács criticized Engels' dialectics of nature, the natural realm lying outside the scope of the things people have made. Lukács used the phrase 'expressive totality' to denote the convergence of thought and praxis. Wholes in human history were the outcome of the intention and practice of a creator, a subject. These subjects were not individuals, but rather broader historical agents, such as classes. In recent history the bourgeoisie and the working class were the major creators of historical forms, their class position being determined by their relationship to the production process. The production process was presently controlled by the middle classes, but they would be ousted by the proletariat who would create their own totality expressive of their aspirations and needs. The process of creation of social forms did not occur healthily throughout human history, but was perverted by features such as reification and alienation (terms which Lukács took from Marx and Hegel and which have since been used widely in western Marxism). Reification refers to the petrification of living processes into static and dead entities which then appear solid and to have a reality of their own. Reification often means that what are in fact social relations come to be viewed as objects. Capital, for instance, which is congealed social labour, is seen to be a thing in itself, rather than part of the social relations of production and exchange. The very distinction between subjects and objects is seen to be the outcome of reification. The existence of objects irrevocably separated from their human subjects is, in Lukács' view, an illusion of the reified consciousness of Kant and others who failed to find the subject which really produces the object. The working class is seen as the concentrated product of alienation in the modern world and the result of a perverted process of human self-creation. Once the working class takes over the process of social production, reification and the alienation from the world which is its result will come to an end. A totality will be created which is more truly expressive of human capabilities and desires than those preceding it.

The tradition of thought from Hegel to Lukács (and beyond) is part of an attempt to place people in the world. For all these thinkers the world is composed of a set of relations and these relations give individual entities their character. Neither things nor people have an essential and unchanging set of properties, but all are bound in a network of relations which gives them their character. A change in one element of the network of relations will reverberate through the whole. A relational view is essentially historical, based around continuous change. Within this network of relations people have an unusual role to play, both as shapers of the physical world and as knowledgeable actors. From Hegel onwards knowledge has derived from a dialectical relationship with the world, whereby the changing relationship that human groups have with things alters their thoughts about themselves and the world in which they live. The central place Hegel gave to the rational apprehension of the universe is replaced in Marx by productive action. Our being as a species derives from sociability and sociability derives from work in the world, people combining in the processes of production, exchange and consumption (Harré 1993). The things that people make embody the sets of relations that went into their making: material culture represents in congealed form both social and object relations. Material culture can seem to us like a series of stable entities, but tables and chairs are the result of moving sets of relations, a moment in the on-going process of production and consumption. The mutually creative relations between people and the world help break down the distinction between passive objects and active subjects. Lukács saw history as a moving stream of objectification and subjectification.

While I am in full agreement with the tenor of these arguments and take much inspiration from them, there is a series of gaps in the ideas relating subject and object which perpetuate the distinction between the two terms. The chief of these is the absence of a theory of material culture which allows things to be a fully active force in human history. In the next three chapters I shall attempt to provide some idea of the active nature of the material world, based around the creation of time and space through social and material relations. The material world is a part of us and not an external environment in which we move and act; it is part of our social force. In order to probe the role of people in the world further I shall now go on to develop the notion of social ontology, which focuses on a social state of being in the world.

Social Ontology

The crucial element in the work of Hegel, Marx and Lukács is the mutual making of people and things, and the role knowledge plays as both a producing element and a product in that making. Hegel and Marx used the subject-object relation to generate the movements of history, whereas Lukács tried to overcome this dichotomy altogether by immersing both subject and object into the totality of historical relations. All three repudiated any real separation not only of subject and object, but of correlative concepts such as mental and physical, or culture and nature. Such repudiation gives us a set of historical views totally different from most of those which exist within archaeology at present. Although there has been some discussion of the dichotomy set up between subject and object in archaeological thought (Shanks and Tilley 1987: 9,11), there has been little systematic attempt to overcome this split. Thus human social forms are either seen as modelling themselves onto the structure of the environment, through solving the adaptive problems it poses (Gamble 1986: 66), or as

evaluating the world through cognitive processes leading to an archaeology of mind (Mithen 1990) or to a pervasive opposition between
nature and culture (Hodder 1990), or are viewed as symbolic forms
creating and transforming themselves in a space abstracted from the
material world (Yates 1990). Here I hope to overcome these oppositions and to concentrate on people's immersion in the world over the
long term.

In order to do this I shall take the idea of making, but shall stress the
history of the material world as well as the human element. The world
created by past generations becomes the arena for socializing future
groups. This world becomes not something people know but something they are, and is thus part of their social creative powers. The
world changes its physical shape as the landscape is remodelled and
resources are used in different ways, and it then enters into human
history as an ever-changing active force. History needs to be written not
just to take account of how people operate in an environment, how
culture shapes nature, but to look at how the transformed world is itself
transforming. Material things have both enabling and constraining
properties so far as human action is concerned. For instance, salination
proved a major constraint to the irrigated farming systems of the
Middle East in the Bronze Age, just as it does in Australia today.
Constraints on human action arising from people's use of the world
must be balanced by the enabling aspects of material things. Both
pottery and metal technologies have provided extremely plastic media
since the early and mid-Holocene, opening up previously unsuspected
dimensions of social being. It makes no sense to separate clay and metal
ores on the one hand from human action on the other in their history
of interaction. Fired clay opened a new dimension into which certain
forms of being human expanded, making use of the possibilities that
this material provided. It is not the objective properties of clay itself
that allowed this to happen, but the conjunction of its physical
properties and social needs. Once joined, the material and the social
cannot be considered separately and pottery becomes part of the
trajectory of long-term social being in many parts of the world; an
habitual, unthought element of life, which provided the basis for a rich
stream of innovations in forms and decoration.

In this context it is worth reiterating a point made in chapter 2: there
is no such thing as social relations; these exist and change only as they
are played out in material forms. Our personae are both social and
material: the world we have transformed in turn transforms us. The

material realm has its own set of properties, which are distinct from social relations, but not separate from them. As the world has its own structure it can surprise us, making some avenues of action unexpectedly difficult, or opening up new horizons. These horizons exist in the landscape that we occupy and in individual material things, creating a sense of the possible and the correct. A social ontology is both an open space to be explored and a set of limits imposed by people and the world. Possibility and limit exist in four dimensions, four moving moments of being: space, time, mutuality and materiality, all of which are both socially created and creating. I see these four dimensions as being shaped into different time-space systems, designating the spatial and temporal unfolding of social action. In this unfolding the temporal dimension is particularly important and forms the subject of chapters 5 and 6. Here I shall concentrate on the other three dimensions, starting with that of space.

Space

Geographers point out that social processes do not occur on the head of a pin, they always have spatial extent and character. The spatial characteristics of social relations also imply temporal modes deriving from the pattern of events occurring in regions and methods of connecting different areas. Space and time are not seen as abstract qualities providing the medium of social action, but rather as dimensions created through the concrete operation of social forms. So, for instance, in recent geographical literature much attention has been paid to the creation of particular forms of time and space in the development of capitalism, whether this be through the circulation of capital and commodities, the creation of uneven development across the globe or modern concepts of time and space in a shrinking world.

The literature on time and space is considerable and impossible to summarize here in any detail (useful general discussions of these themes are contained in Giddens 1984; Gregory and Urry 1985; Gregory and Walford 1989; Peet and Thrift 1989). However, a number of themes stand out which will be useful for my subsequent discussion. The first is the dichotomy between space and place. Harvey (1989: pt III) points out that one of the central problems of modernity is to reconcile an understanding of the widespread structures of space (the world capitalist economy with its ebbs and flows) at one scale with the sense of perspective rooted in familiarity and long experience drawn from being in a particular place. This is not just an academic problem and many of the social stresses of the late twentieth century result from the confrontation between micronationalism and broader political and economic structures. Academically, the split between space and place results in two rather separate literatures.

Studies of place or landscape are concerned with the nature of local experience, which is often studied from a humanist, phenomenological or existentialist perspective (Agnew and Duncan 1989; Cosgrove and Daniels 1988; Seamon and Mugerauer 1989); approaches very similar to these are found in anthropology (Appadurai 1988a; 1988b; Munn 1977; 1983; 1986; 1990). Various concerns converge in the study of place and landscape, centring around the nature of local experience and the notion of landscape as a symbolic form. Cosgrove (1989) points out that the word 'landscape' emerged with the Renaissance and was based on a particular form of viewing arising from perspective and geometry, which allowed landscapes to be laid out in an ordered manner or to be represented in realistic fashion on canvas. In Cosgrove's view all landscapes are symbolic; verbal, visual and built landscapes have an interwoven history.

The literature on space is less concerned with experience and has more to do with economic and social relations relating separated places and times. The main point is that space is not an abstract entity, 'the most solid of all geometries', but constitutes 'hierarchically ordered arenas of social practice' (D. Gregory 1985: 315). Space and time are seen as relational; that is, they only exist in relations between things and practices. Practical action produces time and space, which in turn binds social forms. To use Giddens' terms, time and space are both produced and producing: they are both the outcome and the medium of social action. Time and space are irretrievably linked. Soja (1985: 91) points out that the production of space also constitutes the making of history and that the development of capitalism can be seen as an historical sequence of spatial forms, which soon came to span the globe. Similarly, Giddens (1984: ch. 3) sees different social forms as having various types of extension in time and space, shaping time and space into socially conditioned configurations.

Here a brief consideration of the work of Hägerstrand (1975; 1976) can be used to flesh out some of these points. Hägerstrand tried to understand the routinized nature of daily life, which he saw as having six determinants. The first of these is the corporeality of the body, our means of action in and on the world. Our bodily existence gives us each a personal timescale in our movement towards death. The idea of death brings with it the finitude of all human life, encouraging each culture to see time as a scarce resource. Time is linked to space through the realization that all movement in space is movement in time, and space too has its limitations in that two people cannot occupy the same space at the same time. Finally, the limited nature of human powers means that we can only successfully engage in one task at a time, constraining our uses of time and space. Although influential, Hägerstrand's ideas have not escaped criticism: he has considered the constraints of time and space rather than their enabling aspects and his individuals are still abstracted from the social process – they pursue their own projects but we do not know how they came upon these projects or why they are important (Giddens 1984: 116–8).

The emphasis on the production of time and space accords in some ways with the points made above about the mutual transformation of people and the world. From my perspective, what is missing from the geographical literature is a true notion of mutuality: that people shape the world as it shapes them. The stress in the literature on both space and place is on people as the active element, their physical surroundings constituting simply the raw material to be shaped by the social process. The discussion of place does include some mention of the way landscape shapes experience, but this is usually seen as an influence on symbolic forms rather than on concrete patterns of action.

If time and space are constituted by people, we must ask how is time timed and space spaced, moving conceptually from familiar passive forms of these terms to active ones. By doing so I am deliberately trying to move away from an abstract view of space. Space is not an external medium in which we move and act and which we look out onto as internal subjects viewing the external world. Rather it is something within us, just as we are within it. Each of us shares a general social notion of space, which is a bodily-derived sense of how to operate. Socialization is an initiation into a spatial pattern of activities in a humanly created landscape. The system of reference created by the structure of our acts both creates spaces in which to work and forms us spatially. Our social being derives from the structure of our acts as these extend over space and through time. Our bodies are spatially attuned through the process of socialization and this creates standards for our relationships with other people. Reference sees space as a dimension in which things are done, tasks carried out and skills deployed. Space can then be seen as room-for-manoeuvre, a set of areas in which life can be lived and through which particular patterns of actions are possible.

Room-for-manoeuvre is derived from forms of landscapes which are created so as to enable particular forms of human life and to help to channel future action. As we saw in chapter 2, island Melanesia has a particular physical structure created by the pattern of islands and sea. Entry into this area was made possible by seafaring and skills for dealing with the sea were honed within this environment. The seafaring skills deployed in this set of physical conditions created patterns of movement which gave a basic shape to life. Furthermore, over the millennia the landscape was re-shaped through the movement of animals and raw materials. For instance, patterns of movement and contact between groups influenced the amount of obsidian available, the form in which it moved and the frequency with which it moved. Thus all aspects of the reduction and use of obsidian were predicated upon the patterns of movement of people which helped transfer the material from the source to the areas of consumption. The skills deployed in flaking and using obsidian derived in part from the spatial structure of life. Patterns of movement underlie the system of reference, joining disparate places in chains of action. Much of this action was unthought and the spaces it created were implicit. We can see that over 30,000 years the human spaces of the Bismarck Archipelago changed, with quite different patterns of movement and action 3500 years ago to those of the initial period of colonization. Room-for-manoevure is not only created in obviously cultural products, such as houses, but within the landscape as a whole. Landscapes are social products, but are not first and foremost symbolic constructs or landscapes of the mind. Rather they are spaces carved out by patterns of action, which then help to channel future action. The symbolic aspect of the landscape is derived from the actions carried out in it: a conscious gloss on unthought practice. The notion of reference allows us to look at the landscape as a whole and the patterning of activities across the landscape, breaking down the need to see archaeological sites as special spatial points to be privileged in analysis. It is thus the changing pattern of activity as a whole which should form the basis for understanding the human creation of space.

As a further brief example let us look at Paul Carter's analysis of the spaces created by the European settlement of Australia. Part of these spatial relations derived from the nature of landscape: horizon was all on this predominantly low, flat continent. The horizontal nature of building and settlement also derived from the small size of European populations in the first century of occupation, which tended to straggle across the countryside, rather than build upwards. When suburban living started in the late nineteenth century it formed an unconscious echo of bush settlements: 'Just as huts were strung out along pack-tracks, so, albeit with greater geometrical regularity, quarter-acre blocks were threaded along suburban orthogonals' (Carter 1987: 284). Within less than a century the spaces created in Australia had become part of people's social being, to be repeated without the need for forethought in a new setting. The dispersed and horizontal nature of settlement also fitted within more conscious desires and norms, forming a history of spaces with both deliberate and unconscious elements: 'The detached, self-owned house on its quarter-acre block, surrounded by its high paling fence, is an urban memory of the country farm. The emphasis on being independent and self-contained is common to both' (P. Morgan, unpublished MS, quoted in Carter 1987: 279).

Materiality and Mutuality

The term 'materiality' refers to human relations with the world, 'mutuality' looks at human inter-relations. Materiality and mutuality are linked here for the simple reason that they are inseparable. Full social relations can only be set up through making and using things; full relations with the material world only come about through people working together. Here we are not just looking at how people are directed towards the world but at how the structure of the humanly created world opens up certain possibilities and closes down others. Each generation is socialized within a particular landscape and this becomes something that we are, providing both a sense of possibility and a series of material opportunities and constraints. We approach the world from within and do not encounter it as a foreign object. A familiar landscape is not nature in opposition to our culture, but a web of connections which people have become used to warping in special ways. To use the postmodernist formula: we are always already within the world. People are directed towards the world by the balance between materiality and mutuality, and it is directed towards us, offering not just a stage setting, but both room-to-manoeuvre and bounds on our movements.

Let us consider two contrasting examples of mutuality and materiality. In many societies in present-day Papua New Guinea there exists an unbreakable connection between people and the things they have made or exchanged. In an article which sparked considerable discussion, C. Gregory (1980) made a distinction between gift exchange, which is predicated upon inalienable labour, and commodity exchange, in which the products of labour can be alienated. Because commodities can be alienated from the people who produced them they set up transactions between individuals who remain independent of each other. By contrast, gifts always retain an attachment to the person who produced them and thus create a lasting and dependent relation between producer and receiver. Lasting attachments limit the economic uses to which gifts can be put: in particular, they make capital accumulation impossible. Gift giving creates a complex set of threads binding individuals and groups, linked by relationships of debt (Gosden 1989b). Commodity exchange leaves no lasting social attachments and is aimed at profit through buying cheap and selling dear. Gifts and commodities represent a quite different balance between materiality and mutuality. Gifts use the material world in order to set up unequal relations between people in a system dominated by mutuality. Commodities use people to accumulate material wealth in a system of materiality. However, neither gifts nor commodities represent the only forms which systems of materiality and mutuality can take: these terms are used here as examples. We must also be aware of the complexity of the balance between alienable and inalienable labour in any system of production and exchange (see the discussion on these terms in the correspondence in *Man* 17 and 18 for the many social and economic factors implicated in these different forms of labour).

A dual emphasis on social and material relations exists in all societies in an uneasy relationship. Despite our own apparent concentration on material wealth as the road to success, we cannot see the tension between the social and the material as being resolved in an evolutionary framework in which societies generally move towards increased material production. Today we in the first world emphasize the separateness of economic relations, and of material profit and high consumption as the road to social well-being, but have become uncomfortably aware over the last two centuries that this is at the expense of many forms of social relatedness. Even in the western world things are used for mutuality: meals, drink and presents all help maintain relations between people. No form of life is so one-sided that it concentrates solely on the material or the social.

Whether a society is directed towards the production of things or the creation of social relations encourages the development of skilled action in particular directions. Again to make a crude distinction, if the main social goal is the creation of material wealth then many forms of mutuality will centre around the creation and use of materials. Skills in the production and movement of materials will multiply and the world will tend to be seen as a series of raw materials to be appropriated, giving a particular form to the creation of space. By contrast, an emphasis on power and success through human relationships will stress bringing people together outside the directly productive realm. Mutuality, in general terms, is to do with the ways in which people are combined and divided and this interacts with the spatial structure of reference centred on human relations. Materiality sets up reference around skilled productive action and forms complex links between sites of production and consumption.

In developing these means of looking at long-term historical trends I am trying to move away from a concentration on the institutional structures of society and the economic basis for these structures. Rather than search for institutional structures, we should probe the background dispositions which gave rise to a particular directedness of action. These dispositions can be understood in terms of people's creation of time and space, which in turn derive from the nature of skilled action within the world. Nietzsche called abstract discussion 'the last smoke of an evaporating world'. In order to show how the general ideas outlined above can give us an understanding of long-term change, some application to archaeological evidence is now necessary.

The Neolithic in Britain and Europe

In this chapter we begin the consideration of a case study from the Neolithic and early Bronze Age periods in southern Britain. I shall initially consider the work of Barrett, Bradley and Green (1991) at Cranborne Chase, and this will be complemented by further examples in chapter 5 and 6. The Cranborne Chase work has been chosen as the best example I know of a theoretically informed and thoroughly worked out empirical case study. The theory employed in the Cranborne Chase work shows an explicit consideration of space, time and practice, bringing them close to the position I am developing in this book.

The study of the Neolithic represents a boom area in British archaeology over the last few years. It is also a time period in which archaeologists have challenged old frameworks and views and developed new ones. In the late 1960s and early 1970s, data from the Neolithic period was used to construct a social archaeology using neo-evolutionary ideas, such as those of Sahlins discussed in chapter 2. Renfrew, one of the main inspirations behind attempts to develop a processual social archaeology, concentrated on institutional structures as laid out in the band-tribe-chiefdom-state scheme and saw history as registering the progress from one position to another within this scheme (Renfrew 1975). The Neolithic of southern Britain provided a good example of a chiefdom, becoming more centralized and complex with the advent of the Bronze Age (Renfrew 1973). It was thought that the monuments of the late Neolithic and early Bronze Age were produced through the central organizing power of the chiefs, who could gather together the agricultural surplus which made large building projects possible and who coordinated the mass labour which built the monuments.

Such views have come to be questioned in recent years, both on grounds of data and theory. On the theoretical level it is asked whether the base-superstructure model employed by neo-evolutionary thought is a productive view; that is, whether we can separate out the economic sphere and see developments in subsistence and craft production as the key to increasing social hierarchy. The data on farming in the Neolithic has also come to be seen in a different light. It has become obvious that farming was not adopted overnight in Britain, causing a revolution in social and economic circumstances. For most of the Neolithic period in southern Britain there is no good evidence of permanent settlement; rather, people seem to have moved constantly, leaving little trace of houses or hamlets. Close inspection of seed assemblages from the period indicates a predominance of wild plants, with cultivated cereals forming only a minor portion of the diet. By contrast, new forms of domesticated animals, especially cattle and pigs, may have made a considerable difference to people's lives. Taken together, the evidence demonstrates some continuity with the Mesolithic period, with mobility a key element of life. Rather than settling down and creating a way of life predicated on agricultural surplus, people stayed on the move, although patterns of mobility may have been altered by the new needs of herd animals and small garden plots used to grow roots and cereals (J. Thomas 1991: 18–21).

The Neolithic is now thought to be less an economic revolution and more the adoption of a new symbolic structure, a novel means of representing the world through symbols and rituals (Hodder 1990; J. Thomas 1991). There are great benefits in the move away from neo-evolutionary views which relate people to the world in purely economic forms. However, there are also problems with taking a view centred around symbolic action, as was discussed in the last chapter. In these new models of the Neolithic there is an uneasy relationship between symbolism and practice. It is not that practical action is ignored: a statement such as that of J. Thomas (1991: 11), who says that being in the world precedes consciousness of the world, can be found regularly in the new views on the Neolithic. Rather, there is no fully developed model linking everyday practice to ritual and symbolic forms. The work of Barrett (1987; Barrett et al. 1991) represents the most concerted attempt to situate symbolic forms within structures of practical action, as is discussed below, using the distinction between discursive and non-discursive forms of life. Knowledgeable, discursive action is seen as the starting point in understanding any form of life: 'all social actions are culturally meaningful and find their expression in a symbolic medium' (Barrett et al. 1991: 7). Arising from the problems of linking symbolism and basic forms of practice, two sources of discomfort can be sensed within the new approaches to the Neolithic. Ritual action, so central to these interpretations of the Neolithic, is difficult to separate from the mundane within the evidence: ' "Ritual" is a form of action; archaeological sites may be among the places where such actions took place but this does not mean that they were necessarily dedicated to their performance. Rituals can form part of everyday life . . .' (ibid.: 83). The second uncertainty has to do with problems of social structure. As a result of the demise of neo-evolutionary models, most authors try to 'avoid identifying archaeological evidence with a particular form of social organisation and instead attempt to understand routine social practices maintained within given social conditions' (ibid.: 228). There is, however, little notion of how the public discursive life of the group may have operated in its spatial and temporal aspects, and how this related to habitual forms of life.

Although in sympathy with these new approaches to the Neolithic, I prefer to emphasize forms of involvement with the world which are not directly meaningful. In entering a temporal and spatial world beyond meaning, we also need to consider how meaning is generated and thus how habit and thought interact in the long-term history of groups. The Cranborne Chase study looks at the creation of landscapes through social forces over a period of several millennia and the changing deployment of mobile forms of material culture within these landscapes. It thus provides an excellent set of material through which to consider how time and space are created over the long term through the forces of materiality and mutuality.

Cranborne Chase

The Cranborne Chase study utilizes a relatively small area and a long time-scale in order to explore some of the broader questions of change within British prehistory (Barrett et al. 1991). The study synthesizes archaeological work carried out over 100 years, starting with Pitt-Rivers' excavations at the end of the nineteenth century and ending with the campaign of fieldwalking and excavation coordinated by the authors over the last twelve years. The result combines theory and data in a manner rarely before carried out in Britain. The authors pursue the question of how the landscape has been created between the early Neolithic and late Iron Age periods, which together span over 3000 years. Concentrating on the large monuments such as the Dorset Cursus, they develop the point that over much of the period of interest people configured their activities around monuments rather than moulding themselves to the shape of the environment.

Although the authors do not make heavy weather of their theoretical stance they pursue certain issues consistently and these need examination before considering the data. Much inspiration derives from the work of Giddens, who has influenced Barrett especially (Barrett 1987). Social systems are made up of the play of larger forces and human individuals. Both of these are socially effective in Giddens' view, the broader institutional structure providing the general shape of social action and the individual actors forming the means by which institutions work, shaping these workings as individuals put them into practice (ibid.: 8). Unless human agents are included within our view of the social process, institutionalized practice looks like an abstract force operating outside of human control. Actors change institutional structures through practice in so far as they understand symbolic structures and social codes. Social actions can then be seen as patterns of discourse through which people negotiate matters of importance to their own advantage. Social actions take place within fields of discourse defining the shape of the socially possible and channelling practical actions into meaningful courses (ibid.: 11).

In applying these ideas to the Cranborne Chase material Barrett et al. focus on social reproduction, which probes the way in which people reproduce the material conditions of their life through their actions on the environment and reproduce the social system through maintaining the demands of social discourse. Social action is first and foremost practical action, and this is transformed into discursive knowledge under certain conditions. One particular way in which discursive knowledge is created and put into effect is through ritual. Ritual expresses the symbolic medium which makes all action socially meaningful and can allow some people to control those meanings: 'It is through the highly formalised drama of ritual that dominant readings of cultural symbols are created' (Barrett et al. 1991: 7). These readings are worked out through the landscape. Time and space are not just tools for archaeologists to order sites and sequences, but the matrix and framework within which social action takes place. The landscape was not simply a source of food and other useful things; it was culturally defined and given meaning as people acted within the world (ibid.: 8).

Barrett et al. do not aim to look at changes in social formations, but to uncover changing patterns of practice, taking ritual as a starting point. From this viewpoint, the earlier Neolithic is seen to be dominated by a series of rituals transforming the dead into ancestral figures. Reference to the ancestors is thought to be the means by which access to land and resources was negotiated. Human bones played a central role in a complex series of rituals and appear to have been moved across the landscape many times before they were finally buried. These rituals helped obliterate individuals and individualized authority, stressing instead the strength and continuity of the group. From the late Neolithic onwards there is a long-term shift in the rituals surrounding the dead and a move towards the burial of individuals. Individual burial helps to provide the basis for individual, rather than group, forms of authority and creates the arena within which power and access to resources can be transferred from one generation to the next. The late Neolithic and early Bronze Age landscapes, with their enormous variety of monuments and forms of deliberate deposition, are seen to be the result of complex forms of classification of both the living and the dead. From the middle Bronze Age there is a shift in the social process: rituals to do with the dead no longer dominate and instead the main archaeological evidence derives from enclosed settlements and their surrounding field systems. These changes are not seen to mark a total discontinuity with earlier periods, but to derive out of the greater emphasis on individual authority. Settlements show increasing evidence of the harvesting and processing of food, and the dead are buried with vessels for storing and cooking food. The strategies of authority and inheritance of authority are now thought to revolve around the cycles of human and agricultural reproduction. An emphasis on the dead has been replaced by a concentration on the living.

In their stress on practical action and the unfolding nature of social relations these views come close to my own. There are, however, also significant differences. I would first of all question whether ritual is the only point to start from when attempting to understand the social process as a whole. As I see it, overt public symbolism is employed to cope with more general social problems. The source of these problems lies in the patterns of everyday life, the unconscious patterns of reference which make up the bulk of interactions between people and people and people and the world. Symbolic action is a structure of conscious reference, at once overlaying and deriving from the unconscious referential structure of skilled habitual action. Conscious reference cannot be seen as ritual, a repetitive set of practices to do with life, death and other rites of passage. Conscious forms of reference help to make manifest the problems of unconscious practice. In the Lapita case, the dynamism created by the colonizing process and constant movement through the area was damped down by the wide distribution of similar forms of material culture and the repeated acts which may have been associated with this material culture. Consequently the monuments of the Neolithic and early Bronze Age are not best seen as ritual forms, but as attempts to come to terms with the problems of life during this period. Such a link means that we can compare the evidence from the monuments with that contained within the landscape as a whole, playing one off against the other. The conscious use of material culture makes it open to manipulation and plays of power. However, repetition will cause what is initially thought out to become habit. There is a complex interplay between the unconscious system of reference which causes the creation of particular coping mechanisms. Through time these coping mechanisms become part of habit and can give rise to further problems in their own right. There is a long-term cycle here, with elements of habit becoming conscious and sinking back into habit again. From a methodological point of view we need to start with the broad pattern of evidence across the landscape, which shows recurrent patterns of practice over the long term. This broader picture of the long term can then allow us to place the more scattered evidence of short-term symbolic action into some wider perspective.

What is the general direction and shape of unconscious reference and what are the changes it undergoes between the Neolithic and the Iron Age? The period of the Neolithic to the early Bronze Age seems to me to provide good evidence of an emphasis on mutuality, with things being used to set up and maintain links between people. People were basically orientated towards other people. There is very little direct evidence of productive activity on the landscape, from either the agricultural or craft production sphere, whereas there is considerable evidence of the movement of material. Much of this evidence results from the consumption of food and other items in social settings and the careful deposition of the remains of these activities (J. Thomas 1991). This structure of mutuality was spatially extensive, involving wide-spread similarities in material culture, such as pottery and the long-distance movement of items such as stone axes. Structures involving links between people may well have been volatile, due to ever-changing connections between individuals and groups. The range and complexity of material culture increases in the late Neolithic and early Bronze Age. The middle Bronze Age sees a rapid shift to a structure in which materiality is central. Now there is abundant evidence of production, in the form of field systems, agricultural processing of plants and animals, and lesser evidence of metal and pottery-making. From the middle Bronze Age onwards there exists a much more directed state of being: people focus their actions on a much smaller area and are more involved in localized sets of connec-tions. Evidence of a conscious system of reference is considerably less. This is not due to the shift from a ritual-dominated society to one of profane relations, but perhaps a sign of a less problematical, volatile social world, more constricted in space and more directed in purpose. The following brief excursus into the Cranborne Chase material will look at the structured system of reference as it unfolds over a series of scales and through continued human action. The main point at issue is the relationship of habit to thought over long-term cycles of change.

Cranborne Chase (figure 4.1) lies in central southern England on the borders of Hampshire, Dorset and Wiltshire, some 35 kilometres from the coast. It is an upland area lying between 76 and 257 metres above

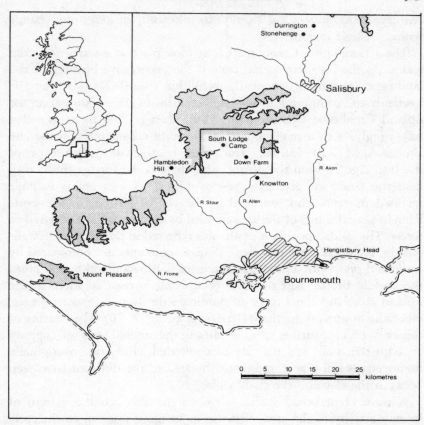

Figure 4.1 The location of Cranborne Chase and the major sites in the surrounding area. (From Barrett et al. 1991, *Landscape Monuments and Society*, Cambridge University Press, fig. 1.1.)

sea level; much of it is chalk downland, although there is a significant area of clay with flints. This contrasts with the lower-lying Hampshire Basin, which has a varied series of clays and sandy soils. The major monument of the area, the Dorset Cursus (see figure 4.2), runs some 10 kilometres along the springline, adding a human reinforcement to the division between upland and lowland. Cranborne Chase is centred on Pitt-Rivers' Rushmore Estate, his centre of operations for extensive excavations in the late nineteenth century. The Chase has been covered by woodland since the early medieval period, thus preserving its many monuments from the effects of modern ploughing. This fact, plus the quality of the archaeological work undertaken there over the last century, makes it an ideal location for the study of long-term change within a single region.

The action within Cranborne Chase took place at a series of spatial scales. At the broadest spatial scale is the progressive opening of the landscape, starting in the early Neolithic (3300–2500 bc) on the lowlands and continuing in the late Neolithic (2500–1700 bc) on the upland Cranborne Chase region. From then on the forest is felled increasingly, with a major phase of clearance taking place in the late Bronze Age (1250–750 bc), creating the relatively open landscapes of the Iron Age. Within the upland area there is the further division of land use based on geology: the clay-with-flints area seems to have retained its woodland longer than the chalk. Indeed, in the post-Roman period much of the area covered by clay-with-flints reverted to forest. The landscape divisions are also reflected in the fauna: throughout the Neolithic on the upland, bone assemblages are dominated by cattle and pigs, with a large percentage of wild woodland fauna. From the middle Bronze Age onwards there is an increase in sheep in the upland area, and these come to dominate the Iron Age assemblages, especially in sites on the chalk (Barrett et al. 1991: 20). The clearing of the forest had the further effect of causing the original loess soil capping on both the chalk and the clay to be eroded, changing an originally homogenous soil type throughout the area to the differentiation seen between the clay and the chalk (ibid.: 17).

A number of broad spatial divisions run through the pattern of human activity in the area, albeit in a changing fashion. In the early Neolithic period much of the study area was covered by forest, with the major concentration of settlement on the lowland. The main focus of the referential system of activities would have been in the lowlands, with only some activities, such as animal herding and flint procurement, taking place in the upland. The broad pattern of evidence has been revealed by fieldwalking (covering some 85 square kilometres) most of the present-day area under the plough (Barrett et al. 1991: 29). This revealed little flintwork (three times as much was found on the lowland), few potsherds and a small number of pits. The major set of evidence comes from large monuments built between 2800 and 2600 bc, which include the Cursus and a large number of associated long barrows, most of which were within 2.5 kilometres of the Cursus (figure 4.2). Some of the long barrows appear to have been built before the Cursus, which was itself built in a number of stages. The banks and ditches of the Cursus were actively maintained for a relatively short period, ending around 2600 bc. In the centuries preceding this date a complex set of spatial patterns was imposed on the landscape, many of which remain to this day. These monumental constructions seem to have taken place prior to the first real settlement of the upland and were hence carried out by groups from the lowland on periodic visits to the downs. This early Neolithic world was spatially extensive and any set of tasks carried out in the uplands was geared towards the more

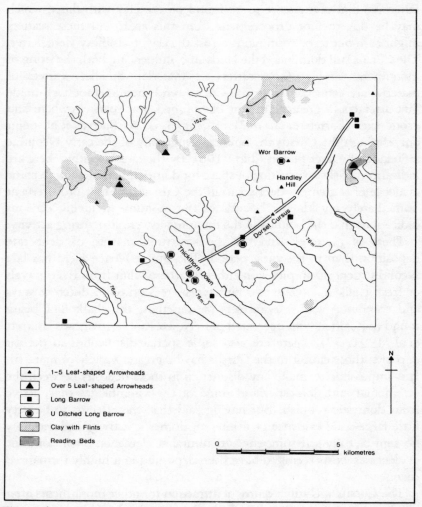

Figure 4.2   The earlier Neolithic period in Cranborne Chase. (From Bradley et al. 1991, *Landscape Monuments and Society*, Cambridge University Press, fig. 2.4.)

intensive activity in the lowlands. Within this extensive world a series of very precise spaces were inscribed on the landscape, which were the focus of activities which show up archaeologically as acts of deposition in the ditches around the long barrows, which continued for many centuries (ibid.: 36–43).

By the late Neolithic there was a quite different use of the Chase. Greater clearance had created a more variegated landscape, hinting that a wider range of activities was now being carried out on the uplands. Extensive flint scatters are to be found on the clay-with-flints, which may be due to flint procurement from this area, and these scatters might turn out to be continuous across the clay if visibility were better. The Cursus still dominated the landscape, influencing both the siting of monuments and surface scatters of material. Smaller scatters of material are connected with the Cursus, and these include well-made flint artefacts, a greater amount of polished flint than elsewhere and exotic axes (Barrett et al. 1991: 64, fig. 3.4). As Barrett et al. point out, through the Cursus the political geography of the early Neolithic influences the later period (ibid.: 106). By the late Neolithic there are indications of the structuring of space for domestic activities, with some evidence of settlement debris within the Cursus and flint procurement immediately outside the bounds of the monument, giving obvious indications that the bounds of the monument were structuring activity.

There is more evidence of the structured nature of deliberate deposition than in the early period. The site at Firtree Field has late Neolithic deposits in pits with either weathered flint from river gravels or fresh chalk flint. The two flint types are worked in different ways and combined with varying sets of materials, the chalk flint being found more often with decorated pottery, axes and arrowheads (Barrett et al. 1991: 77). There are also some spatial distinctions in the pit deposits: those closest to the Cursus have a greater variety of material. It is impossible to make any distinction in these deposits between the ceremonial and domestic, and some of the assemblages may derive from domestic rubbish. But having said this, there seems to be very little large-scale evidence of utilitarian domestic activity and certainly no sign of fully self-sufficient agricultural settlements. Such domestic evidence as exists seems to have been deposited in a highly formalized manner.

The Cursus was still a centre of attraction for other monuments after it went out of active use. The Wor Barrow complex shows the latest stages of the long barrow tradition and the earliest stages of round barrows, showing that in both there was a long and gradual move to individual burial between the late Neolithic and early Bronze Age (Barrett et al. 1991: 87). The one henge near the Cursus at Wyke Down has a series of deposits which change through time, which include the Grooved Ware pottery characteristic of henge sites and human bones. Many of these deposits seem again to have been aligned with the Cursus (ibid.: 105).

The late Neolithic world was even more spatially extensive than that of the early Neolithic. In the upland area around Cranborne Chase forest clearance had opened up the landscape, making it a more obviously human product. The existence of increasing numbers of monuments, the earlier ones influencing the later ones, increases the sense of landscape as a social product. Within this landscape the structure of activities was obviously extensive, any one act being linked to many others taking place far away. The balance between the uplands and lowlands may have shifted, with more activities being carried out in the latter region than previously. This in itself would have created a wider spatial world. On a broader scale there is increasing evidence for both variety within artefact assemblages and the long-distance movement of materials in the late Neolithic. Stone axes, pottery and flaked stone were moving both near and far. Peterborough and Grooved Wares were made of different fabrics and deposited in varying contexts, the former associated with long barrows, the latter with henges. Looking at this evidence in the terms I set up earlier, the balance between mutuality and materiality seems to be firmly in favour of human relations, both on a local and inter-regional level. The movement of many different aspects of material culture set up links between people and the evidence is dominated by structures, such as the monuments, in which social consumption seems to have dominated. The evidence contains little hint of productive activities, but much of the burial of human bones and artefacts from a variety of sources and contexts. These artefacts are combined in spatially complex ways which constrain the room-for-manoeuvre that people had, and this constraint is accepted. We are dealing here with a complex world of reference and restriction, little of which has to do with productivity as we would understand it and which imposes increasing spatial constraint at local levels, contrasting strongly with the spatial openness of the system as a whole.

In the early Bronze Age there is no great opening of the landscape. More of the evidence comes from sites, rather than from flint scatters

(Barrett et al. 1991: 110). The move to round barrows and individual burials found in the late Neolithic increases, as does the diversity of pottery, with Beaker and perhaps early Deverel-Rimbury ceramics joining the repertoires (ibid.: 115–16). This is seen by Barrett et al. as a greater complexity of categorization, a view reinforced by the fact that the pottery types are used in differing depositional contexts. Metal enters the area for the first time and is found exclusively in funerary contexts. In many ways the early Bronze Age can be seen as a continuation of the fragmentation of the late Neolithic uses of material culture and of space.

The middle Bronze Age, on the other hand, has been seen as a period of major transformation ever since Childe. Barrett et al. are at pains to stress, however, that part of this contrast with earlier periods may be due to archaeological visibility: the growth of field systems and enclosed settlements give domestic productive activity a prominence in the evidence it has never had before (Barrett et al. 1991: 143). Ploughing has taken place since the Neolithic, but in the middle Bronze Age this activity became more focused, being repeated on particular spots and created lynchets. A major set of evidence from this period comes from the excavations at South Lodge, first carried out by Pitt-Rivers and renewed by Barrett et al. a century later. Here there is a complex history of human use, with a barrow cemetery and an enclosure existing on the edge of a field system. This went through a number of phases of use, the first of which is associated with Grooved Ware and Beaker pottery and perhaps produced early Bronze Age lynchets. The main field system was then created and associated with an unenclosed settlement. When an enclosed settlement was built, cultivation in its immediate vicinity ceased. The enclosure itself may not have been in use for long and deliberate deposits were made in its surrounding ditches. Similar depositional practices are found in the ditches around the barrows of the cemetery, which went out of use sometime in the tenth century bc (ibid.: 181–3). A similar set of evidence came from excavations at Down Farm near the Cursus, which may have been re-used as a field boundary at this period. This enclosed settlement was reorganized in a major way at least once, with round huts being replaced by a long rectangular building (ibid.: 206–8). In neither the South Lodge nor the Down Farm case do the settlements appear to have been self-sufficient as they do not have provision for penning animals and processing cereals. The enclosed settlements were just some of the focuses of the activities on the chalk, and there may

well be other important unenclosed locations (ibid.: 225). The deliberate deposits formerly found exclusively in the ditches connected with
funerary monuments are now found around the enclosed settlements.

In the late Bronze Age and the Iron Age the landscape was opened
further, so that open space predominated, especially on the chalk, with
only intermittent pockets of woodland. Sheep come to dominate bone
assemblages. Settlements were surrounded by enclosures of varying
types, fields were contained within lynchet boundaries. The evidence
from settlements shows that from this time practice begins at home: the
settlements appear to have carried out a full range of agricultural tasks,
providing enough of the basics of life for their inhabitants. There is
little evidence of burial rites and the evidence is primarily of productive
activities. In many ways this was a much less complex world spatially,
with a greater concentration of activities in a narrow compass: the
settlement and surrounding fields. Human labour was now directed
towards the production of material things, rather than the materials
being used to set up human relationships.

The Neolithic to the Iron Age: Changing Spaces

The Cranborne Chase evidence offers us much insight into the human
creation and use of space. Within the period from the earlier Neolithic
to the early Bronze Age the social world became ever larger. First of all
this was a result of the opening up of the landscape, with deforestation
probably taking place first on the lowlands and then on the Chase; in
the latter area the extent and timing of clearance operated differently on
varying soil types. Clearance of itself gave a different expanse to social
being, affecting the movement of animals, the planting and harvesting
of crops and the procurement of raw materials such as flint. Over the
period of the Neolithic the balance of activities shifted from a major
concentration on the lowland to a more balanced use of the Chase and
lower areas. The greater local expansiveness of social action in the
course of the Neolithic was echoed by a larger set of connections
spanning many areas of Britain and beyond. By the late Neolithic
various forms of pottery were in widespread use – Grooved Ware,
Peterborough Ware and Beakers – polished stone axes were moving far
from their sources and monuments such as the Cursus itself were
established over a wide area. There is much we do not know about
basic forms of practice during this period, but we can say that life was

both spatially extensive and dominated by connections between people. Spatially extensive forms of mutuality represent an unconscious level of social being, but the problems brought about by widespread and unstable sets of connections created responses at the level of conscious practice.

Problems of practice arose in the Neolithic not because the spaces that contained action were too small, but because they were too big. On the local level, in the area around the Chase and the coastal lowlands, forest clearance created a more open landscape than at any time in the postglacial period. On a much broader scale were the sets of connections between people which covered many areas of Britain and were brought about by widely moving elements of material culture. Local activities on the Chase were set within a broad spatial compass, which in turn had a series of paths of action leading out into the wider world. Providing stark contrast to these broad spaces is the internal ordering of the monuments. These can be seen as machines for the creation of space, which make reference between different spatial contexts possible through the creation of spatial order.

The monuments represent a twofold ordering of space. First of all, a construction as large as the Dorset Cursus gave order to the whole landscape. As we have seen, the Cursus influenced the placement of many subsequent monuments, each connected to the rest through their common reference to the Cursus. Secondly, there were very precise forms of deposition carried out within the monuments in which pottery, stone and animal bones were placed in pits and ditches in a regular manner. The activities carried out to create such ordered deposits must have been highly regularized and repeated over a long period of time (J. Thomas 1991: ch. 4). The monuments and forms of deliberate deposition around Cranborne Chase are mutually referential, building up a complex history of interconnections over time. The monuments around the Dorset Cursus are all aligned on that massive construction, even though it went out of direct use fairly quickly. This pattern of concentration is found throughout the whole gamut of activities carried out in the region, whether we are inclined to label these domestic or ritual, using the terms which make sense to us. This is a pattern which continues through to the early Bronze Age and possibly beyond. The activities patterned around the Cursus bring together evidence of far-flung references, as can be seen in the careful combinations of material in the Firtree Field pits, where different flint types were combined with particular types of pottery, axes and arrowheads. The deliberate human restriction of space creates a framework within which reference can take place, within which actions can be related and given coherence. This pattern of restriction and reference is found throughout many areas of Britain over long periods of time. Although such reference and restriction gave rise to daily lived experience and knowledgeable action, it was not itself directly meaningful or thought out. The monuments and their spaces provided a vital ground for experience, and it is with this broader pattern that we should start before looking at the closer patterns of deliberate deposition within each monument or area.

The deliberate system of reference set up by the monuments is not simply to do with the dead or with activities we would label as ritual. The monuments guided conscious acts, but also habitual patterns such as the knapping of flint or the movement of animals. The interesting point here is that these spaces were not simply an external medium in which people acted; rather, the social geography of the monuments became part of what people were. From the late Neolithic onwards we can see a slow transition from a spatially extensive world orientated around contacts between people, to a more spatially restricted world concentrated upon the production of things. The material nature of the monuments and the divisions of the landscape they provided etched ever more prceise spaces into people's social being. The monuments, which were consciously set up and laid out, became part of unconscious practice. There is thus a slow cycle of change. The problem of the extensiveness of the spatial world of the Neolithic leads to a conscious effort to restrict space. This conscious effort involves the building of massive monuments which over generations become part of what people are. The fact that people become attuned to spatial restriction leads to the landscape gradually being set out in more restricted fashion, and this in itself encourages a greater directedness towards the local material world.

The site at Down Farm represents an increased localization and spatial circumscription of activity. In the first phase of occupation there were two buildings within 200 metres of the Cursus, which seems to have been used as a field boundary at this time. The two buildings were unenclosed and may represent a house and ancillary building (Barrett et al. 1991: 206). In any event these represent a greater restriction and localization of activity than found in previous periods, both in terms of the construction of a field system and settlement. The two together formed the nucleus of a referential set of activities, even if it is difficult to discern what these activities were from the evidence available. The enclosure was probably built around 1000 bc and contained a main building and two ancillary structures; there is also evidence of a yard area and a track leading across the site. The site was then reorganized, with one large rectangular construction along the eastern side; this structure may have been a longhouse (ibid.: 208). This site represents a progressive restriction of spaces from two unenclosed structures to an enclosed site with a complex internal structure (see ibid.: fig. 5.28 for details of the sequence of structures). The site represents in microcosm a series of spatial processes being carried out in many areas, which cumulatively changed the shape of the southern British landscape.

We are looking here at a long-term dynamic at work. The unconscious structure of reference in the Neolithic spread productive activity far and wide, making it difficult to find direct evidence of agricultural or craft production in the archaeological record. The conscious system of reference formed by monuments and depositional practices played out over many generations becomes an unconscious part of what people are, and habitual practices became more tethered and directed. There is an interesting interplay here between spatial circumscription and the greater emphasis on material production found from the middle Bronze Age onwards. From this period on there is an increasing concentration of activities in particular areas of the land-scape, and sites start to look more like integrated farmsteads. A crucial spur to this movement was the monuments, which helped inscribe increasingly precise spaces into people's social being. The changing nature of space brought about by the proliferation of the monuments altered the balance between mutuality and materiality, deriving from more spatially concentrated forms of production. From the middle Bronze Age onwards people and things were brought into much more circumscribed and intimate contact and material production came to be central in the life of the group. Not only can we say that space was created and re-created, we can add that the creation of space had consequences for the ways in which people were directed towards the world. Both of these aspects, the creation of space and the engendering of materiality, take place in a temporal cycle. It is to the creation of time that we now turn.

5

Concepts of Being

Durkheim (1965: 488) said that 'it is the rhythm of social life which is at the basis of the category of time'. In this chapter I want to pursue the question of the links between life and time, but rather than looking at the daily life of the group I shall consider how time is socially created over the long term. There are a number of problems to be tackled deriving from points raised in earlier chapters. First of all we need to consider how the background of unthought practice unfolds in time: how practice begets practice unconsciously. We also need to think of conscious practice and to look at how times are enacted and acts are entimed. Last, but not least, we have to look at how material things are used to create and sustain patterns of human temporality both at the conscious and unconscious levels of practice.

As we saw in chapter 1, there has been much recent concern about time. As a starting point for discussion let us look at three theorists who have all thought deeply about human life and time: Husserl, Heidegger and Bourdieu. Husserl will be considered first, as he influenced both the others.

Husserl and Phenomenology

Husserl's philosophy can be seen as a search for a secure beginning for life and thought. Like Weber and Heidegger, an older and a younger contemporary respectively, Husserl wrestled with the nature of European rationalism and its possible future. All three thinkers could see that history was moving on and that the dominant social, economic and intellectual position that Europe had held was slipping. Each had a different response to the problem. Weber engaged in comparative historical work which highlighted Europe's distinctive problems; Heidegger, as we shall see, ended up in forms of irony which increasingly catch the imagination of later generations. Husserl attempted to use the resources of the western rational tradition to build a foundation from which to stave off relativism, seeing his work as both a continuation and a new beginning. Historical problems became more acute for Husserl throughout his life, especially when in his last decade he confronted that most obvious of all signs of Europe's problems: Nazism. As is well known, Husserl and Heidegger, Jew and German, reacted quite differently to Hitler's rise. Husserl's main response was to move away from his early concern with abstract, isolated individuals and towards an understanding of the 'intersubjective constitution of the world' (Husserl 1970: 168). His final work, *The Crisis of European Sciences*, is a painful wrestling with both the direction that Europe was taking and the ways in which a group sense of the world can be built up. It is this last work that will be the focus of attention here, as it is the point at which Husserl's work comes closest to the concerns developed in this book.

Husserl made the word 'phenomenology' famous in this century, but the term had been used as early as 1765 (Kockelmans 1967: 241) and belongs very much to the tradition of western thought. Within this tradition phenomena are defined as things which are perceived, which present themselves to the senses. By extension, phenomenology looks at the nature of appearance and how we can distinguish the merely apparent from the real, bringing up problems both of perception and the status of knowledge derived from perception. Hegel, as we have seen, made much of the term phenomenology, and for him phenomena were not merely appearances or illusions but stages of knowledge, moving in this historical scheme from the acceptance of phenomena by the natural naive consciousness to the more discerning stance of philosophical knowledge.

Husserl had little knowledge of Hegel and came to phenomenology by different paths. Husserl started his career as a mathematician and it is claimed that this gave him his interest in rigorous and well-founded knowledge (Spiegelberg 1960: 76). The contact with mathematics may have had other effects, such as Husserl's reaction against science as the touchstone of the age. Science, in Husserl's view, was based on a series of unexamined assumptions about the world and a form of rationalism concerned mainly with cause and effect; positivist science, starting with Galileo, had developed a thin philosophy unable to deal with moral questions and provide the basis for a rounded form of life (Husserl 1970: appendices II and IV). Much of Husserl's work can be seen to be an attempt to overcome an amoral science through examining its foundations, along with the foundations of all perception. It is in this sense that Husserl's philosophy is radical: it goes to the roots of thought and life.

At the basis of 'Galilean' science lie the idealizations of geometry, which Husserl knew well through his early mathematical training. In much of western thought idealizations, such as geometry, become the basis for knowing the real world. The dichotomy between the ideal and the real finds further form in the distinctions between the natural and psychological worlds and the body versus the mind, ultimately leading to the peculiar western problem whereby the ideal is taken to be more essential than the real. The split between practice and theory was also taken up by Heidegger as a key element of his thought. Sciences, in Husserl's view, were complex combinations of ideal constructs brought to bear on the real. Herein lies what he called 'the mathematization of nature'. Rather than getting caught up in these abstract constructs, he believed that we should return to the starting point for all perception and knowledge, which is 'things in themselves' (Husserl 1970: 95). The famous slogan 'back to the things themselves' was not an attempt to find a single principle as the basis of perception, but was taking us back to the entire field of original, non-idealized experience.

Husserl took the nature of the material world seriously, obsessively probing how people perceive things and how they relate to them. In doing so he made a break with abstract traditions within philosophy and started with everyday life, attempting to build a true philosophy on the 'granite base of mundane knowledge' (Natanson 1973: 6). Husserl's aim was to use everyday experience as a source for a radical questioning of both common sense and philosophical knowledge – 'The ground of experience, opened up in its infinity, will then become the fertile soil of a methodological working principle' (Husserl 1970: 100). For Husserl, experience was concrete, a matter of the senses, rather than being an element of human consciousness shaped by language. The ultimate bearer of meaning was the individual conscious act and language was not a prior necessity for the creation of meaning (Carr 1987: 15–16).

Everyday life arises in natural consciousness, which in turn develops out of a direct and immediate contact with the real. Husserl attempted to capture the basis of our experience, looking at both the acts of perception and the things perceived. Here Husserl shows similarities with positivism in stressing 'that which can be grasped at first hand'. Where he differs in a major way is in subjecting the data arising from sensory perception to scrutiny and in viewing perception as problematical in a manner that positivism never does (Spiegelberg 1960: 130). Consciousness does not, for Husserl, arise from an objective neutral gaze as with positivism, but is directed by individual and communal human interests.

For Husserl pure consciousness does not exist. Consciousness is always consciousness *of* something; it is always directed by intention. Consciousness arises in the living body and we are each of us related to objects through our body. We are also combined into communities with different modes of directedness towards objects. 'The world exists not only for isolated men but for the community of men; and this is due to the fact that even what is straightforwardly perceptual is communalized' (Husserl 1970: 163). Different cultures ('the Chinese, Negroes in the Congo') have different lifeworlds, which according to Husserl can be seen as different forms of directedness. At the level of minutiae intention shows how the different aspects of an object which present themselves to sight, smell, taste, touch and hearing are connected and given an identity so that the full object can be presented to consciousness. The existence of different forms of directedness towards the world seem to bring Husserl close to a relativist position. However, the move towards relativism is halted by the idea that all lifeworlds have common characteristics in that they are based on spatial shapes, motion, sense-qualities and so on. It is the focus on these common characteristics that puts us on the way to objective science, in Husserl's view. The world for Husserl has regional categories and spatio-temporal modalities arising from different cultural manners of intention. A vast comparative survey of these local forms can allow us to pick out their common characteristics, which provide the basis for an immense series of novel and *a priori* truths.

These novel truths, arising from mundane existence in all parts of the human world, provide the foundation upon which Husserl wished to build. Husserl's search for a non-relative, non-historical source of all life is part of what Bernstein (1983: 16–20) calls a reaction to Cartesian anxiety (see Husserl 1977). Bernstein uses this phrase to

life and thought, Heidegger takes a whole series of everyday things such as hammers and door knobs, looking at the role they play in our lives and how knowledge of the mundane world is generated. For Heidegger, hermeneutics begins at home.

The decline in the quality of our thought within the theoretical tradition is linked by Heidegger to a more basic decline in our relationship to the world. A central theme of Heidegger's was the growth of what he called a 'productionist mentality' over the last 2500 years, which has altered our relationship to the world (Zimmerman 1990 discusses this point in detail). The changed relationship is not an intellectual shift, but an alteration in the ways in which the world manifests itself for us. For instance, Heidegger said, in the medieval period people saw material things as the creatures of God and something to be approached with piety and feeling, whereas now the world is manifest as raw material, something to be taken advantage of and to use for our ends.

The key to understanding our relationship with the world lies in technology. The roots of our modern word technology lie in the Greek word *techne*. '*Techne* belongs to bringing-forth, to *poeisis*; it is something poetic' (Heidegger, in Krell 1977: 294). But modern technology has lost this poetical aspect. It is rather a challenging: it challenges nature to bring forth energy and people are challenged to stand by as labour power. Everything is seen as raw material, as a standing reserve. In order to understand its properties and potential as a raw material, nature is approached as an object of research. Physics attempts to understand phenomena as a coherence of calculable forces. Technology is seen as an instrument, as the cause of known effects. But alternatively it could be seen as a bringing-forth, as revealing the nature of the world, and this would place technology close to art. The lack of a proper connection to the world lies at the heart of the absence of satisfying forms of thought, according to Heidegger. And the blandness of both thought and being are made manifest in the forms of public life which exist in the twentieth century. The new nation-states have given rise to a perverted political process, a philosophy without feeling, communications media used for the manipulation of public opinion and forms of mass entertainment designed to dull our sense of life. Heidegger talks scathingly of the 'They', the anonymous public world in which blandness and boredom are all. His escape from an anonymous and unthinking public life was to be achieved through a return to piety and a feeling of care towards the world.

Central to my account of Heidegger is the shift his thought represents from knowing to being. Crucial to his account of Being is the German term *Dasein*, usually translated as being-there. Being for each of us is not a disembodied state of knowledge, but a particular physical situation, a special place in the world, a being-there. A peculiarity of *Dasein* is that it is a being for which Being is an issue: we want to know the hows and whys of existence. Human Being is self-interpreting. The hermeneutic method is crucial as this can explore how interpretation derives from our position and actions within the world. Such explorations of interpretation can challenge our views of ourselves and the world in fundamental ways. We must start our investigations of practice from within those practices and using the traditional under-standings of practice. But those understandings may have passed over crucial features of practice, and we must be prepared to radically overhaul our notions of space, time, language and so on. The hermeneutic circle, when pursued with an open mind, is likely to lead in unexpected directions. At the heart of Heidegger's work is the call for a new beginning in understanding the relationship of thought and life. Heidegger saw knowing as another element of doing and strove for a non-mentalist vocabulary to express this relationship.

Heidegger believed that the way out of our present relationship with the world is complex. That way is essentially philosophical, or rather thoughtful. Heidegger stressed thought against philosophy. He came to see the philosophical tradition of thought on the world as part of the problem. Philosophy had become a hardened and solidified tradition which did not have the lightness of touch or the fluidity necessary to connect ourselves with Being. We should, then, give up the philosoph-ical tradition and go back to thinking. Thought that starts anew and questions all that has gone before is the only way out of our manipulative, reasoning stance to the world. Questioning helps relate Being to people. It is through thinking and questioning that Being comes to language. 'Language is the house of Being. In its home man dwells. Those who think and those who create with words are the guardians of this home' (Heidegger, in Krell 1977: 193). Plato and Aristotle saw thinking as *techne*, as making and doing. But really thought should have no end or purpose. Unlike calculative reason, thinking Being has no result, no effect, it simply satisfies its essence in that it is (Heidegger, in Krell 1977: 236). Mystical and directionless, thinking Being is quite different to most modern thought which takes place within the public realm where opinion-makers hold sway.

Heidegger believed that we must create our own opinions and not accept our views from the anonymous mass. Original thinking is closely connected to original forms of language. Our search for a new and more immediate relation to Being was in effect a search for elementary words which keep their impact when expressing Being.

Heidegger's primary question was 'what is the nature of everyday practice?' His basic answer was that everydayness comes from a set of skills for coping with the world in creating and manipulating equipment. When we say that people are in the world we are not just making a statement about spatial position, like saying that the water is in the glass, but are talking about involvement, which is closer to the notion of being in love or in business. Being in the world is a state of involvement, which is clearly quite different from having a view or a theory of the world. Our attempts to cope with the world create an understanding of what is possible, a series of states of readiness which together create an open-ended but finite range of possibilities for action. Many of these possibilities are canvassed unthinkingly, we simply get on with life rather than bringing thought to bear on many of our tasks. If we hammer in a nail, 'The hammering itself uncovers the specific "manipulability" of the hammer' (Heidegger 1962: 98); it is not something we think about consciously. Dreyfus suggests the blind person's cane as an example of the unconscious involvement of people and the world:

> We hand the blind man a cane and ask him to tell us what properties it has. After hefting and feeling it, he tells us that it is light, smooth, about three feet long and so on ... But when the man starts to manipulate the cane, he loses awareness of the cane itself; he is aware only of the curb (or whatever object the cane touches); or, if all is going well, he is not even aware of that, but of his freedom to walk, or perhaps only what he is talking about with a friend. Precisely when it is most genuinely appropriated equipment becomes transparent. (Dreyfus 1991: 65)

It is only when things do not work that we have to pay attention to them and bring understanding and thought into play. This is not a question of canvassing mental images, but rather of making the range of possibilities inherent in a situation manifest. Language is one of the more complex and satisfactory means of making things manifest: it is not simply sounds or marks which have mental images attached, but rather is part of the flow of practice. Theoretical approaches to problems which abstract from particular situations and try to work from general principles are one form of thought and language and are good for some purposes but limited for many others. Symbolic logic is the result of a progressive decontextualization and impoverishment of daily being and cannot be seen as the quintessential human achievement.

Everydayness has its own essential structures, the chief of which is temporal. Time is central to coping with the world. Time is not a successive sequence of 'nows', a series of points to be measured moving from an infinite past into an infinite future. Heidegger, by contrast, felt time to be a structure of occurrence, a style of existence. Time is a human dimension and unfolds in action. Here Heidegger comes close to Husserl's views and his terms protention and retention. Past, present and future are all evoked in action in complex ways. For Heidegger time occurred as three ecstasies, the past, present and future. The main emphasis of existence is towards the future, which drags us towards it and in the process shapes both present and past. The present is a point of oscillation between the possibilities created by the past and the potentials held by the future. A tendency to live for the future is at the heart of one of Heidegger's most famous concepts, that of Being-towards-death, where the value of life can only be brought out fully by the thought of extinction. One of the routes out of the inauthentic life of the present is the perspective offered by death, which alone can make us conscious of life's full meaning. Heidegger here makes a division between public and personal time. Public time is large and open, perpetuated by institutions longer-lasting than the individual; it is often measured and distanced from individual experience. Personal time is all too obviously bounded, leading each of us towards death. Heidegger felt that it was too easy to become involved in public time and to forget our personal finitude. This sort of existence was inauthentic and it was only through becoming fully conscious of the nature of Being-towards-death that we could come completely to know ourselves in the world and take up a proper attitude towards the world. This attitude is one of care. Here Heidegger's work, with its talk of authenticity and inauthenticity, became extremely influential in the later existentialist movement.

Heidegger's thought is characterized by a sheer longing for a sense of oneness with the world. The longing and anxiety which make *Being and Time* such a powerful work can easily be seen as a reaction to the fragmented experience we have in the modern world. Humanism, which was centred on the thought that people are rational, provided too slender a basis for comprehending the whole of human being and the world historical unfolding which is Being. Heidegger used history to cast the modern world into an unfavourable comparison with the pre-Socratic Greeks. In many ways this gives history a structure which would have been familiar to the Greeks. The present is seen as the Age of Iron coming after the Age of Gold, in which we were at one with Being.

Potentials and Problems of Heidegger's Thought

One of the first uses of Heidegger's thought comes from the observation that understanding derives from practice, or more particularly *our* understanding derives from *our* practice. This observation immediately involves us in a set of hermeneutic connections, rather more complex than Giddens' double hermeneutic. Giddens sees social science as the meeting of 'two frames of meaning': 'the meaningful world as constituted by lay actors', together with the second-order understandings of social scientists (Giddens 1984: 374). Working from Heidegger's conception we can see that our knowledge of the world is a derivative form of our everyday practice, developed primarily in the process of coping with everyday life. In order to understand our own forms of knowledge we have to examine that knowing as a particular form of making manifest the problems of our world. This involves probing our use of material culture, forms of mutuality and structuring of time and space through action. To know forms of life other than our own we have to understand how we operate, as well as looking at the structure of the Other. It is often said that understanding the Other will highlight the particular features of our world, allowing us to know ourselves better. However, the distance between ourselves and other social structures can only really be understood from within the context of our own lives. This supplies some measures of the gap between different forms of life. In this view archaeology (or any social science) must take cognisance of our practice and the knowledge it creates, rather than starting with the practices of others. This is a form of reflexivity that is deeper than that normally talked of in post-structuralist thought, which looks mainly at the form of language we use and the narrative structures we employ to tell the story of the Other. Heidegger's linking of thought and life makes our life the starting point for understanding all other forms. Although we cannot step out of our practices, our spirals round the hermeneutic circle may provide a whole set of unexpected perspectives opening up the possibility of change.

As well as changing our models of thought, Heidegger has much to offer on a substantive level in our attempts to understand the flow of life. His stress on time is particularly attractive to any historical discipline interested in the temporal structure of life. However, the major weakness of Heidegger's thought from the perspective of this book is that although Heidegger concentrates on the nature of human being – Dasein – he looks much less at the world with which Dasein is involved. Hedegger's work lacks any empirical analysis or attempt to understand actual historical change, how people changed the world and it changed them. This is because, whilst reacting against much of philosophy, Heidegger remained a philosopher, and retained many of the traits of thought he criticized. Dasein was never given context and the remarks on the growth of the productionist mentality hardly constitute substantive history.

Heidegger contrasted public with private time, where the latter held the possibility of salvation. Our lives can be given back point and purpose by a consciousness of finitude. We have to make life meaningful because it is inherently precious, and this sense of life can only be supplied by its negation, death. A caring attitude to ourselves and material things may save us from the bland and formless time of the modern public world where measurement and calculation is all. 'Questioning is the piety of thought' (Heidegger 1977: 317). Piety and care can re-establish our relationship with the world, thus creating both new public and private forms. Because of his disdain for the public world Heidegger engaged in no real analysis of it. To this disdain was added a tinge of fear, after his involvement with the Nazi party, an affiliation he never repudiated. A sharper empirical analysis is contained in the work of Pierre Bourdieu, whose thought holds many parallels with Heidegger's (Bourdieu 1990a: 5).

Talk about Practice

The work of Pierre Bourdieu has many facets to it, but Bourdieu is probably best known for his general ideas on practice. In some ways in tune with historians interested in 'history from the bottom up',

Bourdieu has focused on general patterns of life and society as a differentiated whole. Indeed, much of his work has been concerned with how differentiations are made and maintained within the social mass and how some sectors of the population are systematically excluded from the centres of social power through the use of art and education. These concerns with mass action have led him off in two directions. First, he has tried to develop a general theory of social action, around the idea of 'habitus'; and second, he has obsessively explored his own privileged position as a social analyst, the sorts of knowledge his position has led him to produce and how knowledge of this type can be used in forms of social demarcation. These dual interests have directed Bourdieu's thought away from the dominant post-structuralist interest on discourse, and he has focused instead on practical action. But, on the other hand, these same interests have put him in the forefront of those concerned with reflexivity and the position of the analyst, another dominant topic for the post-structuralist movement. Here it is not possible to survey the whole of Bourdieu's work; instead I shall concentrate on the material which pertains most closely to being-in-the-world and our knowledge of that being.

In order to focus on patterns of general action Bourdieu has built a theoretical framework which tries to avoid a sole emphasis either on subjective states and individual creativity, or on objective social structures which mechanically generate individual acts. The latter model derives from a cast of thought he labels 'objectivist' and takes structuralism as his prime example. This is distinguished from subject-ivist modes, such as phenomenology or existentialism. The history of post-war thought in France can be characterized by a move from Sartre's existentialism centred on individuals making their own choices in an indifferent universe, to Lévi-Strauss's 'universal structures of the human mind' which generate and subordinate individual acts (Bour-dieu 1990b: 1–4).

It is worth noting at the outset exactly why and how Bourdieu uses key terms such as 'objectivist'. One of the most original features of Bourdieu's thought is that he emphasizes not just the things observed – actors, social relations and structures – but also the position of the sociologist/ethnographer as observer. Hence he uses the words 'objec-tivist' and 'subjectivist' to describe the observer's point of view and the expectations held, before starting research, as to the sorts of data he or she will observe. Bourdieu takes structuralism as the prime example of the objectivist viewpoint, the example he pursues most doggedly.

Structuralism is, first and foremost, a relational mode of thought. The structuralist view is best exemplified by Saussure's view of language as a system of objective relations (note the use of the word objective), of which speakers are not fully conscious, but which generates speech. Saussure's view puts this logical construction before individual or group history: language as a system predates our individual uses of it. In Bourdieu's view this is a *logos* not a *praxis* (terms which parallel Heidegger's distinction between theory and practice) and derives from an outsider's view of language (Bourdieu 1977: 1). His point is that people learning a language in a classroom, rather than through speaking, are more likely to see language as a formal grammatical structure than as an essential part of life. The outsider's view is at the heart of objective forms of thought such as structuralism and has been since the days of Saussure. Anthropology, dealing as it does with other cultures, has been especially prone to the outsider's view and the objectivist stance. Anthropology has a consequent tendency to produce maps of social action, rather than an understanding of real space. It is only the stranger who requires a map; those who know the terrain use their knowledge to guide them. The problem for anthropology is not just that it is the view of a series of outsiders, but that the crucial features inherent in an outsider's view are not explored by anthropology itself, which tries to downplay its own world view. The intellectualism inherent in all forms of academia tends to slide from the 'model of reality to the reality of the model' (Bourdieu 1990b: 38).

Opposed to objectivism in Bourdieu's scheme is subjectivism. The existentialism of Sartre sees practice as an individual and free project, with each action a confrontation without antecedent between the subject and the world. Individual praxis is given primacy over history and any determination by the group. Sartre is only outdone in subjectivism by the rational actor theorists, of whom Elster (1983; 1985) is the main example. As Bourdieu says, those who see society as composed of a series of rational acts find it both difficult to account for the forces which hold the wider matrix of society together and for actions which are reasonable but not the product of reasoning (Bourdieu 1990b: 46).

It is just this form of social action, which makes intuitive sense without having been thought out, that Bourdieu is trying to capture. Subjectivism is of no use here, as it cannot give an account of why the social world is necessary: if individual experience is primary, who do we need to generate meanings for, with and against other people? Bourdieu attempted to come to terms with these different facets of experience through his most famous concept, that of habitus. Habitus is

> systems of durable, transposable dispositions, structured structures predisposed to function as structuring structures, that is, as principles which generate and organise practices and representations that can be objectively adapted to their outcomes without presupposing a conscious aiming at ends or an express mastery of the operations necessary to obtain them. (Bourdieu 1990b: 53)

The key aspect of habitus from our point of view is that it is not consciously mastered, but is built up from experience. Habitus represents the sedimentation of past practice in the human organism so that it unconsciously guides future practice. Habitus is a link between past and future which is unconsciously transmitted. The idea of habitus bridges the methodologies of subjectivism and objectivism (but not, as we shall see, subject and object). Forms of subjectivism such as phenomenology concentrate on primary experience and look at the familiarity of the subject with the taken-for-granted-world, but cannot explain why the world is familiar and can be taken for granted. Habitus, on the other hand, explains familiarity (Bourdieu 1990b: 25), as it shows how actions and perceptions are unconsciously inculcated in the individual body and the social body in a way which creates consistency, although not sameness, in life. Structuralism outlines the relational schemes underlying life, but has a tendency to see life as rule-bound, viewing action and thought as the outcome of pan-human dispositions operating irrespective of social context. Habitus offers a similar view of relational schemes underlying human practice, but is a generative scheme creating dispositions to act within which individuals can choose their own strategies. Habitus produces practices which are unpredictable individually, but limited in their diversity (Bourdieu 1990b: 55).

A constant example which Bourdieu refers to throughout his work is the Kabyle sense of honour (the Kabyle were an Algerian group amongst whom Bourdieu did his early fieldwork). The notion of honour, and more particularly the equality of honour, underlies many of the relations between Kabyle men. An initial honourable exchange (of gifts, words etc.) implies the possibility of a reply or a return gift and it contains a recognition of the partner. Recognition in itself is a finely judged business. By challenging an inferior, a man dishonours himself by stooping too low. The challenge to a superior may not be taken up and the lack of reply becomes a snub and a confirmation of inferior status (Bourdieu 1990b: 100). Figure 5.1 represents a simple generative model laying out the choices deriving from a small number of basic principles (Bourdieu 1990b: 101).

These choices and the principles underlying them are not consciously recognized by the Kabyle. In any case, these simple principles do not convey the full flavour of Kabyle male life. Degrees of honour are expressed in men's deportment and physical being. These must be correctly judged. Gift and riposte are a matter of style as well as substance, and the timing and nature of reply or refusal are vital in producing conduct others judge to be correct. The stakes in this game can be high (a misjudged move may end in death), so that urgency and stress make correct judgement more difficult. However, a social persona deriving from degrees of honour can be read in the body of the partner and innumerable unconscious cues can help a man towards correct action if judged aright. Little of this judgement is conscious, but derives from the habitus, inculcated from birth. Thus knowing the abstract principles of challenge and response can only help a man so far, sketching out the limits of acceptable action and giving a certain predictability to exchanges. However, the limits are fairly broad and there is room for both stylish and graceless response. The habitus is socially derived, but how it is acted upon on particular occasions depends on command and external accident.

Habitus is a series of relations between different elements of life, and it is possible to see here the influence of structuralism. Although Bourdieu worked with a structural model he rejected Lévi-Strauss's

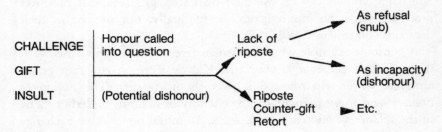

Figure 5.1 Bourdieu's model of honour amongst the Kabyle. (From Bourdieu 1990b, *The Logic of Practice*, Polity Press, p. 100.)

view that there are universal structures of the human mind, or indeed anything such as human nature (Robbins 1991: 178). Cultural groups, social classes and fields of activity (art, politics, sport etc.) all have their own forms of habitus enjoining and generating socially recognized patterns of actions. Although all elements of life are ultimately related, there is no final and dominant relational structure.

Habitus, then, is a general, concerted but unconscious harmonization of social life, a second nature. Habitus is not so much a state of mind, but a state of body. The human body is the nexus of the habitus, which organizes movements through space and time through forms of deportment and movement. As Bourdieu (1990b: 69) puts it, 'Arms and legs are full of numb imperatives.' 'Hexis' is the name Bourdieu gives to the embodiment of habitus. Hexis is the body politic realized, as divisions of gender, class and age are found inscribed in the body (Bourdieu 1990b: 70). The acquisition and activation of bodily action is not consciously learned or taught, but picked up during the child's early years and built on throughout life. The child in relating to the mother's and father's bodies learns unconsciously about gender divisions and divisions of labour. 'What is learned in the body is not something one has, but something one is' (Bourdieu 1990b: 73). These divisions are reinforced during ritual, where attitudes of mind and body are struck. Bodily movement is also channelled through the material world, during which time dispositions are enforced and reinforced.

The other major area of practice which Bourdieu concentrates on is rather closer to home: the activity of research. Bourdieu sees science (which he defines along the lines of systematic and discursive knowledge) as having its own unconscious habitus as well as procedures which are consciously learned. The unconscious aspect comes from the researcher's position within his or her own society, which in the European case is determined by class structures, together with the shape of the academic field. The notion of field is crucial to Bourdieu's views as a whole and derives from his structuralist background. A field is a geometric space in which points are connected by a series of relationships, in which the whole is more than the sum of the parts. The importance and influence of each point derives not from its own characteristics, but from its position within the field of relations as a whole. Understanding a field of human action is therefore a geometry of knowledge, delimiting the fields and the connections within them. When looking at the production of knowledge two sets of fields have to be mapped. The first of these, as mentioned above, is formed of the positions in which researchers are placed both within society itself and internally within academic institutions and power structures. The second is that of the concepts of science, made up of a network of ideas and values with its own changing shape and structure. A third field, which is in some senses external to the fields producing knowledge, is the relations of practice and action forming society itself.

Much of Bourdieu's recent work has been concerned to explore the structure of the social fields producing knowledge and discourse and the relationship of the observer to the observed, the links between the fields of knowledge and the structure of society. In one of his more accessible works, *Homo Academicus* (Bourdieu 1988), he has mapped the terrain in which he himself moves: the French academic world. In parallel with his attempt to place academia within its broader social matrix, Bourdieu has tried to chart that broader world and the manner in which society as a whole makes social judgements. He uses the concept of taste as a means of distinction, particularly as it is applied to forms of artistic expression. In *Distinction* (Bourdieu 1989) he shows that working-class and middle-class people have their own internal standards of decency, which the other class fails to meet. Views of decent behaviour derive from class habitus. Different and conflicting standards of taste in art and social life both arise out of and reinforce class divisions, dividing 'us' from 'them'. Bourdieu sees society as a series of forms of habitus, which look at each other and address each other from their own point of view. Academics and educational institutions can be seen as inculating particular points of view about social norms and values, especially socially dominant middle-class values. The production of knowledge has nothing to do with objective observation and the compilation of facts, and everything to do with class-based views and patterns of action.

The need to understand academic habitus is especially pressing as it produces knowledge about other forms of habitus and is one of society's ways of discussing itself. Following Bourdieu's division between the social and the intellectual fields, two tasks are necessary: the first is to look at the type of understanding produced by the observer's viewpoint; the second is to understand the position of the producers within social fields as a whole.

In pursuing the first point Bourdieu stresses that practice is the aspect of life most opposed to discourse. Analyses produce 'mere totalization' (Bourdieu 1990b: 82), a model which collapses the space and, more particularly, the time of practice. Arriving after the event, the observer views it as a whole and can move backwards and forwards in time during the analysis. For the participant immersed in the action as it unfolds, time is a vital part of the social game, and the urgency of events dictates not just what people do, but the timing of their actions. There is an antinomy between the time of the leisured observer and of the pressured social actor, the rhythm and tempo of the action being an integral part of its meaning (Bourdieu 1990b: 81). Such a tempo is difficult for the analyst to recreate, operating in abstract logical time. Furthermore, the very instruments of communication – writing and speech – impose a linear sequence on events which may originally have been more confused and layered. The real measure of the gap between the actor and analyst is that if an actor were to take up a purely theoretical stance, the truth of action would be lost. It is practically impossible to be both actor and analyst at the same time.

There are many parallels between Heidegger and Bourdieu: both react against abstract theoretical forms of thought, which derive from an outside observer's view. Bourdieu is particularly critical of structuralism in this regard, which he sees as the mechanical generation of action and thought through a set of rules, which ignores the predispositions to action contained in the body and the real exigencies of practice. The real time of action, vital to its unfolding, is collapsed down to logical time through which oppositions are worked out. Bourdieu also rejects structuralism's notion that all people generate knowledge in the same way due to the structure of the human brain. Knowledge only arises through practice: present-day academic knowledge derives not only from the intellectual field in which we operate, but also from relations of class, which inculcate class-based forms of discrimination and interest.

Of the two thinkers, Bourdieu is the more practical, having carried out a large number of investigations of the relationship between practice and knowledge. However, although he has stressed the importance of understanding the temporal structure of action, Bourdieu has produced no theory of human time. For such a theory we must turn to Heidegger, who took from Husserl the notions of protention and retention and immersed them in the flow of daily life. A major gap in the thinking of both Heidegger and Bourdieu is the lack of a real consideration of material culture. Both are extremely aware of the material settings of everyday life, but neither has produced ideas linking bodily action and material things in the on-going flow of life, because Heidegger paid insufficient attention to the real settings of life and Bourdieu has no real theory of time. Taken together, their thought has many possibilities which need to be rounded out by a consideration of the interaction of people and things in the creation of time. It is to the creation of time, and to our understanding of time on the basis of archaeological evidence that we must now turn.

Practice in Time

Let us begin our discussion by starting from the premise that time is the crucial dimension in all human action: it is the means by which present practice structures future action. From this point of view there are no natural patterns of time. The divisions between day and night or the passage of the seasons represent a biological background to be played with culturally, in the same way that gender is the cultural use made of sexual differences. The natural economy tied to the rhythms of the earth disappears as a myth. Natural rhythms are used culturally. Looked at as a human construction, time is not a sequence of 'nows', a mere series of moments in a linear flow. Human time is rather made up of protention and retention, to use Husserl's terms, and has within it a directedness towards the future, as Heidegger saw. All action takes place in anticipation, which is derived from past experience. In chapter 4 I used the term 'reference' to explore how every act is connected to a whole series of other acts in space. We can now see that this structure is also temporal, linked together by forms of anticipation and memory. Reference is thus a structure of space and time, linking human projects. We need now to consider how the creation of time and space takes place in the long run.

Richard Bradley (1991) has explored the relationship between the time-scales of human practice and the time resolution of the archaeological record. He takes as a starting point Braudel's threefold distinction between the *longue durée*, which Braudel sees as the time-scale on which society relates to the environment; social time, which is the history of social groups; and individual time, the history of events (Bradley 1991: 210). (Braudel's ideas will be discussed more fully in chapter 6.) Bradley goes on to argue that there are elements of social time which do not fit into this scheme, as they are so long-lasting that they fit better with the *longue durée*. Art styles, monuments and forms of deliberate deposition are all seen to belong to this long-lasting category. The longevity of such forms is due, in Bradley's view, to their connection with ritual. Ritual is formalized and sometimes deliberately conservative, which helps to take social formations out of time and make them appear natural. Ritual and its material media can be so enduring that they show up well on the time-scales over which archaeological evidence is created. Using a distinction employed by Sahlins (1985) between societies based around prescriptive rules and those based around performative structures, Bradley puts forward the notion that ritual is most commonly to be found in social forms where compelling rules enjoin repetition of social acts. Ritual derives from prescriptive structures. Performative structures are volatile and reproduce themselves as change. The move from the landscape of the early Bronze Age dominated by monuments to the field systems of the middle Bronze Age, discussed with reference to Cranborne Chase in chapter 4, may be due to the shift from prescriptive to performative structures (Bradley 1991: 212, 217).

Bradley illustrates his argument by reference to Stonehenge, a monument with a 1500-year history and which showed a striking continuity of layout throughout its history, being enclosed by a circular ditch with two entrances and having a central area occupied by a round arrangement of uprights at every phase. At the start of its history Stonehenge was one of a number of causewayed enclosures on Salisbury Plain which were connected with the remains of the dead. It subsequently became a henge, with a ring of pits dug concentrically with the earthwork and cremations placed in its bank and ditch. It also received deposits of maceheads and decorated pottery, which have distributions right across Britain. It was one of a large number of henges with a common ground plan, such as that found at Durrington Walls, 3 kilometres away. During the next stage, the first stone circle was built and the alignment of the monument may have changed from an orientation on the moon to being directed towards the sun. In the early Bronze Age, when round barrows with rich burials were being constructed in the area, the large stone monument known today was put in place. In its construction, for example in the use of mortice-and-tenon joints, this appears to hark back to earlier Neolithic wooden types of henge. The construction of such a large monument when all other henges had gone out of use is seen by Bradley as a vain attempt to mask a period of crisis. That the attempt was vain is shown by the abandonment of the monument shortly thereafter, when it became isolated within a network of fields and land boundaries (Bradley 1991:214–16).

The sequence of Stonehenge presents 'an appearance of massive continuity . . . against a background of drastic change' (Bradley 1991: 217). Deliberate reference to the past through the monument is seen as a means of creating stability in an otherwise volatile social world, and the very continuity of the monument helped it to persist. However, our understanding of the exact use of the monument is subsidiary to Bradley's major point, which is that ritual time is much closer to the chronological resolution of the prehistoric evidence than mundane time. Bradley's explicit discussion of long-term structures is part of a growing emphasis on long-term change (Bradley 1990; Hodder 1990). His emphasis on ritual takes us away from general patterns of practice into the area which Heidegger called public time. It is not enough to say that ritual represents a long-term continuity against a background of shorter-term practices. We need to look at all areas of life and the times they create, habit and public time alike.

Practice produces and structures time. The exact nature of the structuring process depends upon the patterns of reference within which acts are embedded. So far we have looked at reference as a spatial structure: an act which is carried out in one place dovetails with acts in many different locales. The set of connections between activities is implicit in each individual act; it provides orientation which does not have to be consciously thought out. Reference also has a temporal dimension, creating chains of action. Any process of production and consumption unfolds as a chain, a series of steps in which the next action is implicit in the present. Lemonnier (1990) makes a similar point in discussing his notion of *chaîne opératoire*. Many of the chains of action we carry out are habitual, taking place without thought. However, habit is not mere repetition, but rather recursiveness using the knowledge of the past to create future action: a structure of retention and protention. Bourdieu sees habitus as hexis, as something learned in the body. This is only part of the story. The stream of action does not just derive from the sedimentation of past acts within the sinews of the human body, but is also contained within material things, the physical properties of which trigger anticipation. A structure of recursiveness thus derives from the interaction of the human and the material. Action can be unthought when it hits no snag, but when a series of actions is unexpectedly successful or an unanticipated failure occurs, then thought is needed. Properly creative action will be a continual blend of thought and unthought, with habit sustaining the main flow and thought coming in when that flow is interrupted. The present is a creative moment because it is a point of oscillation between past and future, monitered in thought and enacted in habit.

Practice produces time. But we need to go a step further. *All* practice produces time. From this it follows that there will be as many forms of time as there are types of practice. These time-scales derive partly from the nature of the materials being worked with: pottery, metal and wood all have different time-scales contained in their production, necessitating different structures of action. On the other hand, the relative stability of material settings into which people are socialized, formed by the landscape as a whole, ensures that practice has some stability and coherence. The bulk of life has a particular structure of recursiveness, drawing on the resources contained in human bodies and material things. The mass of unthought practice gives life a general forward movement and direction.

But there is more to life than unconscious structures of recursiveness. Time and action can be consciously manipulated, as anyone who has worked in a factory is all too aware. We must consider the notion of public time, which is the conscious use and manipulation of materials, spaces and times. Public time is a concept running through much of the discussion in the following chapters. Heidegger sketched out the notion of public time, but his distaste for modern forms of public life prevented him from painting a full picture of what public time is or could be. Public time is not an arbitrary creation. It only has meaning and power if it derives from habitual time-scales and the problems created by habitual action. Public time is derived from the mass of unconscious times and from attempts to solve the problems of habitual practice. In the last chapter we saw how the orchestrated spaces created by monuments were an attempt to give manageable dimensions to the expansive world of the Neolithic and early Bronze Age. The monumental landscape helped shape the direction society as a whole took, in that the repeated actions within those orchestrated spaces gradually went from being conscious to unconscious. Public time derives from and draws its power out of the structure of habitual times. But repetition breeds habit and public time is continually becoming naturalized, conscious action shading off into unconscious. There is no fixed dividing line between public and habitual time, but a moving relationship whereby habitual problems give birth to a conscious response which over time becomes part of what people are, rather than something they know. The interaction of public and habitual time is a powerful force, which is itself a source of power, the point at which conscious thought meets elements of life and which makes the social seem natural.

Life is composed not of one or two times, but many. Time, like space, is produced through all social practice. Time comes from everywhere and effects everything. Time has a spatial element, in that the places in which time is created affect the nature of time and the interaction of different times. The times of human action can be clustered or dispersed: actions leading from one to another may take place in the same spot or be spread widely across the landscape.

Times of action have a spatial structure; they also have a harmonic form. I distinguish three forms of time: harmonious, disjoint or concatenating. Harmonious times are formed when different areas of practice flow into each other easily and smoothly, intergrating actions with different time-scales and periodicities. Disjoint times are formed of a series of cycles of action which constantly cut across each other like waves on a choppy sea. Concatenating times occur when actions with different periodicities are brought together into an accelerating rhythm with an ever faster and unstable pace. Our own world could be seen as a prime example of concatenating times. The ways in which times of action are combined has much to do with the exercise of power: the restriction of elements of practice and their distributions across space will make for disjoint or concatenating times, where practices do not flow into each other or build into unstable rhythms. The control of practice partly depends on the material media employed in action and how far time and space can be partitioned and have their rhythms altered. Concatenating and disjoint times exist where they cannot be contained by social resources.

Looking back at the example of Stonehenge raised by Bradley, we can see that the public time that Stonehenge represents can only be understood against the background of habitual times operating in the early and middle Bronze Ages. We can consider this problem by returning to Cranborne Chase, which allows consideration of the matching between habitual and public times.

The Times of Cranborne Chase

It is obvious from the preceding discussion that a number of times must have been in operation at Cranborne Chase. In attempting to understand these times I shall start with the proposition, advanced in the last chapter, that the Neolithic on Cranborne Chase, and in Britain generally, represented a structure of mutuality, whereby material things were used to set up links between people. I shall now add to this the further idea that a structure of mutuality is inherently more unstable than a structure of materiality. In a social world where everyone is trying to set up as many links as possible, there will be constant change and instability. The unstable links will be part of people's social being, as will the standardized forms of material culture used to regularize those links. A problematical social situation will require a considerable emphasis on public time, which can be seen in this instance as the development of means to solve the problems caused by changing links between people. The widespread similarity of material culture and of monumental forms can be seen as a means to restrict and order space. Just as important, artefacts and monuments are means of providing pattern to recursiveness.

Once monuments were constructed they became indelible marks on the landscape (Barrett et al. 1991: 1–2). As Bradley points out for Stonehenge, it is the very continuity and antiquity of the monuments which give them their power. The monuments form a cultural means for creating recursiveness, a means of controlling action through creating particular anticipations of the future, giving pattern to some of the rhythms of lfe. So as to see why this order was necessary we need to view the monuments against a broader background of patterns of action in the landscape. Barrett et al. (1991) attempt to place the monuments in context, but their concentration on ritual and deliberate action does not provide the basis for linking public time to habitual practice.

What did the broader system of practice involve? The answer to this is contained within the landscape and the changes we can observe in it. The first and longest of these changes is the progressive opening up of the landscape from the Neolithic to the Roman period, with some reversion to forest after that. The deforestation of itself created different patterns of action. As we saw in the last chapter, the centre of social gravity shifted from a concentration on the lowlands in the early Neolithic to a more balanced distribution of activities between the Chase and the lowlands later on. Within the Chase the nature of activities also shifted over time, with a concentration on sheep-rearing on the chalk by the Iron Age, plus a possible greater preponderance of cereal cropping there than on the clay-with-flints. During the late

Neolithic the clay-with-flints became an important source of flaked stone material, presumably due partly to the greater amount of clearance which made the flint more available and because of the importance of flint in the tasks of that period. The creation of open country out of woodland humanized the area to an increasing degree through the prehistoric period, opening up different sets of possibilities at different times.

During the Neolithic evidence of the production of food is conspicuous by its absence. The lack of evidence for subsistence derives from the dispersed spaces and times of production. There may well have been regularity in the movement of animals, but such movements do not show up archaeologically. The Cursus may mark the boundary between the upland pasturage and the lowland arable (Barrett et al. 1991: 223), providing a precise human definition of the spaces crossed on these movements. There is evidence of traction ploughing well back into the Neolithic (Barrett et al. 1991: 225), but no evidence of field systems before the early Bronze Age, and fields only become widespread in the middle Bronze Age. Neolithic ploughing was not repeatedly undertaken on the same spot and created no lynchets. Similarly, the lack of settlement evidence before the middle Bronze Age suggests mobile settlement and a dispersed pattern of the preparation and consumption of food. As we saw in chapter 4, the Down Farm settlement represents an increasingly spatially restricted set of activities, quite unlike any found in earlier periods. For the Neolithic and early Bronze Age we seem to be dealing with repeated movement which may have had little regularity to it. The streams of action to do with the growing, processing and consumption of food, as well as actions like flint procurement and knapping, were dispersed across the landscape in patterns which are at present difficult to discern. Despite the extensive fieldwalking carried out as part of the Cranborne Chase project there is still much that we need to discover about the use of the landscape as a whole. This will come not just through further data-gathering, but also from schemes of thought which make it possible to link together different patterns of activity in space and time.

Let us look now at the broader landscape and the foci, in terms of monuments and settlements. The public time of the monuments helped bring together the more scattered times of different parts of the landscape and connections further afield. The dispersed system of reference in the early Neolithic may have produced problems of space, but there is no evidence for a disharmoy of times. The monuments were set up to deal with problems of space, but they created disjoint times, for the very regularity of action contained within them clashed with the more irregular times of practice. Apart from the seasonal movement of animals, there is no indication of temporal regularity in food or craft production. By contrast, the monuments were much more regulated and their possible use for charting the movement of astronomical bodies, such as may have been made of the Dorset Cursus to observe the setting of the midwinter sun, would have highlighted their involvement in the creation of time (Barrett et al. 1991: 56). Over time the activities carried out at the monuments sedimented down into habitual practice within the bodies of the human actors. As the intense set of references contained in the monuments became increasingly restrictive, the sets of habitus connected with restricted action strengthened. By the middle Bronze Age this led to a greater concentration of a whole range of activities on particular parts of the landscape and an increased focus on the spatial and temporal coordination of production. The gathering together of spaces and times was one way out of the disjoint times of the late Neolithic/early Bronze Age world and led to a different ordering of the landscape.

The reorganization of space and time from the middle Bronze Age onward enjoined the repetition of productive action on particular spots on the landscape. The repetition of acts such as ploughing created field systems and the coordination of domestic activities led to settlements. The middle Bronze Age does not represent the switch from a ritually dominated landscape to one with a secular ordering, but rather a solution to the sheer weight of different times and spaces which had accumulated by the early Bronze Age. The repetition of acts in restricted areas also became more of a part of people's social being. Eventually, the problem gave way to a cure and the space and time of production were brought together within a limited compass. Such a novel coordination of tasks changed the balance of social action away from mutuality and towards materiality. The newly linked chains of production were harnessed to a new end: the production of increased amounts of material things. Society had attained a new temporal trajectory and subsequently faced the problem of concatenating times as activities ran together in self-reinforcing chains around the central motive of material production.

Public times always create a set of rhythms different from those of habit. The deliberate manipulation of action possible in public time makes for faster change in this area of life. For this reason, there is always likely to be a clash between public time and habit, which will either lead to disjoint or concatenating times. Public time is also intimately connected with power: the public manipulation of material things allows for the manipulation of people. However, as we shall see in chapter 6, power is inherent in all relationships, so that we should not see power as a form of dominance of the few over the many. The rise of a small privileged group only occurs under certain conditions of materiality and mutuality. We should also bear in mind the complex connections between public time and habit, which have a cyclical form affecting the nature of power relations. Problems which first arise in the area of conscious practice – in this case the monumental spaces of the early Bronze Age – can set up conflicts with habitual action. The clash between habit and public time can, as we have seen, change the nature of habit, but it can also bring the structure of public time into question. The interaction of public and private times involves the most potent forces operating in society. Habitual action makes social forces appear natural: habit forms a second nature. Public time, which represents the purposeful manipulation of people and things, can only be taken seriously if it derives from the problems of practice. However, if through public time, too much of the basic structure of our social life is brought to light, thought can undermine habit. Public time and its manipulations obviously involves the exercise of power. It is to the sources of power we turn in the next chapter. In considering power we also need to deepen our thoughts on time, by adding extra layers to the creation of temporality and considering long-term trends. A consideration of the long term will help knit together the nexus between the habitual times of practice, public time and power, throwing new light on each of these terms.

6

Problems of History and Meaning

In October 1868 the *New Zealand Gazette* announced 'that the time corresponding to the longitude of 172° 30′ East from Greenwich . . . has been adopted as the mean time for the Colony . . . in accordance with a resolution of the House of Representatives' (quoted in Pawson 1992: 238). Up until this point New Zealand had a variety of local times, despite being a small country. Each local time was supposedly based on longitude, using Greenwich as a base, but due to the lack of transit instruments necessary for time determination, local times were imperfectly known and the scarcity of public clocks meant that local times were not always kept to. Thus Christchurch and its port of Lyttelton, just a few kilometres apart, often had varying times, causing problems for steamer passengers. The main impetus to the standardization of times in New Zealand was the introduction of the telegraph, a vital means of circulating information within the country and of gaining rapid access to fluctuations of price on the world market, especially important to a country dependent on imports (Pawson 1992: 282–3). Similar moves to standardize local times had occurred with the introduction of the railways in Britain in the 1840s and in the United States thirty years later. These various moves were codified on a world scale by the Paris International Conference on Time in 1912, when time zones were set up using Greenwich as the zero meridian and agreeing upon a means of transmitting time signals around the world using the radio telegraph (Pawson 1992: 285).

The setting up of standardized local times, and the combination of these on a world scale, shows the manner in which time and space are linked in the measured public times of the modern world. The New Zealand example also demonstrates the connection between time, power and knowledge. New Zealand Mean Time was introduced to facilitate transmission of information by telegraph – information which was vital in order to maintain New Zealand's place within the world economy and to regulate activity in different parts of the country. Before the telegraph, prices had been 'subject to violent fluctuations due to a scarcity caused by incomplete communication and imperfect information' (McIlwraith 1911: 32, quoted in Pawson 1992: 282–3), and its introduction made it possible for New Zealand's farmers to respond rapidly to world changes in price. The creation of world time was fundamental to the global economy we know today in which commodities, capital and information can move ever more rapidly round the globe (see Harvey 1989: part II on flexible accumulation). An emphasis on measured time and regular hours of work and leisure is basic to capitalism (Thompson 1967). The New Zealand experience was also part of a broader process in which measured time creeps into a central place in every day life. Again in reference to New Zealand in the nineteenth century, Pawson notes that 'During the last twenty years of the century, when national trade statistics by product are available, net totals of 456,907 clocks and 403,346 watches were imported. Even if half the imported clocks went to businesses, it seems likely that most households in 1901 owned a clock as there were then only 158,898 occupied dwellings nationwide' (1992: 284). The regulation of individual routines through time was thus well established at the beginning of this century and represents the start of the endemic spread of the 'hurry sickness' (Young 1988: 260). This disease also came to affect the non-European populations of places like New Zealand, which previously had moved to different sets of temporal rhythms (Sahlins 1985: ch. 2).

The fact that the times by which we live are both conventional and created does not need further emphasis. However, the New Zealand example brings to the fore a three-way link between time, knowledge and power. The moves by New Zealand's legislators to standardize local times helped regulate the internal economy of New Zealand, but also to tie the country into the global economy. The creation of world time rigidified a process of measuring time which had started at least with the first Greek city-states. The division of the world into time zones was necessitated by a growth of a social and economic form, industrial capitalism. The birth and eventual triumph of measured public time came about within particular circumstances of power and domination. In this chapter I shall explore the link between time and power. These two terms have surprising congruence: I put forward in the last chapter the idea that time is the product of all social interaction. Foucault and others have said exactly the same about power. The interactions between time and power can provide new definitions of the social process and, as both arise through involvements with the world, we can give a material definition to both sets of terms.

Before confronting the notion of power directly we must consider one extra theme. A paradoxical effect of the creation of world time over the last century is to make evident the diversity of cultural and personal times existing on different parts of the planet. Not only are different forms of social time seen to exist, but the idea has been put forward that time exists on different levels. Such a notion obviously has attractions for archaeology, which attempts to look at long-term time-scales, as well as shorter-term changes. The link between time and power noted above opens up the possibility that if time operates at different levels, so does power. We now need to consider some of the problems of differing time-scales, before tackling the problem of power, and going onto link power and time through exploring some archaeological examples. The notion of different levels of time has been developed within historical writings over the last fifty years, before being introduced into other disciplines. I shall first of all explore the notion of different levels of history, before considering how these can be linked to problems of time, power and knowledge.

The French historian Braudel is the best-known proponent of the idea that time operates on different levels. His notion of the *longue durée* (long duration) is rightly of interest to archaeologists as it seems to accord with the structure of the archaeological evidence, which precludes us from picking up the lives of individuals or short-term events. Much recent positive discussion has been dedicated to Braudel (Bailey 1983; Bintliff 1991; Hodder 1987; Knapp 1992), as well as Bradley's (1991) more cautious approach, discussed in chapter 5 above. As is well known, Braudel separates out three levels of history: the history of event, the history of conjuncture and the history of the long duration. These three forms of history could be glossed as episodic, cyclical and structural (Knapp 1992: 10). The history of event is the least problematical from an everyday perspective, as it deals with the individual characters of history and the effect of their actions. The history of conjuncture focuses on economic and cyclical human forces, such as the movement of prices or demographic trends. Here ideas such as those of Kondratiev are important and allow careful statistical compilations and manipulations to throw light on trends and cycles (Braudel 1985: 80–5). The long duration underlies both these forms of history and derives from people's place in nature and the effect that a particular set of spaces and material settings had on them. The long duration is human history moving at its slowest, and movement is structured around long-lasting topologies of population density and their linked patterns of food-getting and disease. For Braudel, the long duration must provide the starting point from which total history can be built, representing a long-lasting rhythmical structure out of which derive the quicker pulses of cyclical history and the rapid episodes of everyday life.

Two basic ideas underlie Braudel's scheme. First, that group history is quite different from individual history: the long duration is the history of a social group as a whole, and this has its own structure and effects separate from shorter-term events. Second, that this big history is determinate and that we can only start our understanding of human life from long-lasting structures. In Braudel's view, the individual will not allow us entry into structural history. This is because structural history is more than the sum of its individual parts: it has some vital efficacy of its own. Really effective long-term history is, for Braudel, beyond the knowledge and reach of the individual and cannot be deduced from the actions of any one person.

Braudel's scheme is both compelling and controversial. The very richness of his writings derives not just from his unparalleled command of detail, but from his attempt to see societies as acting on differing social levels. However, the implications of the stress on the long duration have come under increasing attack over the last few years, not least from within the *Annales* school of which Braudel was a member. In common with many other areas of historical writing, the *Annalistes* have turned in recent years to an increasing concentration on narrating individual histories. This reaction is part of the general debate about the relationships between individual actors and larger historical forces. Braudel's history is seen to make individuals the dupes of long-term social processes, having no effectiveness of their own in shaping the course of broader social forces. Braudel's works, such as that on the Mediterranean (1975), have been criticized for not combining different levels of history satisfactorily and for not bringing together the 'durable phenomena of history' with faster moving events. Le Roy Ladurie

(1979: 111–16) has added that the lack of links between different historical levels makes it hard to explain discontinuous change, and that events may well create break points in structures which move life suddenly from one social form to another.

The main problem with Braudel's work from my point of view is not simply that he finds it hard to incorporate the individual, but that his notion of the long duration is insufficiently theorized. His structural history is trying to provide a social basis for understanding the long term, but instead tends to privilege biological and physical factors over the social. The basis of human history is formed by the interaction of people and their environment, whether this is the landscape and its effects on food and population, or the microbial environment with its changing patterns of disease. The concentration on physical factors in the creation of long-term patterns and social or economic effects on conjunctures and events means that the different levels of history are acting under differing impetuses. Combining the longer and the shorter term, when the former and the latter have their own structures of cause and effect, is impossible. On the one hand, the long duration springs from physical factors; on the other, conjunctures and events are seen as social and economic trends. While it may be true that long-term trends underlie all other elements of history, it is hard to see from Braudel's work exactly how the long and the short interact. This may well be because Braudel concentrated most of his attention on his most original creation: the long term.

One recent critique of Braudel's work is contained within the work of Ricoeur, which constitutes one of the most extended and insightful discussions of time in recent years. Ricoeur forms a counterpoint to Braudel, less empirically rich, but more theoretically informed. In *Time and Narrative* (1984; 1985; 1988), Ricoeur contrasts Aristotle's view of time as inherently measurable with St Augustine's exploration of personal time, a contrast I mentioned earlier. For Aristotle, time is related to movement without being identical with it. Time is bound up with the before and after in movement and the numbering of that before and after. Such sequences and their measurement are only possible when there is an intelligence to establish and measure the nature of before and after (Ricoeur 1988: 15). Ricoeur uses Aristotle's thought broadly as an example and originator of the tendency to see time as measured. Measured time becomes cosmological time and can stretch from a nanosecond to the whole life history of the universe. Opposed to cosmological time is Augustine's view of time as personal.

Augustine saw that the present moment of attention refers to both the past of memory and the future of expectation. It is easy to see from this statement how Augustine's thought influenced Husserl and Heidegger (Ricoeur 1988: 21). Kant also felt the influence of Augustine, which is present in his view that time and space are parts of the ways in which our intelligence orders and makes sense of the world. Kant saw time as a 'collective singular'; something which everyone uses to order the world, but which each of us experiences in our own way.

For Ricoeur personal and cosmological time tend to blot each other out, to occlude the other. Although we may all view time in both its personal and cosmological dimensions, it is difficult to think and feel both types of time at once. Our means of making sense of the conflicts of personal and cosmological time is through narrative: 'time becomes human time to the extent that it is organised after the manner of narrative; narrative, in turn, is meaningful to the extent that it portrays the features of temporal experience' (Ricoeur 1984: 3). Narrative's therapeutic function in bringing together these two different times derives in turn from Ricoeur's general view that life is only made liveable through language. As discussed in chapter 3 above, such a strictly hermeneutic view excludes the role of material things in creating the spatial and temporal structures of life, as well as omitting all elements of life which are not directly meaningful. If we follow Heidegger's view that much of life is dominated by unthinking routines, and knowledge is only employed when these routines encounter problems, then we must accept that much of life is beyond the scope of meaning.

Ricoeur's grounding in hermeneutics and meaning leads him to see our main temporal task as creating meaning from the intersection of big cosmological time and small personal time (Ricoeur 1988: 245). Because of this view Ricoeur sees Braudel's stress on the *longue durée* as an escape from the problems of personal time. Ricoeur translates Braudel's writings on the long duration into a form of narrative history, claiming that long-term group time has no special existence and can only be discussed using the narrative strategies of quasi-characters, quasi-events and a teleological ordering, all of which are drawn from individual time (Ricoeur 1984: 208–25). In his view, the long duration becomes a stretched-out form of personal time, which loses Braudel's insight that the long term has a power and efficacy of its own.

In drawing my own view out of the tangled skein of ideas on time I shall start by reformulating Kant's notion of time as a collective singular. I too see time as a collective singular, not because, as Kant thought, it is one of our brain's basic ordering principles, but because it is created together and experienced singly. Time both unites and divides us. Each of us must live our own life, but the shape and structure of each person's life is created out of forms of group time. The notion of a collective singular can reveal an infinite number of times from the purely personal back as far as we want to trace our present forms of group life. Although time as a collective singular has infinite depth and many different forms, I shall echo Braudel in distinguishing three main levels. The first of these is the time of our lives, the time of personal existence bounded by birth and death. Following this is a public time of consciously manipulated symbols and meanings: both Ricoeur's narrative forms and the setting up of world time represent the setting up of different forms of public time. From this point of view, Ricoeur's work appears as one of the most insightful explorations of public time and its structures. We can see over the last few hundred years the growth of certain narrative forms such as the novel and the regulated public times of work and leisure, which have been arenas of conscious manipulation and conflict. These public times are not sufficient unto themselves as narrative and symbolic forms, but have to do with everyday practice and the material settings in which this takes place. Ricoeur talks of the relations between practice and narrative, but has no model of practice or its relationship to telling. Beyond conscious public times are the larger group resources of recursiveness, pulling features of the past into the present and creating projections towards the future. Longer sweeps of recursiveness are solidly material, as it is the enduring nature of material culture that makes possible life on a scale greater than that of the individual. These different levels are not totally separate but interpenetrate in complex ways. Individual life is grounded in habit, which derives from larger and longer structures of recursiveness. Each has its own forms of effectiveness, and although we can say in general terms that we are most conscious of the structure of own lives and least of the long term, it is also true that facets of individual life remain hidden and that some elements of the long term can lie revealed.

Public times represent the main arena for the operation of forms of power, poised as they are between the individual and the naturalizing forces of the longer duration. Public times gain their power through seeming natural and having a degree of rightness in the eyes of all the actors. Feelings of rightness derive in turn from the material settings within which people are socialized, stemming from their concordance with longer term forms of recursiveness. The long-term creation of time is the most hidden, accepted and therefore powerful social arena of all. Long-term time thus represents a powerful set of forces which, when manipulated aright, can aid acceptance of the current state of affairs, but if mishandled can highlight the arbitrariness of social forces and the necessity for change. The long term is closely connected with power, and before examining examples of long-term continuities evident from archaeological evidence we need to undertake a brief excursus into the problems of power. Nietzsche and Foucault together are two of the most influential writers on power in the last 100 years. There is much to be argued with in their writings, but their views cannot be ignored.

Times of the Body and Times of the Head: Nietzsche

Nietzsche's thought forms a major element of a critical stream within the western intellectual tradition, feeding into the writings of Heidegger and thence into post-structuralism. His criticisms of rationality and Christianity have found an increasing echo through this century and his idea of the world as an aesthetic effect, a text, is everywhere. He is also modern in tone, sharing with a great deal of recent popular culture a desire to shock those with secure middle-class values. Much could be (and has been) written about Nietzsche, but here I am only concerned with one subject: the link between power and knowledge, both in the creation of history and in writings on history. Nietzsche's thought finds a recent echo in the work of Michel Foucault. Nietzsche and Foucault, considered together, have done much to open up the scope of history writing and to change its nature. Archaeology, as a discipline attempting to comprehend different forms of history from that which can be constructed from written accounts, has taken considerable interest in Foucault in particular (Miller and Tilley 1984; Tilley 1990), though paying less attention to Nietzsche (Bapty 1990). Also of interest, but as yet unremarked, is the tension in both writers between words and the nature of the material world. Although both emphasize the constructed nature of reality, they are reluctant to disavow the material qualities of things and the effects that these have on historical action.

When approaching Nietzsche's writings one question that immediately assails the reader is, why be interested in the thoughts of a racially bigoted misogynist who provided some inspiration for Nazi thought? Leaving aside the fact that Nietzsche's anti-Semitism may be more apparent than real and that the use the Nazis made of his thought may have been repulsive to him (Kaufmann 1974, ch. 7), Nietzsche is a disturbing thinker – and in this he resembles Heidegger. At best one can feel ambivalent about both of them; it is impossible to decide whether one likes their work or not and in many ways this is an effect for which both strove. Nietzsche has touched a number of the raw nerves of the twentieth century and attempted to disrupt what would otherwise be comfortable habits of thought. His disruptive qualities make him impossible to ignore, although sometimes embarrassing to explore. Such exploration has been made easier by recent commentaries such as that of Nehamas (1985), who handles Nietzsche so subtly that one gets the feeling that he may have extracted more from Nietzsche's writings than is actually there.

The first thread I want to pull out of Nietzsche's work (and which can be followed through to Foucault) is his relational view of the world. Nietzsche sees the world as an infinitely dense series of interconnections. The things in the world do not exist alone, but derive their properties from sets of relations with other things. Nietzsche does not deny the existence of objects, but he does argue that there are no isolated objects; no things-in-themselves. The world's connections are not static, but always in a state of flux. 'All Being is for Nietzsche, a becoming. Such becoming, however, has the character of action and the activity of willing. But in its essence will is will to power' (Heidegger 1979: 7). Things do not have power, they are power. And the set of connections composing the world are governed by continual jostling and the struggle of everything against everything else. Force must be resisted, every thrust met by a counter-thrust. Power has no particular direction or goal and its one rationale is self-gratifying expansion (Eagleton 1990: 247).

The jostling, competitive, warring nature of the world means that the sets of relations which compose the world are in a continual state of flux. The things which we take to be separate entities do not have essences, core sets of unchanging properties which make them what they are. Things are instead constituted by interconnections and are as unstable as the seething mass which contains them. Instability is as true for human subjects as material objects. We are unstable and fleeting, constituted as individuals by an effect of grammar which rules that objects must be counterposed by subjects, rather than through real necessity – 'our grammatical custom which adds a doer to every deed' (Nietzsche 1968a: 484). Lacking essential properties, things do not have simple origins. We cannot write history by taking things as they exist today and tracing them back in a linear fashion to the point at which they came into existence. It is impossible to write the history of individual entities and we must rather understand the changing sets of connections which create seemingly stable entities as passing effects. The complexity of history in turn creates the multifarious nature of things: 'all concepts in which an entire process is semiotically concentrated elude definition; only that which has no history is definable' (Nietzsche 1968b: 516). Objects are the result of historical connections, not their cause.

Simple histories should be replaced by genealogy, which charts the contingent, complicated and motley character of past events. In its everyday usage genealogy refers to the construction of family trees drawn up by interested parties, often those within the family whose past is sought. Family members start with certain assumptions about which people to include in the tree, usually themselves and their nearest relatives. If different starting assumptions were used, other genealogies could be constructed. Competing genealogies are not necessarily better or worse; they simply cut reality in different ways. Each genealogy attempts to follow a tangled skein of connections and manifests its own will to truth, its own picture of the world. No description can depict the world as it actually is: there is too much to include and selections have to be made. An attempt to provide an accurate and complete account of the world would have to posit 'an eye that is turned in no particular direction' (Nietzsche 1968b: III, 12, quoted in Nehamas 1985: 85). History, like all forms of knowledge, is produced by interested parties in pursuit of their own ends.

Just as the character of things derives from their interconnections, so do our views of the world. There is no single view, all views are from a viewpoint and have their own perspective on the world. Nehamas points out that one of the central paradoxes in Nietzsche's thought is that while emphasizing that each view is one among many, he sees some as better than others (Nehamas 1985: 3). Although different views are not all reconcilable, or all true, they are not all false. Just because a view is an interpretation does not make it false, but at the same time there are no overall standards for judging truth. Views of the world can be judged good or bad depending on how life-enhancing they are. The world is composed of such a dense and infinite set of connections that we can only appreciate part of it. Truth is how we arrange the world and make it a world that we can live in. The main point of much of Nietzsche's work is to encourage views which are life-enhancing and criticize those which block the flow of life. Life, like all things in the universe, is shaped by the will-to-power, and views of the world also derive from that will and work to enhance that power in particular ways. Knowledge is inextricably linked to power, deriving from our life interests and helping or hindering them. Dogmatic views, such as those of science or Christianity, try to take forms of knowledge deriving from particular forms of life and impose them upon everyone. These perspectives try to pretend that they are not views but the truth and, as such, universally valid. Christianity and rationalism are not equally useful in helping all people live and, in fact, dam the flow of life for many. Much of the blame for the origins of rationality is attributed to the Greeks, who started by flowing with the forces of life in a Dionysian manner and ended up as cool rationalists with a calculating attitude towards the world. Socrates in particular is seen to be to blame: 'a cave of bad appetites', who sought a cure for this in rationality at any price (Nietzsche, in Kaufmann 1982: 477–8).

Also important for Nietzsche and his subsequent influence has been a stress on the body. The body provides some unity for both the self and life. Our bodily being situates us in the world in a particular way: a different biology would yield us up another universe (Eagleton 1990: 235). Our body is the source of all our sensibilities, even those which we see as the most refined: 'But the awakened, the enlightened man says: I am body entirely, and nothing beside; and soul is only a word for something in the body' (Nietzsche 1971: 61). The body is not itself a unity but provides the necessary condition for a unified life – 'The body is a great intelligence, a multiplicity with one sense, a war and a peace, a herd and a herdsman' (Nietzsche 1971: 61). The body is organized coherently and therefore allows conflicting desires, thoughts and actions to exist. Different and incompatible habits exist within the body and guide it at different times. The unity of the self is not something given, but something which must be achieved. The art of life is to achieve unity as a conscious process, an outcome of the will-to-power to find the best form of life. Power, in this view, is not a negative repressive force but the source of creation and unity. Its source of raw material is the body. Of recent years there has been much discussion of the body as an object of history; and the centre of many of these discussions is the work of Michel Foucault.

Foucault

Foucault was much influenced by Nietzsche, in his attempts to capture the full tangle of history for which he used the notion of genealogy, and in the centrality of power to Foucault's work (Rabinow 1984: 71–100). Foucault takes the themes of power and genealogical history and pursues them in a much more concrete form than Nietzsche. Even so, it seems to me that his history is not concrete enough; but this is a point to which I shall return after having considered some of the themes of Foucault's work. Foucault's writings were extremely wide-ranging and the secondary literature on him is vast (Tilley 1990). I have therefore chosen one piece of work through which to introduce some of the crucial points in his discussion of genealogy and power: the first volume of *The History of Sexuality* (Foucault 1981).

The History of Sexuality is not really about sex, but about power; and in Foucault's work power is seen to derive from discourse. Sexuality is located in the broader context of changing forms of discourse between the medieval and the modern worlds. The medieval tangle of powers gave way to the power of the state which worked through regulation, arbitration and demarcation, a series of forms of rationalism. In the move to the modern world the rule of law becomes the central codifying power. During the eighteenth century, according to Foucault, the law took charge of people's bodies. Power, in this view, does not emanate from a single point, but oozes out of every pore of the social system: 'The omnipresence of power . . . it is produced from one moment to the next, at every point, or rather in every relation from one point to another. Power is everywhere; not because it embraces everything, but because it comes from everywhere' (Foucault 1981: 93).

The modern view of sexuality, according to Foucault, is centred around confession, a practice which started in medieval monastic life but which is given modern forms. The result is that we talk compulsively about our silence concerning sex.

> The question I would like to ask is not, Why are are we repressed? but rather, Why do we say, with so much passion and so much resentment

against our recent past, against our present, and against ourselves, that we are repressed? By what spiral did we come to affirm that sex is negated? (Foucault 1981: 8–9).

In order to answer these questions, Foucault feels we need to follow the complex interplay between truth and sex. China, Japan, India, Rome and the Arab world all produced an *ars erotica*, in which truth is understood through experience and accumulated with pleasure. Only the West has fostered a *scientia sexualis* in which confession about sex is codified in scientific terms and the truth is revealed through the skill of the confessor. At the centre of this structure of discourse is the suspicion that sex harbours a dark and fundamental secret (Foucault 1981: 69). The craven, guilty, confessing West is compared unfavourably to the more open enjoyments of other cultures.

Foucault is trying to undertake an 'analytics of power' to examine how different sets of discourses arise about sex, irrespective of whether these are connected with demography or psychoanalysis. These discourses do not arise due to conspiracy; they are not coordinated and coherent, but rambling and contradictory. They are nevertheless powerful. In the seventeenth century there arose two forms of control over the body. The first came from the view of the body as a machine, which must be disciplined to optimize its capabilities and maximize its usefulness. The second focused on the body as the propagator of life and the species. Both were vital to a nascent capitalism (Foucault 1981: 139). For the first time in history the fact and nature of living was brought within the realm of specific calculation, and sex was at the centre of much of the new discussion on life and its meanings. These points fit in with the strands in Foucault's work which look at how people are created as subjects, and specifically how the nature of power is connected to the human body.

Although he emphasized that power is everywhere, power has a very 'top down' look within Foucault's survey of sex. This is partly because he concentrates on the origins of discourse rather than looking at practice: discourse is seen to be dominated by the state, science and the church, and imposed on those below. There is little suggestion here of *hexis*, embodied forms of habitus, of the numb imperatives in arms and legs of which Bourdieu speaks. Because power is seen as discourse, and not practice, it is hard to perceive how power can be resisted, because we get little sight to the ordinary, everyday life from which resistance can start. This fits in with the criticism that is often raised that Foucault provides diagnosis, but no cure: he can show the predicament we are in, but not how to get out of it (Berman 1988: 34–5).

In the end Foucault's is an outsider's view, an objectivist view in Bourdieu's terms, emphasising oppressive forms of knowledge, but little of the texture of lived experience. Both Nietzsche and Foucault share a distaste for the regulated life of the modern world, a theme also found in Heidegger's work. All societies create relations of power, but power in the modern West is used for regulation and repression. Our public institutions and private practices are not simply repressive, but have the cumulative effect of deadening our feel for life. Foucault highlights these themes and the long-term creation of links between power, knowledge and the human body. *The History of Sexuality* as a whole traces the long-term creation of sex and the human subject from antiquity to the modern period (Foucault 1987a; 1987b). It is to the long term that we now turn, and to the links between power, knowledge and practice, before considering three attempts within archaeology to understand long-term change: Bradley's *The Passage of Arms* (1990), Hodder's *The Domesticaiton of Europe* (1990) and Thomas's *Rethinking the Neolithic* (1991).

Power, Symbolism and Time

The main points I take from Nietzsche and Foucault are that power arises from all aspects of social action and that power and knowledge are closely linked. In the last chapter I defined time and space as arising from every action within the social process. Nietzsche and Foucault define power in relational terms, as deriving from the sets of interconnections which make up the world. Time also derives from relations; it is not an abstract measured medium, but sets of relations of recursiveness linking past and future through the present. These joint definitions create considerable unity between time and power. Both these elements of life are by no means the same thing, but they do have the same all-pervasive aspect. Linking time and power represents a considerable advance in thought, as within recent forms of archaeology it has been difficult to frame definitions of power in terms which make it amenable to investigation through the archaeological evidence. In the neo-evolutionary scheme power had a definite top-down look. The chief ordered production, organized redistribution and benefited from exchange. The base of the social pyramid only moved under impulses from the apex, representing a resistant but malleable mass. More sophisticated views of power helped bring down this view of society and took on the notion that power is inherent in all social action. However, in tune with the general emphasis on meaning, power has come to be seen as ideology and has not been given any direct material definition (Shanks and Tilley 1987: 72–3, 180–1).

The three-way link between time, space and power can help make power materially manifest. Equally important, linking these terms can help temporalize definitions of society. If all social operations involved the exercise of power, and power and time are linked, then the whole social process can be seen as an essentially temporal structure, a process of the unfolding of power relations. This view gets away from a crucial disadvantage of the neo-evolutionary scheme: that its categories of society were static. Movement occurred in the change from one stage to another, for instance from tribe to chief, but it was difficult to incorporate the process of becoming into any category considered alone. By contrast, if power derives from relations between people and things and these relations always involve change, then power becomes a moving moment of the social process.

The forms of involvement in the world which create time and space have different dimensions to them, and so must power. All ordinary everyday relations, such as those of gender, age and class, are structured by power. There is first of all the inertia caused by the mass of habitual practices which, while by no means homogeneous, give an overall direction and flow to life. These are contrasted with public time, forming a consciously referential structure through which time and space are deliberately created as a means of coping with the problems of habitual practice and open to manipulation. Those who see power as ideology concentrate on public time alone, missing the real connection of this sphere of life with habit, which also makes resistance to power difficult to understand. It is too simple to see public time as the area through which domination is exercised and habitual practice as the site of resistance, but there is some truth to this formulation. A straightforward distinction between conscious domination and resistance through habit cannot be made because public time is deeply ambiguous. Public time is not the planned creation of individuals but arises from habitual practice. The forces of habit legitimate and bound public time: it is only within habit that feelings of the rightness of the world are created. If public time is manipulated in such a way as to cut across habitual practice, habit becomes the source of resistance to manipulation. However, through long repetition public time can sediment down into bodies and things, creating new forms of habit. There is thus a complex interplay between problem and solution, manipulation and emancipation. Where habit and public time meet there is instability, which is the source of both much social creativity and pain.

Our consideration of different levels of time has led to the notion that both time and power operate on a number of levels. If power is linked to time and time has a number of levels to it, then power cannot be seen as all of a piece, but must also operate at different scales. In order to develop this and the other points made above, let us turn to an archaeological example. In the last chapter we looked at Bradley's (1991) consideration of Stonehenge as a public legitimating device operating over 1500 years. We can move on to a more extended consideration of the long-term forces in society, more extended both in terms of the treatment and the time-scales considered. This arises from both Bradley's (1990) work on structures of deliberate deposition in operation between the Neolithic and the Iron Age in Europe, and Thomas's (1991) on the nature of Neolithic life.

Deliberate Deposition: A Long-Term Structure

Bradley (1990) looks at forms of deliberate deposition in hoards, graves and river finds from the Neolithic to the Iron Age in order to work out long-term continuities in these areas and consider how these continuities were used to create change. He looks at a sequence of change over 4000 years, providing an excellent opportunity to review different forms of power and time. In exploring Bradley's work I shall follow the argument advanced earlier. The Neolithic to the early Bronze Age can be seen to be dominated by mutuality and forms of consumption designed to set up links between people; from the middle Bronze Age onwards this switches to a system structured around materiality and production, a form of life which provides a continuing dynamic in the Iron Age when material and social relations take on new forms of centralization and standardization. In the following discussion I accept Bradley's basic premise that forms of deposition from the Neolithic to the Iron Age represent a continuous but changing tradition. By the late Neolithic the tradition already had immense time depth. Although people may not have known how long these forms of deposition had been taking place, they would have represented a structure of recursiveness of infinite depth from the point of view of the individual. This raises the dual question of how this long structure of recursiveness operated within life as a whole, and how it was maintained.

Bradley starts his survey from two basic points. First, he stresses that each class of deposit, such as hoards, graves and water finds, cannot be looked at in isolation, but must be considered all together as a structured set of differences. Second, that these structured sets of differences unfold as a system over the long term. By playing each deposit off against the rest we can learn a lot about the forces which drove deliberate deposition over four millennia. In my terms they create a conscious system of reference overlying unthought practice. In Bradley's view, a central fault line running through the deposits is the difference between sacrifice, in which animate objects are offered up to influence spiritual and natural forces, and offerings, where inanimate items are discarded for reasons of social power (Bradley 1990: 37).

Bradley compares developments in different parts of western and northern Europe. He stresses similarities between Britain, Brittany and southern Scandinavia in their slow adoption of farming resources and the monumental landscapes that were initiated at the beginning of the Neolithic in all three aras. The monuments formed centres of deposition in pits, ditches and chambers. To provide continuity with the previous examples, I shall concentrate on Bradley's discussion of the British evidence and I shall complement Bradley's work with that of Thomas (1991), who has provided a detailed analysis of a number of monumental landscapes in southern Britain.

The deliberate deposition of artefacts and rubbish in pits, tombs and water can be traced back at least to the beginning of the Neolithic. After the widespread occurrence of causewayed enclosures early in the Neolithic, different regional traditions were set up. In the Midlands and the north of England individual burials were made under circular mounds which contained items such as belt fittings, beads, pins and stone tool types made on local flint. Peterborough Ware is as common in these deposits as polished stone axes are rare. The area within which these burials are found has few henges, cursuses or communal tombs (see figure 6.1). In the area where henges are found, axes are common both within monuments and as votive deposits in rivers and bogs. Bradley sees the axe as a central symbol in the British Neolithic, having both a practical function for forest clearance and symbolic power

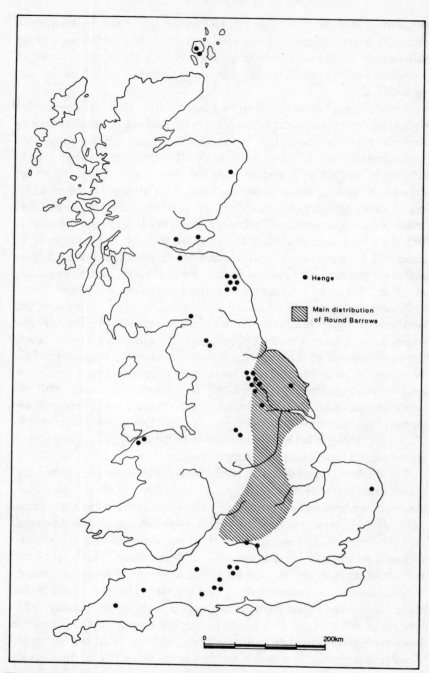

Figure 6.1 The distribution in Britain of Neolithic round barrows compared with that of henge monuments. (From Bradley 1990, *The Passage of Arms*, Cambridge University Press, fig. 14.)

deriving from that function (Bradley 1990: 94). Axes moved far from their quarries and foreign axes were often found in large amounts in areas which themselves produced axes, demonstrating that the movement was not due to utilitarian considerations of supply and demand. However, the deposition of axes varied from region to region, being relatively uncommon in areas with individual burials. Grooved Ware dominates the deposits in many monuments, where deposits are often made in a highly structured manner (Bradley 1990: 69). Thomas (1991) has emphasized the complexity of deposits within many of the monuments. For instance, within Woodhenge wild animals dominated deposits in the outer ditch, pigs were the main animal in the outer pits and cows were most common in the inner pits within the henge. Human remains were mainly found outside the henge (J. Thomas 1991: 71–3). The repetition of such deposits which are carefully structured in space in many monuments indicates a considerable need to deal with the problems of space, as we have seen. Furthermore, much of the debris may well be the remains of mass consumption of food, a set of social events which led to a precise spatial distribution of the remains of feasting. The combination of the structure of the monument and the mobile elements of material culture and refuse opened up rich possibilities for spatial combinations.

The twin systems represented by the single burials and the monumental landscapes operated separately for over 500 years. Here we have two quite different approaches to dealing with the problems of practice. There are also variations in the region with a monumental tradition. Two contrasting areas are surveyed by Thomas, the Upper Thames valley and Avebury. The overriding difference is the number and complexity of monuments in the Avebury area compared with the Upper Thames. Avebury also seems to have had different depositional practices from the rest of Wessex, such as pits in which Peterborough and Grooved Ware are associated, unlike the rigid separation found elsewhere, as on Cranborne Chase. Avebury also seems to have been a source of raw material in the form of flint. Hackpen Hill has a series of indentations which may indicate flint extraction (J. Thomas 1991: 163), and this process of extraction and working seems to have increased in the later Neolithic. Axes were also exchanged more in the later Neolithic, showing the growth in the movement of material (ibid.: 171). Other aspects of the economy were also unusual in the Avebury area, as indicated by the large areas of cleared land, and sheep may be more predominant in this area than in others (ibid.: 163). The area also displays some heterogeneity in material culture, which may be due to the large number of exotic contacts and differential activities within the region. The pottery at Windmill Hill comes from both clays in the Kennet valley and from the Marlborough Downs (ibid.: 165). The chambered tombs, such as that at West Kennet, show similarities to tombs in the Cotswolds and the deposits at Windmill Hill provide evidence of high densities of animal bone, which Thomas sees as evidence of feasting. Taken altogether this evidence is considered by Thomas to show the existence of a number of interrelated groups in the area, which had a wide range of contacts in material culture, as shown by pots and the tomb types. The Avebury area may have supplied high-grade flint to the Mendips, the Cotswolds and the Upper Thames valley. In exchange for flint they may have been able to 'extract exotic goods, social knowledge (including methods of tomb building), personnel and corvée labour from their western contacts' (ibid.: 168).

In the late Neolithic these contacts intensified and this period saw the construction of some of the most famous of Britain's prehistoric monuments, including Avebury itself and Silbury Hill (see figure 6.2). By around 1880 bc all the major monuments were complete and avenues were built to join up several of the larger constructions, such as Avebury and the Sanctuary. 'Possibly this phase saw the rise to dominance of a single group, briefly controlling a proto-state social formation' (J. Thomas 1991: 174).

Quite a different situation is found in the Upper Thames valley. As we have seen, one of the chief contrasts is that this area is less dominated by monuments than Avebury. Early Neolithic settlement is sparse, with a series of flint scatters downstream from Oxford. In the earlier Neolithic the upper reaches of the Thames may have been used only on a seasonal basis, being settled on a larger scale in the later Neolithic period, developments paralleling those on Cranborne Chase. The area south of Abingdon is seen by Thomas as a core area from which the northern stretches of the upper Thames was settled (J. Thomas 1991: 155, fig. 7.4). The causewayed enclosure at Abingdon is the one monument which might belong to the later fourth millennium. Indeed, the bulk of the dates come from a later phase of the monument, between 2700 and 2500 bc, and many of the other barrows and mortuary enclosures seem to have been built around this date.

One of the chief characteristics of this area is the large number of relatively small monuments: Cranborne Chase has one large cursus, the

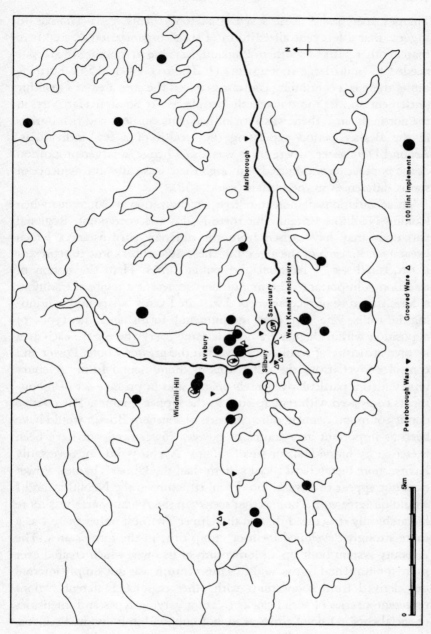

Figure 6.2 The distribution of monuments and artefacts in the Avebury region in the later Neolithic. (From Thomas 1991, *Rethinking the Neolithic*, Cambridge University Press, fig. 7.8.)

Thames area has at least seven small ones. This leads Thomas to suggest that a less centralized form of social organization existed here than in other parts of southern England, less able to mobilize the labour needed to build large monuments (J. Thomas 1991: 155). Furthermore, there is a continuing contrast between the core area of Neolithic settlement and its more northerly periphery. At Stanton Harcourt, in the northerly area, there was a major henge monument and rich burials in the Beaker period expressing the wealth of a few individuals. Around Dorchester, where there was also a henge, a larger proportion of the population was buried, although there was still some evidence of status differences in the burials (ibid.: 158).

These variations demonstrate that generalization is dangerous when looking Neolithic Britain. But there is also a deeper point. Regional variations may have arisen from the different circumstances which existed *within* each of the areas, but these differences come to represent a structured set of habitual and public times. Here the notion of tradition is important. The monuments represent a regional tradition, a basic structure of recursiveness distributed across space and continuing in time. The fact that monumental forms and the types of deposition within them were not the same everywhere gave each area its own structure of recursiveness within the greater whole. Power and control derived from the differences in monumental form: Avebury represented a particularly densely spaced and impressive set of monuments compared with regions such as the Upper Thames. The relative density of monuments in different parts of southern Britain would have been as important as a source of power. Power need not have been exercised by individuals or small groups: Avebury did not necessarily have a more hierarchical social system than the Upper Thames. Power does not appear to have a 'top down' structure in the Neolithic, and I would disagree with Thomas that society in the Avebury area was more hierarchically structured than in the Upper Thames; rather there was a more strongly developed form of group time in the former area. The Avebury system built up a momentum of its own, which created ever more monumental forms, and this momentum was not simply internal but derived from connections with other regions. Different regions represent a series of social clocks creating varying types and intensities of social time. Disjoint times arose not only within individual regions, but between regions. These together formed an unstable system of structures which all collapsed by the middle Bronze Age. The large scale of the changes from monuments to field systems shows that they arose not from the problems experienced in any one area, but throughout the system as a whole. Such large-scale changes take us back to Braudel's notion that large historical processes are the most effective. Whilst agreeing with this to some extent, we can also see that large history arises from social circumstances, not from people's relationship to the environment.

Varying intensities of ritual practice also encouraged differential movements of materials, as can be seen from the early Neolithic causewayed enclosures, where the most elaborate sites (such as Hambledon Hill, the Trundle and Whitehawk) produce the richest artefactual assemblages. These differences were not static phenomena but mutually structuring: the public time of one place had considerable effect on the times and cycles of life of other areas. It is also of considerable importance to note that although the times and spaces of the monuments did open up the possibility that some groups could manipulate the social process, this possibility is limited by the fact that public time is structured on such a large scale spatially and temporally that deliberate manipulation was always constrained. The possibility that public time could produce a power base for individuals or small groups was limited: power was to do with relations within the group as a whole.

These regional traditions structured the post-Neolithic history of southern Britain and influenced the reception of metal into Britain with the beginning of the Beaker period. The tradition helped facilitate change. The Beaker period in Britain saw the rapid introduction of metal, which was manifest in different forms within the two different Neolithic traditions. The single graves come to be dominated by daggers and small tools. They never contain axes. On the other hand, bronze axes are found in henges, hoards and in rivers. The exotic origins of bronze made it suitable for replacing the stone axes, moving over long distances. However, although metal first appeared in a manner structured by Neolithic traditions, metal deposits developed new structures of their own. Metal opened up new avenues for deposition, but this novelty was incorporated into the existing structure of deposition. A greater distinction came to be made between grave deposits and hoards on the one hand and between deposition in water and dry land on the other. These distinctions strengthen in the late Bronze Age when the deposition of metal reaches its peak. Weapons predominate in rivers and bogs and may well be associated with human remains, providing a hint that weapons and water were connected with the disposal of the dead (Bradley 1990: 108–9). As Bradley notes, it was by the late Bronze Age that the past had lost its hold, the old monuments had been abandoned and settlement evidence comes to the fore.

Looking at southern Britain more generally we can see greater similarity between regions from the middle Bronze Age onwards. In many areas large monuments come to be replaced by field systems, some of which start in the late Neolithic period. It has only recently become obvious how widespread and early in date many field systems are: recent work has turned up extremely extensive and deliberately laid out systems in many parts of the country (Fleming 1988: ch. 8). Given the fact that work to discover field systems is only recent and that so many must have been destroyed, the examples so far discovered must represent only a small fraction of the systems which originally existed. Field systems by no means created a standardized social landscape, but they do provide evidence that in many areas new forms of recursiveness came to dominate, and these had to do with repeated sets of agricultural practices carried out in the same confined spaces year after year. The extreme regional diversity seen in the late Neolithic declines, together with the emphasis on the creation of public time. Bradley's work provides an insight into this decline of public time.

The novelty of the middle Bronze Age was to link habitual practice and productivity. From now on habitual action was centred around making and refining things. An emphasis on materiality set up a new dynamic in which things were used to create more material things, and installed this process at the centre of social life. There was much less stress on relations between people and the human emphasis is found mainly in the movement and deposition of bronze. By the late Bronze Age, bronzes were deposited regularly in watery locations and on dry land in hoards and graves. Bradley sees both a dual structure to the deposits and two sets of motivations. The votive deposit of weapons in water sprang from social competition, a form of pot-latching in which gifts thrown away represent the simultaneous giving of a gift and destruction of wealth, the latter limiting the ability of others to respond (Bradley 1990: 138). The impressive deposit of weapons in water formed a very effective type of conspicuous consumption. It also had effects on the metal supply. The main innovation of Bronze Age deposition was the lack of creation of complex spaces and times in the process of deposition. Bronze Age deposition, whether in water or in graves, seems to have occurred at a single point in space and may not have involved the coordinated actions of number of people spread over space and time, as in earlier period. The forms of power created by such acts of deposition may have helped increase the influence of one group within the whole. This is a measure of changing group structures brought about by the new emphasis on materiality. A further change with a similar cause is that up until the early Bronze Age many things deposited did not have inherent worth. Rubbish was a favoured material put into many pits and ditches, although this was complemented in some areas with stone axes and pots which may have had some intrinsic worth. From the middle Bronze Age many elaborate bronzes were thrown away and, as Bradley notes, these forms of destruction may have had material as well as social effects. The difference between the Neolithic and the later Bronze Age forms of deposition is the lack of emphasis on space in the latter. The amount and type of material seems much more important than the elaborate spatial distribution of deposits. Space is less of a social problem than the amount of material deposited. In both cases, public time derives from practice, so that changes in public time derive from changes in practice. The fact that the overall structure of the evidence across the landscape can be linked to forms of deliberate deposition means that one set of evidence can be pursued to provide insight into the other.

There were also problems with the supply of bronze at different periods, and these were dealt with through the hoards in which bronze was recycled. Recycling activities go up as the supply of bronze declines and are thus more common at the end of the Bronze Age (Bradley 1990: fig. 34). There is also a geographical structure to hoarding: the massive hoards containing a jumble of different types in the metal-producing areas can be constrasted with the smaller and far more structured hoards in regions where supply was more constrained. Taken together, river deposits and hoards reinforce Bradley's point that different deposits have to be seen as a system. The major effect on the metal supply may not have been utilitarian considerations, but votive deposition in rivers. The votive deposits had their effect on the cycles of production, which show up archaeologically as hoards. One class of find cannot be understood without the other.

The Bronze Age system was replaced by a greater complexity of deposits in the Iron Age. Iron was only accepted reluctantly, because it did not have the exotic connotations of bronze and did not represent a technical evolution from an inferior to a better metal type, but resulted from the breakdown of the Bronze Age system. Iron Age deposits proliferate beyond those made in graves and water and see an increase in standardization of the objects deposited. This greater standardization of objects, such as coins and ingots, may well reflect more regularized relations between people. Standardization is connected to the greater centralization of some areas of life created through the setting up of oppida in the late Iron Age as centres of production and exchange, which represent new forms of control within the landscape. As well as change, the Iron Age sees the cycle of deposits coming full circle with a return to the emphasis on sacrifice found in the Neolithic. In Bradley's view the Neolithic concentration on sacrifice and fertility is to be understood as a means of coming to terms with the novelty of domestication, planting, breeding and herding. The early Iron Age sees an unparalleled reorganization of farming and the agricultural land-scape, returning problems of fertility and food to the centre of the social agenda (Bradley 1990: 199). Once again the problems of change were dealt through the medium of a tradition with an antiquity of several millennia.

The long tradition of deposition can be seen as a response to a continuing set of problems set up in the Neolithic. The different forms of monumentality and deposition which existed until the early Bronze Age represent a long duration. The disjoint times within and between regions which existed by the early Bronze Age led to the downfall of the whole structure and the setting up of field systems with their well-defined spaces and emphasis on production. The greater materi-ality created by this shift is reflected in new depositional practices which did not deal with the problems of space and time, but focused on the destruction of material wealth. New forms of power may have started to grow from the middle Bronze Age, which gave a small group increasing influence over the rest. By the Iron Age we see the growth of centralized settlements involved in production and exchange, as well as the possibility of social divisions reflected in standardized forms of material culture. The very existence of a continuing tradition implies that although much change occurred from the Neolithic to the Iron Age certain problems stayed the same. The small-scale, relatively decentralized societies of this period experienced a core set of problems to do with the material and social life of the group. The tradition responded by combining people and materials in recurring ways over a period of millennia. Ultimately the system of deposition did cease in the early medieval period, at which point life was restructured in a fundamental way.

My answer to the question of why the tradition of deposition initially came into being is that it derived out of a form of public time set up at the beginning of the Neolithic. This leads us to consider a question that has hung over archaeology for the last 150 years: what is the Neolithic? We can move towards an answer to this question through a consideration of a new answer provided by Hodder (1990).

The Domestication of Europe

In *The Domestication of Europe* (1990), Hodder takes as his main problem the structures of power and meaning in Neolithic Europe. The basic theme of the book is contained in the title: the domestication of plants and animals between 10,000 and 4000 years ago in the Near East and Europe was not just a physical process, but also a symbolic and social process involving the taming of the community to allow it to live in new forms. The book fixes on a series of struggles and dichotomies, central to which is the conflict between the individual and the group, as events versus structures. Such dichotomies were played out through new forms of symbolism arising at the period when agriculture started. Symbols are seen as the 'secondary connotations evoked by the primary associations and uses of an object or word' (Hodder 1990: 13). Symbolic structures are used to create general concepts and schemes which order the whole of life, and in Hodder's view these are often organized in a series of oppositions, such as death:life, wild:domestic, male:female. Social relations and symbolic schemes are mutually producing: symbolism derives from social relations of kin, gender and age, and symbols form the matrix within which these relations are conceived and worked out (ibid.: 13). Hodder is particularly interested in the way society and symbols are both produced and producing over long time-spans.

In the case of Europe this interplay is traced from the Palaeolithic through to the end of the Neolithic, providing a contextual analysis of changes within this one set of cultural traditions. Hodder sees society and its symbols as ultimately deriving from a really long-term division between nature and culture, in which the desire for a cultural order arises in basic fears and needs for protection from social and natural forces. A contextual reading for Europe thus grades into a universal human reading: 'The culture/nature duality is the very stuff of all human society' (Hodder 1990: 30). This dualism, seen as the difference between the domestic and the wild, is thought by Hodder to have been produced in Europe during the Palaeolithic period through the particular cultural forms of the exercise of power.

> I have suggested that the construction of the cultural in relation to the wild derives from a single process – the creation of social and cultural prestige through the separation and control of the wild. But at different times in different ways this single process is given different expressions. (ibid.: 289)

The Palaeolithic attempt to control nature for reasons of social prestige led to the setting up of two opposed terms – the *domus* and the *agrios*. By the Neolithic the domus is associated with the house, the domestic sphere. The notion of domus has to do with a whole series of domestic activities, such as the preparation of food and the rearing of children within a stable space; the very core of the newly stable farming ways of life. But the house also becomes the centre of symbolism to do with controlling social and natural forces. Oppositions between men and women are worked out anew, as well as between life and death. The domus does not operate alone, but is joined to its opposing paired term: the agrios, the wild. 'Agri-culture' is seen as culturing the wild. 'The "origins of agriculture" are connected, via the domus-agrios opposition, to the more general social and cultural process of domestication' (Hodder 1990: 86). From the late Palaeolithic period onwards, wild resources are used extensively; plants and animals were removed from the wild and brought within the cultural sphere. These moves increased people's dependencies on a small range of species and brought about genetic changes in the animals and plants, which in turn made them dependent on people for propogation and survival. All of these changes took place within a symbolic context centring on the house, through which both nature and society were domesticated. The house formed a centre of symbolism, the site of paintings, figurines and pots, which also reflected a central concern with death. The dead were buried in the floor of houses, domesticating the natural process of death, which was seen to have a whole set of fears attached to it (ibid.: 36). The disciplining of these fears also helped to hold social forces in check, through demonstrating the power of society to control nature (ibid.: 292).

The process of domestication started in the Near East and spread through Europe, changing continually as it went. These changes brought about three Neolithics, each with their own variants of the domus-agrios opposition. The Near East and south-east Europe built villages, often of mud brick, and these relatively dense communities struggled with tensions between the genders and the fear of death. Central Europeans built large longhouses in clearings in the forests and emphasized transitions between the internal domesticity of the house and external natural forces contained within the forest. Western and northern European communities adopted the novel resources of farming late and incorporated these gradually within traditional Mesolithic practices. The major effect of farming was to extend the range of communities, from a concentration on coastal marine resources to cultivation of plots inland. In these areas there was no sudden adoption of sedentism, but a gradual reduction of mobility over a millennium or more as the garden plots became increasingly important to life. Since it would be impractical to try to cover all the areas looked at in Hodder's wide-ranging book, I will concentrate here on the area from which my previous examples have been drawn: Neolithic Britain.

In Britain, as we have seen, there is little settlement evidence (presumably due to the mobility of people) and Hodder therefore sees the domus principle as working itself out through tombs. The main problem of the domestication of society in Britain, as Hodder sees it, is the working out of conflicts between individuals and society. Early in the Neolithic the rituals associated with tombs and burial help to submerge the individual and reinforce the group. Human bones move within tombs and between different parts of the landscape: long bones predominate in long barrows, whereas skulls are more common in causewayed camps. Monuments were linked through the movement of human remains and these movements helped to integrate the landscape. Humans were also linked in symbolism to other animals. Cows, in particular, may substitute for people, with cattle bones often being treated in the same manner as human bones: articulated, disarticulated, burnt and unburnt bones of both species are found in the same places and contexts (Hodder 1990: 250). Tombs are axially ordered. Megalithic chambered tombs have an obvious central axis formed by the passage with chambers off the central axis. Non-megalithic tombs are often constructed along a central fence crossed by a series of smaller fences (ibid.: 245). The linear ordering found from the early Neolithic onwards comes to dominate the whole landscape in some areas in the later Neolithic. Massive bank barrows, avenues and cursuses pull together individual monuments in areas such as Avebury to form an integrated landscape. Hodder sees this as the domus principle moving out from tombs to enculturate the social environment as a whole (ibid.: 255–6). The amount of effort needed to produce such a humanly ordered landscape increases from the early to the late Neolithic, perhaps indicating larger forms of social organization moving from the family and the lineage to some supra-lineage form of organization.

At the end of the Neolithic emerges the Beaker phenomenon, which in Hodder's view represents the re-appropriation of the agrios principle and a gradual change of the structure from within. Beakers 'represent a development of a process in which the domus is gradually trans-formed from within by appropriating the ideas of the individual, the warrior and the wild' (Hodder 1990: 268). This takes place through separating burial and the domus principle, as this principle becomes increasingly associated with henges and the contexts in which Grooved Ware was deposited. Henges and the domus became increasingly separate from burial practices, which were shifting from the communal to the individual. The emergence of the individual in the form of a cadre of male warriors is part of a dialectical process between the group and the individual. The gradual clearing and taming of the landscape during the Neolithic meant that the wild could re-surface in a controlled domesticated environment, providing the springboard for the Bronze Age. Change is seen as internal, due to a dialectic of structures, rather than caused from without by environmental change or soil exhaustion. Internal changes were set in train by the first oppositions between nature and culture made during the Palaeolithic and given a particular symbolic form in the Holocene by the communal tensions of farming.

Embedding symbolism within practice also has the major advantage that we do not need to give particular meanings to the forms of symbolism used in the past, but must seek to understand them as part of the overall flow of life. In setting up the oppositions between domus and agrios, as the principle moving element in early and mid-Holocene European society, Hodder takes ideas from the present and applies them to the past, raising the immediate question as to how he can know such principles operated many millennia ago. Hodder deals with this problem by acknowledging that the terms he uses are created in the present, but also by saying that out present ideas may have very deep prehistoric roots. The principles of domus, foris (the outside, the foreign) and agrios are still with us today, handed down from early farming communities, and these notions echo back and forth between the Neolithic past and the present in which archaeological interpretation is made. The echoing quality of the ideas makes them impossible to pin down: they are not simply of the past or the present, but reverberate between the two contexts. However, such a view and the complex question of whether such interpretations are correct can be avoided if no necessity is felt to give meanings to the symbolic structures of the past, but rather to see them as a particular element of the flows of life in the past. Further, a view structured around conscious and unconscious reference helps get away from a distinction between economic forms of action on the one hand and symbolic forms on the other. A distinction between symbolic and practical is inherent in Hodder's argument, where the former is seen as more potent than the latter. In my view, conscious and unconscious reference have different forms of cause and effect which are intermingled in a complex manner; and although the public manipulation of conscious reference originally derives from problems in practice, symbolic forms can take on a dynamic and shape of their own.

The consequences of the Neolithic have been much discussed since the nineteenth century, but discussion has been mainly in terms of economic changes which have had social effects. Hodder reverses the arrow of cause, seeing the social and symbolic as at least as important as the economic. This is an extremely important polemical point, reversing the usual concentration on economic forces and the effect of the environment which make the social forces peripheral. However, to concentrate solely on symbolism is to swing the pendulum too far back in the opposite direction.

I would see the Neolithic as neither social nor economic, because of the impossibility of separating these two terms. Rather than talk in terms of economic base and social or symbolic superstructure, I see the Neolithic as setting up a new balance between public time and habit, which of itself created new forms of mutuality and power. The Neolithic in Britain did not suddenly bring about a sedentary way of life, create agricultural surpluses or promote huge population growth; but it did have profound consequences in the practical sphere. The British Neolithic, which represents the slow acceptance of novel resources by marine-orientated hunter-gatherers, created problems of what we might call 'tethered mobility' experienced by hunter-gatherers with crops and herds. These new forms of mobility created a novel structure of involvement with the material world and unprecedented forms of mutuality. Not only were group problems encountered on the local level, but there seems to have been a new structure of widespread contacts which promoted the dispersion of the novel material media of the Neolithic. The monumental Neolithics found in Britain, Brittany and southern Scandinavia are evidence of both problem and solution. The monuments and the materials deposited in them are used to finesse the new structure of space and time deriving from a novel system of habitual reference. But the chains of repetition and recursiveness set up by these new forms of public time were at first also unusual.

The real novelty of the Neolithic lies in the new relation of habit and public time. It is the first period in which the materials used to create public time came to dominate the archaeological record. This dominance obscures the real dynamism of the period, which derives from a multi-levelled interaction of habit and public time. This interaction was diffuse and complex. Public time, in many ways, moves at a quicker rhythm than habit, but the strength of the material forms created by the Neolithic enabled public time to become long-lasting.

Different time-scales are in operation here. Habit changes slowly, whilst some elements of public time move more quickly. A monument, even a large monument such as the Dorset Cursus, may be constructed relatively quickly, but then last for millennia, structuring activity all around it. The relatively quicksilver operations of public time can set up resonances which outlive particular structures of habit. This peculiar temporal relationship between public and habitual was crystallized at the beginning of the Neolithic. Over thousands of years the traditions of deposition build up authority of their own, which gives them unequalled problem-solving powers and the scope to embrace change. We can see a long-term tradition as a cultural treasure, a recursive form of infinite time depth from the standpoint of the individual participating in the tradition. By the early Bronze Age the monumental and depositional landscape had become so complex that it was unsustainable. But is important to note that while considerable changes occurred in the middle Bronze Age the tradition of deposition did not finish, but helped to deal with these changes. By this period the depositional tradition had built up a legitimating power that only time depth can provide. We are faced with something of a paradox. In general habit changes more slowly than public time. But given the right media and social conditions, public time can create immense strands of recursiveness, such that each act calls upon a tradition of immense time depth. The most obvious parallel we have in the western world today is the church. Like Braudel, we can distinguish different forms of the creation of time. These do not form discrete and separate levels, but a set of combined effects. All forms of time can be linked to aspects of power, whether this be the conscious manipulation of public time or the naturalizing influence of long-lasting traditions.

The Neolithic not only initiated new short-term forms of public time, but provided the conditions whereby some of these forms could be perpetuated over extremely long periods, thus sinking from conscious manipulation into habit. Changes occur from the Neolithic to the Iron Age, but the constant problems of material and social relations remain. However, these problems were not entirely new and derive in turn from patterns of history prior to the beginning of the Neolithic. One of the great strengths of Hodder's book is to show that really long-term continuities may have existed between the Neolithic and what went before. In order to appreciate the novelty of the Neolithic, or even to decide whether the Neolithic was new at all, we need to go backwards in time and look at the very long strands of practice represented by the Palaeolithic.

7

Species Being:
The Very Long Term

In this chapter we return again to the question posed in chapter 3: what does it mean to be human? But as well as repeating this question, I shall pause to consider why we should want to create and tackle a problem as large as the global characteristics of human beings. The answer lies in the creation of a world system and the considerations of global history it evoked.

A minor theme of this book has been the setting up of the modern world system over the last few centuries and the need to study processes at a world scale. In the last century a series of disciplines were created which attempted to understand the world through setting up a series of principles seen to operate in all times and places. Geology formed something of a model with its development of uniformitarian theories, based around processes in operation in the present. Uniformitarian approaches were applied widely in the human and natural sciences and enjoyed great sucess in uniting and explaining the diversity of the world. However, the basic laws and models were derived from a general distillation of specific cases observed in the world. Real events and occurrences have particular time-scales built into them, but generalized laws exist in abstracted spaces and times (Fabian 1983: 13). As we saw in the last chapter, people like Nietzsche, Heidegger and Foucault have reacted against the creeping rationalism brought about by the growth of general principles and this has caused a move against abstract theory. Later twentieth-century post-structuralist thought has, in turn, viewed any attempt to return to grounded lived experience as an impossible romantic dream. Instead, the schizophrenic processes of late capitalism are considered to have whipped up a froth of life which is all style without substance, surface without depth. Life has become alien to those living it, anarchic, anomic and inescapable. Harvey (1989) argues against the hopelessness of post-structuralism and sees the forms of thought of late capitalism not as postmodernist, but as a continuation of the tendency found since the birth of capitalism for all cultural forms, including academia, to mirror fast-changing economic and social conditions. The recent stress on styles of life rather than substance derives, in Harvey's view, from such elements of present capitalism as the short production runs which create an ever-changing variety of goods, together with the financial instability caused by an electronic global communication system.

We have on the one hand the broad, theoretically based and empirically orientated schemes of science versus the reaction against such totalizing thought (Jay 1984) contained in the multiple narratives of post-structuralism. I shall take a position halfway between the large general narratives of uniformitarian science and the small particular forms of telling of post-structuralism. As previously noted, thought arises so as to cope with the problems of the world in which we live. We *do* live within a global form of life. From this it follows that questions of how different elements of humanity relate to each must be posed and answers must be attempted. Therefore large narratives to do with human unity and diversity are necessary: the modern world-system has made totalizers of us all. On the other hand we must be aware of casting the world in our own image, and generalizing on the basis of aspects of life we are most familiar with in the West. In building global models we are in danger of taking the processes and relations found in the West as deriving from human nature, and this may carry the implication that different forms of life are unnatural or less developed than our own. Part of our investigations must always involve probing the structure of our thought; thinking about why we see the world as we do and what causes and effects thought will have in terms of the network of power relations that embrace the world. A central problem which arises from generalizing forms of western thought is that global processes are seen to operate in abstract measured time. This causes us to be oblivious of the differences found in forms of human time. Time is not the medium through which human relations unfold: action in the world produces time. The very temporality of life and thought means that we cannot accept uniformitarian principles as formulated over the last two centuries. Change is inherent in human life: but this fact should not lead us into those strands of recent thought which say that change is so endemic and formless that we can say little about it.

To embrace questions on the scale of global being does not mean we have to reduce the vast variety of human times to one big measured sequence. Long spans of time can and must be tackled, as they set up discussions of the nature of the diversity of life in the world today. However, truly temporalized principles are needed in order to appreciate the true diversity and variety of life in the present and the past. The past throws the present into perspective and what we are looking for is a thread to join both, which helps us appreciate both the enduring qualities of human history and its changing nature. Questions concerning humanity as a whole are not the search for a single truth, a single set of principles or an unchanging essence, but part of an attempt at coping in a difficult global situation, which may throw light on how individuals and local groups can exist in a global world structured by unequal sets of relationships. Archaeology is part of a perilous, but necessary, search for the things that bind and divide human groups locally and globally.

Let us start our questioning about human characteristics by considering one of the most important fields for considering humanness: primate studies. I shall use the critical voice contained in the work of Haraway (1992), who has surveyed work on primates and its use in defining human characteristics. Haraway presents a full and critical account of the practice of primatology in this century, as a discipline which has often studied animals in order to find out about people; and in the process she examines the story of the origins of humanity. This is complemented by a second, more focused, study by Cheney and Seyfarth (1990) of a particular group of primates, the vervet monkey, in which they pass explicit comment on the light monkeys' behaviour can throw on human life and thought.

Human Origins and Human Unity

Haraway considers the narrative forms used in studying primates and how these derive from flows of power within the academic community and the world at large. She notes that primates form a border zone between people and nature which is richly productive of ambiguity and hence meaning. Her stance is a partisan one, explicitly feminist and anti-racist, which sees primatology as part of a series of global forces in this century. The forces of colonialism, found in Africa in the pre-war period when the first primate studies were carried out, helped structure the topics of gender and race tackled by primatologists. Post-war decolonization of many of these same countries has helped to change the field conditions in which primatologists work and the sorts of topics they tackle. Primate studies existed within a network of wider forces which both changed the physical conditions under which field studies were carried out, and helped to create new views of gender and class. Not all forces have been external to primate studies. The very fact that these studies have been carried out has helped in changing definitions of race and gender.

> Late twentieth-century primatology may be seen as part of a complex survival literature in global nuclear culture. . . . Primates existing at the boundaries of so many hopes and interests are wonderful subjects with whom to explore the permeability of walls, the reconstitution of boundaries, the distaste for endless socially enforced dualisms. (Haraway 1992: 3)

Stories about primates are both enmeshed in a global culture and a means of working through and redefining some of the discursive elements of that culture.

Haraway covers many topics. Here, I shall concentrate on one central theme: the origins of humans and human behaviour. Primatology is the life history of an order which includes humans, and part of the tales told by primatologists are bound up with origins of the order and of ourselves (Haraway 1992: 5). Haraway concentrates on the narrative structure of the tales told by primatology. A concentration on narrative, she insists, does not dismiss science as mere storytelling, but looks at how possible worlds are reinvented in the struggle for the present world. Stories are part of the practices of power, and primatology is to do with redefining the boundaries set up by two main dualisms: those between sex and gender on the one hand, and nature and culture on the other. One of the purposes of Haraway's book is to reconstruct the primatological narrative so that these oppositions are done away with, making new narrative forms possible.

We pick up Haraway's retelling of the search for human origins in the middle of this century, when accounts of the beginning of human life had come to be structured around the figure of Universal Man. In 1948 the United Nations, itself part of the institutionalization of global life, released a Universal Declaration of Human Rights followed in 1950 and 1951 by statements on race. As Haraway notes, these statements were made by a body speaking for the world as a whole and were published at a time which had just seen the demise of European fascism and colonialism and was about to see the birth of multinational industries, the Cold War and decolonization (Haraway 1992: 197). The Constitution of the United Nations stated that the Second World War was made possible by a 'doctrine of the inequality of men and races' and the statements on race and human rights were made as part of a move to counter such a doctrine of inequality. These statements were written by white academics concerned to show both the mental and physical equality of all present races and the plasticity of culture which led to a kaleidoscope of different ways of life. The main message was that inequality could not be derived from variety. Discussions over the unity and variety of human behaviour immediately brought up questions of the origins of the things that make us human. The liberal humanism which informed the UN declarations derived from and reinforced more general social and academic views. Haraways shows that the work of Washburn was an important vector, both influenced by the general currents of thought at the end of the war and subsequently providing data supporting the propositions of equality contained in the Universal Declaration of Human Rights.

In Haraway's view, Washburn's work links concerns with human unity to an investigation of the origins of human forms of action. Washburn, as a physical anthropologist, was looking for a 'master behavior pattern of the human species' which could be linked into biology. Each major evolutionary shift in the primate world was seen to be due to a primary adaptational complex which resulted in a behavioural transition. Hence it was the modification of hands and feet for grasping, together with stereoscopic vision, that divided the primates from other mammals; apes diverged from monkeys on the basis of pectoral modifications for brachiation. Bipedalism was the crucial factor in dividing off hominids from the rest: the hands could be freed for tool use, and tool use created both mind and body. Around 1950, when Washburn started to pull together his synthesis of biology, behaviour and human origins, recent analyses of the pelves of South African australopithecines had established that they could walk up-right. An upright posture provided the possibility for working with the forelimbs to create technology. Washburn's work, through the idea of a primary adaptational complex, provided a framework within which physical structure could be related to cultural form. 'With the primary humanizing adaptational complex, the animal adopted the behavior to remake itself. . . . In this framework, culture means first of all tools. Culture remakes the animal; this is the universal foundation of human unity and the structure of the persistent western dualism of nature and culture' (Haraway 1992: 208). The creation of culture distanced nature, while at the same time culture was the means by which nature was exploited for human ends.

But Washburn's views went further. Exploitation took a special and essential form: the hunt. From his early interest in bipedalism and tools as the key to human life, Washburn gradually moved to a much more precise hypothesis – that hunting formed the original and basic human adaptation. Australopithecines were intermediates in this scheme; it is only with the advent of the genus *Homo* that the hunting of large animals started. The idea of hunting provided a means to move from biological definitions of a group, clustered round the notion of population, to a social definition in terms of the structural and functional characteristics of the group. A population was a unit with a common ancestry, which was contiguous in space, had a joint ecological role and behaviour and was reproductively continuous over many generations (Simpson 1958: 531–2). Onto this concept Washburn grafted ideas taken from current social anthropology and psychology on structure and function, through the hunting hypothesis (Haraway 1992: 213). Hunting was important not just as a form of subsistence, but because it brought about new forms of social cooperation. Cooperation was essential between males in the process of hunting and subsequently between males and the rest of the group (the women and children) through sharing the results of the hunt. Through hunting, the human group became both divided and united. There was a strong sexual division of labour, with man the hunter the main provider, but also more complex forms of cooperation through food sharing, which took the form of swapping plant foods gathered by women for meat hunted by the men. Hunting provided the basis for universal forms of human behaviour through bridging the biological and the social.

As we have seen, the model was developed in the middle of the century in a climate which used science to argue against racial differences and particularly racial superiority. The universal nature of hunting gave all people the same behavioural origin and the same set of capabilities. Hunting was not only connected with the birth of human characteristics, but seen to be a long-lasting element of human history, encompassing 90 per cent of our existence as a species. This view makes the differences seen between cultures and races today a recent phenomenon, a superficial variety masking deeper unity. However, as Haraway stresses, the emphasis on unity submerged and helped remove from critical thought one particular difference: that of gender. The social world man the hunter inhabited was based around the family, with an outgoing male figure providing for more sedentary women and children. Much of the criticism of this model, both on the theoretical and empirical level, has focused on the issue of gender, particularly after the publication of the 'Man the Hunter' symposium by two of Washburn's former students (Lee and DeVore 1968). The notion of male dominance central to the man the hunter model came partially from primate studies and was seen to be a linking element between hominids and the other apes. For instance, DeVore saw that male dominance animated baboon society, ensuring a coherent group structure and thus group survival (DeVore 1965). Although hominid groups were seen to be more open and flexible than any other primate and centred round a home base, there was thought to be a continuity between baboon and human social life in the existence of male dominance. Gender inequalities were naturalized and seen not as the product of history, but as deriving from human (or even primate) nature.

Emphasis on the universality of human characteristics and the long continuities of human history are understandable in an immediate post-war climate. But in the last thirty years concerns about human unity have been partly eclipsed by the problems of gender. Obviously since the late 1960s there have been various counter-moves. which attempt to ground different stories of human evolution, many of which centre not on race, but on gender. Gender is concept developed specifically to contest the crystallization of sexual differences into particular social roles. Gender looks instead at how men and women are socially constituted (Haraway 1992: 290). A major plank of the argument is that gender cannot be grounded in biology and that sexual dimorphism in the present and the past represents not a single dichotomy, but a changing constellation of traits, which singly and in combination are difficult to connect to behavioural correlates (ibid.: 340–4).

Changing views of human nature and society have been reflected in differing attempts to interpret the archaeological record. I shall consider these briefly here, returning to the topic later in the chapter when considering how to rewrite the long-term human continuities of the Paleaolithic evidence. Since the first discovery of combinations of stone tools, animal and hominid bones in various sites in southern and eastern Africa, attempts have been made to provide behavioural models. One of the most influential has been the formulations of Glyn Isaac. Looking at the early evidence from East Africa, Isaac felt that central foci on the landscape would have formed an essential component of foraging patterns. Isaac saw a division of labour possibly by sex, with the males foraging for meat and the females for plant food. Plants and meat were then combined at a home base through the practice of sharing. Home bases could also have provided the locus for the care of young and other maintenance activities. In Isaac's view home bases were central to the development of early hominid foraging behaviour; and the extension, the cooperation that made home bases possible lies at the root of what makes us human (Isaac 1978). This model has been widely discussed and criticized and the main empirical point of much of the criticism has been that the combination of bones and stone tools may not be evidence of central foci of activity. Rather they may simply be the points on the landscape at which carcasses were butchered (Potts 1984). Potts has argued that an efficient way of exploiting carcasses would be to cache stone tools and move the animals to the tools. The resulting accumulations of stone and bone would soon resemble Plio-Pleistocene archaeological sites. Caching of stones has been observed amongst chimpanzees, and these sites demonstrate patterns of behaviour linking hominids to other animals, in contrast to Isaac's view of them as evidence of the elements that make us distinctively human.

Potts' conclusions open up a new range of possibilities for modelling behaviour in the Plio-Pleistocene period. Stone and bone accumulations may not represent home bases and therefore not be points on the landscape at which females waited for male provisions. Some of these possibilities can be glimpsed by looking at Zihlman's (1984) work, using the pygmy chimp as an exemplar of aspects of early hominids' group life. In Zihlman's model hominids lived in complex and flexible groups, both sexes were broad generalist foragers and were involved in extensive sharing of the range of foods they brought to the group. Groups were matrifocal and the long-lasting nature of infant dependency made female gathering and sharing crucial to the perpetuation of the group. In this version of human history, the move to humanity is due to a greater complexity of social life and sharing than ever found before (ibid.). Although, as Haraway cautions, this notion is in danger of universalizing the 'woman the gatherer' model, which brings with it the same set of dangers as man the hunter, in casting present-day relations far back into the past (Haraway 1992: 347). Bearing such caveats in mind, Zihlman's ideas open up the possibility of a more balanced history in which both sexes are active and the translation of sex into gender that we are familiar with in the present is not a constant of human evolution, but a recent historical product.

The story of the interpretation of human evolution, as Haraway tells it, sees a move away from a concern for racial unity, which made gender invisible, to a more explicit consideration of the problems of sex and gender. Both sets of narratives are rooted in broader contemporary social movements: the emphasis on racial unity was a response to pre-war fascism, whilst gender and sex have been highlighted by feminist currents of thought over the last thirty years. Neither tale is objective or innocent, but neither is a total construct told in ignorance of the evidence as we know it. Later accounts of human evolution break down the gap between nature and culture, seeing the origins of society in society itself, giving both sexes an historical role, rather than privileging the partial activities of one sex. An account such as Zihlman's has much in common with recent primate studies which stress the role of primates as informed social actors and allow weight to be given to the activities of both sexes. In exploring the problem of species being let us now consider one such study, as it makes explicit comparisons between monkey's and human's capabilities. This study is contained in the book *How Monkeys See the World* (Cheney and Seyfarth 1990).

Monkeys and Minds

Cheney and Seyfarth's study is concerned with vervet monkeys (*Cercopithecus aethiops*). Between 1977 and 1989 they observed eleven groups of vervets living at the western end of the Amboseli National Park in Kenya. Vervets have a similar group structure to others of the Cercopithecidae sub-family, such as baboons and macaques, with a group of stable females and mobile males, who always migrate away from the group they are born in and may move several times during their lives. The group is based around the females and their dependent offspring and represents a set of aligned matrilines (Cheney and Seyfarth 1990: 20–2). Cheney and Seyfarth's study was set within a particular theoretical framework sometimes known as cognitive ethology, which concentrates on intelligence, with particular emphasis on the evolution of the human mind. Vervets can throw light on human capabilities through contrast, highlighting the things that we can do and they cannot. The gap between us and them helps to focus attention on the social and evolutionary forces which created human intelligence. Cheney and Seyfarth's approach to the development of cognitive capacities was to look at groups of monkeys in the field, rather than through laboratory experiments. Field-based studies tend to concentrate on the social relations of animals, whereas those in a laboratory examine animals' capacities to handle objects. As Cheney and Seyfarth note (ibid.: 5), laboratory and field workers measure different things under different conditions. The laboratory allows precision, control and repeated tests, but it does abstract the animal from environments in which their capabilities are developed and exercised.

The division between laboratory and field work runs parallel to, and reinforces, a theoretical divide in approaches to primate mental capabilities. On the one side there are those who stress that selection pressures for intelligence arise from social interactions within the group. According to this view, primates learn to think in order to cope with and influence the actions of other members of their group. The social origin of intelligence became influential as an idea through papers by Jolly (1966) and particularly Humphrey (1976), whose basic idea was that social interactions are so complex and changeable that they tax cognitive capacities to greater extent than any other area of life. The interactions of the group are the evolutionary nursery in which intelligence grew up. The counter-idea is that mental capacities grew through manipulating the world, and in particular through the growth of tool use. Washburn provides a good exemplar of this view: 'It follows that the structure of modern man must be the result of the change in the terms of natural selection that came with the tool-making way of life' (Washburn 1960: 62) – although, as we have seen Washburn did not concentrate on tools alone, but rather considered technology a catalyst which helped create the hunting way of life and the forms of social interaction which were the result. Cheney and Seyfarth take as an explicit theme of their work the social origin of intelligence hypothesis, examining the links between sociability and cognition in vervets (see Byrne and Whiten 1988 for broader discussion of the tools versus sociability debate).

In pursuing these links between social life and intelligence Cheney and Seyfarth outline a particular model of mind and cognition, deriving partly from the intermingled histories of ethology and comparative psychology and partly from broader questioning about mind. In considering theories of mind, they contrast the views of the behaviourists with those of the mentalists (Cheney and Seyfarth 1990: 7–9). The former either deny that any mental processes, such as thought and consciousness, exist and that these have been mistakenly inferred from behaviour; or they take the more modified stance that mental events, if they exist, cannot be defined and measured, only behaviour can. The mentalists maintain that there are mental events and that these shape and direct behaviour; mental operations represent the world and allow it to be manipulated and connected up in thought: the mind has true causal power. Cheney and Seyfarth adopt a compromise position. They study behaviour but admit the possibility of mental states in animals, as well as humans. In their view mental representations not only exist, but are related to each other in a syntactical structure, like that of language. They thus 'adopt a definition of cognition as the ability to relate different unconnected pieces of information in new ways and to apply the results in an adaptive manner' (ibid.: 9). Their book sets out a complex argument pursuing the nature of mental capabilities of vervet monkeys, focusing on how far these capabilities arose within the interactions of the group and the light that the nature of vervet cognition can throw on the human mind.

Cheney and Seyfarth start with the question of how vervet groups are structured, how mental capacities can be indicated by actions in groups and derive out of group action. As mentioned above, groups are composed of matrilines, but not all matrilines are equal. The rank of the matriline tends to be due to its size, with dominant females in the largest matriline more sought after as grooming partners. Grooming establishes social bonds and there is competition to groom high-ranking females. Rank is also influential in alliances. Females play a major role in group defence and high-ranking females are most likely to be aided in fights.

It is in considering the knowledge vervets have of social ranks that Cheney and Seyfarth start to explore their categorizations of rank. Not only can vervets distinguish the ranks of a whole series of animals relating to them, they can also transfer this knowledge and understand relationships which do not include them. The existence of knowledge that can be transferred from one situation to another hints at more general principles of classification. Let us take an example given by Cheney and Seyfarth. A high-ranking female (ranked 2 out of six adult females) approaches two monkeys grooming each other, who are both of lower rank (for instance, ranked 4 and 5). Although both females are subordinate to the approaching female, they are not both equally likely to depart.

> From 1985 to 1986, in 29 out of 30 interactions that took this form, the higher ranking female (female 4, in our generic example) did nothing, while the lower-ranking female (female 5) moved away . . . It is female 4, of course, whose behavior is most interesting. She acts as if she has made the following computation: "We're both subordinate to female 2, so *someone* has to move away. However, female 5 is more subordinate than I am, so I can stay put." . . . To do this, she must not only know her own status relative to females 2 and 5 but also their status relative to each other. In other words, she must recognise a rank hierarchy. (ibid.: 81–2)

The ability to recognize the nature of the relationships between others is complemented by memories of the structures of group action. Vervets appear to remember who cooperated with them in the past and this helps structure their future behaviour: they act in a reciprocal fashion. Put in the terms I have been using in this book, they act with some anticipation of the future.

The range and subtlety of group behaviour is further instanced by the calls vervets use. Up until recently monkey calls and human language were seen to be divided by a huge gap of intention. Monkey calls were thought to be instinctive and given in response to specific stimuli (the alarm cry which warns others of an eagle was thought to be automatically elicited by the appearance of the bird). Human language, of course, is seen to be under conscious control and can refer to absent states of affairs or even to things which have never existed. Cheney and Seyfarth's book is part of a growing body of work that shows the degree of conscious control monkeys have over the sounds they produce. This conclusion is reached in part because vervets cries vary with the social context: they can recognize other individuals and assess social relations through their cries. Vervets produce a range of noises and within the group grunts are common. Different sounds effect the behaviour of others. 'Grunts to a subordinate, grunts to a dominant, grunts to an animal moving into an open area, and grunts to another group all elicited responses that were consistently different from each other' (Cheney and Seyfarth 1990: 117). Vocalizations also transmit information about the social and the natural environment. The authors conclude, not that vervets possess language parallel to our own, but that the noises they make are under conscious control and do contain information. This information can change the behaviour of others and this seems to be deliberate on some occasions. However, there are limits. Unlike chimps, the vervets seem to have no abstract concepts, such as colour. All their cries are tied to the situation and the lack of generalization from the specific to the abstract stops them before the borders of language.

In coming to an overall assessment of the actions of vervets, Cheney and Seyfarth agree with the proposition that primate intelligence developed, and is most used, in the context of the group. What we would label intelligent behaviour is much less evident in their interactions with the material world. Vervets can anticipate a range of group situations and how these are likely to develop, but they are much more limited in their anticipation of other species. Compared to our own patterns of sociability, group life is also impoverished. Food sharing is rare, vervets do not cooperate in order to learn and they find it hard to transfer the skills they have learnt in one area of life to another. There is also no hint of introspection in vervet life, no suggestion that they review their own, or others' actions to come to general conclusions on the basis of particular events. Cheney and Seyfarth conclude that vervets are social specialists in the same way that beavers are dam-building specialists. They are very good at what they do, but have no means of extending their mental and physical capacities honed in the group to other areas of life (Cheney and Seyfarth 1990: 310–11). The social hypothesis for the development and exercise of intelligence in vervets would seem to be demonstrated. Can we take the vicissitudes of group life as the point of genesis of intelligence in all primates, including ourselves?

Tools or Sociability as the Motor for Long-term History?

In using any study of primates to throw light on human developments we must be aware of the criticisms Haraway has made of over-simplified attempts to construct the gap between nature and culture, whereby animals represent the natural world from which humans emancipated themselves through developing cultural forms. We also cannot take a particular modern primate species, or primates in general, to stand for human ancestors, the world we have lost through culture. However, a study such as Cheney and Seyfarth's which concentrates explicitly on intelligence and group behaviour in a primate species, is useful food for thought about human capabilities.

As we saw briefly above, and as Byrne and Whiten (1988) discuss in some detail, there are two sets of theories for the origins of the human mind. The idea that intelligence has arisen as a means of coping with group life has been counterbalanced by the thought that it was tool use and technology which first concentrated the mind and which lies at the heart of what makes us human. Like all debates of this scope there has been no resolution, although it must be said that the tools hypothesis gains increasingly fewer supporters as time goes by (Wynn 1990: 99). Rather than take one side or the other, I want to question the terms of the debate, or rather the central term which is the concept of mind. Throughout this book I have made the point that many of the forms of thought of the West can be seen as devices which help distance us from the world. The concept of mind is the greatest of all the distancing devices. This sweeping claim will seem more reasonable when we consider that the notion of mind lies behind the division between knowing subject and known world. The mind represents an inner space which can receive information about the world through the senses and create representations of the world in thought. The mind creates a series of shadowy representations of the world which are often mistakenly taken to be the essence of human life. Action is controlled by thought, in this view, and the complexity of our acts is seen to be a direct result of the complexity of the cognitive processes going on in the mind. The mind is the source of action, change and evolution. A recent discussion of mind in an archaeological context makes great play of inner/outer metaphors and of the idea that the mind's operations are central to life. Mithen (1990: 1) feels that learning, decision-making and problem-solving are unique human characteristics and that this has given us a behavioural flexibility unparalleled in other species. This viewpoint necessitates some notion of the mind in which decision-making takes place. Mithen (ibid.: 26) follows a view of Fodor who divides the mind into input systems (the senses) and central processing systems (Fodor's views are rather more complex than Mithen's account suggests: see Fodor 1982). Not only does this definition clearly echo the way computers are set up, it helps distance the centre of life, which exists inside our heads, from the source of information, the material world. The real action of life takes place in the mind, where cognition is about improving one's knowledge of the world so that better decisions can be reached. As a means of critiquing notions of mind and any possibility of an archaeology of mind, let us return to what insights the study of vervets provides.

As we have seen, the concept of mind is central to Cheney and Seyfarth's study of vervet behaviour. 'To attribute beliefs, knowledge and emotions to both oneself and others is to have . . . a *theory of mind*' (Cheney and Seyfarth 1900: 205, original emphasis). In the authors' terms the advantage of acknowledging minds in others is that this allows a greater range of anticipation of, and influence over, their actions. To be able to look into the minds of others (which can only be done once minds are acknowledged) is to be able to see their beliefs, their ignorance and predispositions to act in general and specific ways. Attributions of minds to others demands the ability to give attention to both one's own thoughts and those of others simultaneously and to recognize a possible discrepancy between one's own knowledge and that of others.

Using this framework, Cheney and Seyfarth see that the crucial feature of vervet behaviour lies in the fact that although in many situations their anticipation of the actions of other vervets is very good, this is mirrored by a very poor anticipation of the non-social world. One instance of anticipation in social circumstances is the vervets' ability to deceive others. Deception is based upon the premise that another individual's actions will be altered in a more advantageous way if they are deceived than if they are apprised of the correct state of affairs. Practising to deceive involves a double anticipation: how others would act if they knew the true state of affairs and how these actions would be altered if they could be fooled. There is evidence that vervets practise deception both through withholding important information and by passing false signals (Cheney and Seyfarth 1990: ch. 7). The ability to deceive is even more developed in other species such as the chimpanzee (de Waal 1989: 47–8). Deception shows advanced states of anticipation in social circumstances generating considerable subtlety in primate behaviour.

However, in vervets, at least, this is contrasted strongly with a considerable lack of anticipation in circumstances outside the group. Cheney and Seyfarth constructed field experiments to test vervets' powers of deduction. In one they placed the stuffed carcass of a

Thompson's gazelle in a tree not far from the monekys' sleeping trees. Thompson's gazelle is a species often hunted by leopards, who also frequently place their prey in trees. Leopards also eat vervet monkeys. Although the experiment was repeated, on no occasion did the vervets appear to connect the gazelle with the possible proximity of a leopard (Cheney and Seyfarth 1990: 284). Similar experiments were performed using clues to other species which prey on vervets, but on no occasion did this create alarm. It is only at the sight of the predator itself that vervets raise the alarm. This implies that the fine discriminations and clues to the future which activate behaviour in a social group do not operate in the non-social environment. Furthermore, there is little sign that vervets or other primates involve the material world in social interactions. Food sharing is rare in most species and although tool use is now widely documented, it is rarely used in cooperation between more than one individual. The main exception here seems to be chimpanzees, and de Waal documents in words and photographs captive chimps' cooperative attempts both to escape from their enclosure and to gather leaves from trees protected by electrified wire (de Waal 1989: 26–8, 200–3). We can consequently say that anticipation in most primates is far better developed in social situations than in relation to the rest of the world.

Such a conclusion might seem, on the face of it, to confirm the hypothesis that in evolutionary terms intelligence was born from coping with the social group. By extension, the link between tool-making and intelligence seems to have little to recommend it. However, I shall come to a different conclusion, one more in tune with the argument of this book. Rather than opt for an either/or answer – tools or sociability – I feel that it is only when the material and the social world were firmly linked that human styles of life came into being. In contrast to vervets, humans have very good anticipation concerning both the human and the material world. Furthermore, these anticipations are linked. We know how to involve material things in our social strategies and how to combine socially to be practically effective. Our social relations are material and our material relations are social. Anticipation extends throughout the conjoined material and social worlds in complex ways. Our actions, material and social, are not effortless or always effective, and for this reason we have the well-developed sets of anticipation and recursiveness that we call intelligence. In this view human social life arose not when culture divided from nature, but when we became able to immerse ourselves fully in the world. Vervets might have a split between the social order and the natural world; we do not. Human groups are not placed within an environment, but immersed in it, having a quality of involvement found in no other species. This involvement leads to the creation of time in the form of joint anticipations of the human and natural worlds. Here were can see how materiality and mutuality are linked: a fundamental juncture giving shape and trajectory to life, providing a means of creating history.

From this vantage point we see how a notion of mind is insufficient to provide a full insight into the long span of human history. The theory of mind provides no possibility for understanding human involvement in the world, much less its temporal structures. Mind locates the real action of life in an inner space away from the world. Cognitive processes are more or less adept at manipulating the information at their disposal. The inner-outer dichotomy leads us away from the idea that it is the two-way involvement of people and things which constitutes human history. In looking at the differences between people and vervets we should ask not whether the latter have minds, or a concept of mind, but rather what are the gaps separating vervets from the world and from each other that are not found in humans? For vervets, with their limited sets of anticipations, time divides their actions, causing forgetfulness and breaking what we take for granted as the flow of life. In the human world we have means of binding the combined actions of individuals to produce a complicated group life and connected material forms which together persist in time. The enduring nature of material culture prolongs anticipation and creates group time beyond the range of the anticipations of the individuals. Vervets are a series of individuals joined into a whole by mutual need. Human groups bind space and time in ways that make the whole more than the sum of its parts. The depth and endurance of such forms of binding cannot be reached through concepts of mind.

Dialectics, as we saw in chapter 4, is seen as an attempt to overcome one-sidedness. Theories of long-term human history have either concentrated on economic or physical factors, such as technology, adaptation to the environment or hunting, or on the social and symbolic elements of life, such as the growth of cognition, cooperation or symbolic behaviour. Not only is it impossible to divide the practical from the symbolic, but to privilege one over the other is one-sided and provides too slender a basis for understanding life as an unmutilated whole. In order to illustrate this point we can now consider, extremely briefly, some ways to think about the long-term history of people and the world, using evidence from the Palaeolithic.

The Palaeolithic and Species Being

In the following sketch I shall again start from the distinction between habitual forms and public time developed over the last two chapters, where habit is the unthought flow of action, providing a basic shape to life, and public time is a conscious working out of the problems generate by habit and the source of consciously manipulative power relations. If truly human behaviour comes from the interaction with the world which involves both habit and public time, when did the interaction of these two times begin and what sort of history can we chart of their unfolding?

Let us start at that very beginning, Bed 1 at Olduvai, which is not a single point of origin, but a broad span of time on the boundary of the Pliocene and the Pleistocene. The evidence from this period, because of its scanty nature and the interest that it holds, has been much debated. A recent critical review of the evidence from Bed 1 (1.85–1.70 Mya) by Potts (1988) throws light on the question of whether public time existed in this period. Potts sees evidence for the existence of a series of central spots on the landscape which were repeatedly revisited by hominid groups. 'In habitats that resembled modern savanna mosaics, tool-making hominids carried artefacts and parts of carcasses to specific places on the landscape' (Potts 1988: 300). The individual tools used at each site were extremely simple, but fitted into a rather complex round of activities. These central places were not like the locations used by chimps for nut cracking, as these are close to the nut-bearing trees. Instead the locations used by the hominids indicate some spatial complexity of behaviour, with the products of different activities carried out on various parts of the landscape being brought together at central spots. At these spots carcasses were processed, and it may be that stone tools were cached specifically for this purpose. Caching of stone tools for use in the future indicates developed forms of anticipation of the world and the nature of cooperative group action. Presumably anticipation was enhanced by the repetition of acts over time, so that spatially complex behaviour was made easier by the fact that patterns of movement across the landscape were repeated. Potts sees spatial complexity and temporal repetition in terms of forms of cognition which set these hominids apart from all present-day primates (ibid.: 305). I would prefer to believe that these creatures had the ability to use the world in a fashion that enhanced anticipation. This was a landscape of habit as much as thought, which entailed relatively complex chains of actions which structured the nature of the group as it re-ordered the world. I would agree with Potts that there is no need to see a sexual division of labour or anything like a modern human group structure as existing at this time, but the nature of involvement with the world does indicate that forms of group life may have existed that are not present in any modern primate. Potts also stresses that his study does not provide us with an invariant pattern for all hominid life in this period. Different areas and different time periods within the Plio-Pleistocene may have witnessed quite different forms of life.

Although we are not looking at any basic hominid pattern, we can see that there are forms of involvement with the world, both in the production of tools and patterns of life across the landscape, which indicate long chains of habit linking different spots on the landscape. This may go together with some greater sense of the group than seen in non-human primates, although it is difficult to see in the evidence as it exists at present any well-developed sense of public time.

If we now take a huge leap in time we can use Gamble's review of the Palaeolithic evidence from Europe to look at the history of habit and public time on that continent. Gamble sees a major change occurring between the lower and the middle Palaeolithic periods, which carries with it the implication of new forms of action. The former period produces off-site archaeology, with stone tool scatters across the landscape and commonly found in river valleys, whereas the Mousterian brings about the first use of caves, together with the first repeated use of open sites. There is also the first evidence of spatial patterning within Mousterian sites, such as the layout of hearths and activities of production and maintenance (Gamble 1986: 390). Gamble sees the repeated use of sites and the spatial structure within sites as deriving from logistical planning and the ability early humans had to think their way through the landscape. Patterns of thought and interaction were limited by the closed networks of mating and interaction (ibid.: 391). Much more open sets of relations are found in the following period, after around 40,000 bp. The Upper Palaeolithic is seen by Gamble to represent a huge opening up of social relations through alliance networks which may well have covered much of western Eurasia (Gamble 1982). New forms of social relations are evident in the profusion of innovation in material culture, which includes a whole series of new tool types, a greater range of material used as tools, cave art and mobiliary art.

From my point of view, these are not evidence of new forms of social relations on their own, but a dual emergence of new forms of habit together with a more developed sense of public time. As with the Neolithic evidence, the media for dealing with the problems of the group's social and material relations, such as rock art, are the most striking aspect of the archaeological evidence, but this is not the place to start. Considerable change is evident in the arena of unthought action during the Upper Palaeolithic. Dennell (1983) has detailed many of these changes. First of all, there is an expansion of the techniques used every day. According to Dennell (ibid.: 81), in the Mousterian four basic techniques were used: percussion, whittling, scraping and cutting. During the Upper Palaeolithic these were complemented by other actions, such as pressure flaking, drilling, twisting and grinding. Some of these required complex forms of manual coordination, for instance drilling, which needed repeated movements of the hands in opposite directions. The range of raw materials used after 40,000 bp also increased, with stone, bone, wood, skin, ivory and antler being evidenced in the archaeological record. Given the filtering effect of preservation these may be a small part of the things originally in use. The number of individual components used in a single object was much greater, and this was evidenced not just in composite tools, but by items such as the necklace found in a grave in Sungir which was made up of 3500 drilled ivory beads (ibid.: 86). Of great importance for the present purposes is the fact that the stages of manufacture increased considerably in the Upper Palaeolithic. A bone harpoon required a number of sets of stone tools to detach an antler splinter, shape it into a blank and then create the barbs. Separate sets of tools and techniques would have been needed to make shaft and to form the hafting (ibid.: fig. 11). The Sungir necklace involved a major investment of time and a considerable number of different tools in its production. Just as important is the fact that finished technologies interlocked with each other in much more complex ways than in the Mousterian, allowing more integrated forms of gathering and hunting. Plant materials would have been needed for making nets and sewing clothing, and nets extended the range of animals, birds and fish which could be caught. Each new species caught added new raw materials in bone, feathers and fur.

All these factors taken together represent a huge increase in the structures of anticipation involved in daily action, creating quite new forms of time. The long chains of action needed to produce and use particular items were added to by the spatial complexity implied in the bringing together of different raw materials from varying parts of the landscape, as well as in deploying new technologies such as nets. All these forms of action involved greater coordination of individuals within the group. Artefacts were not created by relations between single individuals and materials, but through new forms of group interaction, competition and cooperation. Actions had to be coordinated in time and space, bringing about a whole new set of group relations. Deepening involvement with the material world increased the scope and depth of mutuality. Transformations in material and social relations can only be understood when taken together. More forms of habit were retained by the human body and more cues to action were provided by material things; both were contained within and promoted groups with a longer temporal and larger spatial scope.

The new social and material relations did not develop because people could think further into the future or construct broader spaces in their mind than even before, but mainly because people could create broader forms of time and space *without thinking about it*. Habit carried them further in space and time. But the new complexity of group forms also set up a series of clashes in time and space, which needed resolving through the most remarked-upon elements of Upper Palaeolithic life: cave and mobiliary art. These form the first real archaeological evidence of public time; that is, attempts to deliberately manipulate people and the world. These new coping mechanisms entered into the habitual forms of life and their enduring nature became part of the ways in which wider-ranging and longer-lasting forms of group life were created. But public time also created a new set of forms of power manipulation, and the conscious manipulation of human and material relations created a new dynamic. Public time was both a means of dealing with the problems of habitual action and a set of pathologies causing more problems: both medicine and a new disease. The dual dynamics of habit and public time, which blend and clash, started to create history in the form of a rushed forward movement. Exactly what forms of life existed in this period and how habit and conscious manipulation interact needs much further investigation.

Conkey (1991) has provided an extremely thought-provoking discussion of aggregation sites and the relations of power and gender which may have existed. Her approach nears my own in its concentration on activity streams and the human relations involved in these streams. Conkey attempts to identify the contexts of Magdalenian life in which gender may have been at work. Her main focus is large aggregation sites which contain a record of groups larger than the household, and she notes that one feature of attempts to create an order beyond the household is that age and sex differences are played upon. Gender relations are thus a prime structuring principle in the network of social relations. These relations also use material culture as an active and constituting medium and not as a passive vehicle for attaining utilitarian ends. Gender relations can then be sought in material culture. The site of Cueto de la Mina is composed of a rockshelter and a small cave, excavated in 1904. It lies 1.8 kilometres inland from the Bay of Biscay. It contains evidence of a multitude of activities: engraving bone and antler tools, working sea shells, processing vegetation, working hides, the butchering and processing of animals, to mention only a few. The resources gathered in the cave came from the coast, woodlands and the plains, and a journey of several days would have been necessary to obtain some of these items.

Conkey does not offer specific gender attributions in analysing tasks, but instead attempts to provoke thought in two directions. The first is to question the gender attributions that have been made for artefacts found at Cueto de la Mina. Around 200 pieces of worked bone and antler were recovered from the site, some of which have been seen as harpoons used for male hunting practices. Conkey (1991: 76) raises the possibility that the holes and barbs on these objects could have been used for cordage, producing sets of lines for nets and ropes. As well as providing a critique of the unconscious bias towards identifying male activities on the part of many archaeologists, Conkey looks at the chains of activities that may have been carried out at the site and the forms of organization lying behind them. She points out that at any point in time dozens of people may have been coming and going at Cueto de la Mina, engaged in a range of tasks, which would have necessitated a partitioning of people and a division of labour and space. In addition, tasks would have interlocked, such that the products of one set of activities would have supplied raw materials for another, forming complex sets of references. Artefacts are not simply raw material for classification or evidence of production, but can show us how streams of activity are embedded socially and the relations set up through these activity streams. Conkey's article brings out the complexity of habitual behaviour that lies behind the archaeological evidence from Upper

Palaeolithic sites. This bespeaks a complicated coordination of people and activities in time and space, mediated through the existence of consciously manipulated symbolic forms. This is far from Bed 1 at Olduvai in time and in the type of action which took place, but it is also far from our own world. Long streams of habit which meet and clash with public time create a new form of history, one which changes through time but which never goes away. We are both separated from and connected to the world of the Upper Palaeolithic.

The scheme sketched here for the Palaeolithic overcomes the dichotomy between ecological and social explanations, which often sees ecological relations as the key to evolutionary pathways until the Upper Palaeolithic, during which period social factors take over. The process which gives rise to the warring duality of habit and public time provides a central thread to be followed without denying change. The differences between the middle and the upper Palaeolithic have raised controversy over why, when and how changes happened (White 1982), but most accept a fundamental shift in human affairs at this time, even if a number of key traits of technology and settlement can be traced from the Middle into the Upper Palaeolithic. The key differences between the two periods revolve around the complexity of human action found after 40,000 bp. I have attempted to indicate how this change arose through the juxtaposition of habit and public time, as well as how public time arises from the newly elongated chains of habitual action. Continuity throughout the Palaeolithic exists because at all periods habit underpinned the sense the group had of itself. Discontinuity occurs because the relationship between habit and group sense undergoes sudden changes, which derive from an increasing depth in the involvement of people in the world.

8

Towards a History of Temporality

Patrick White once said that there is another world, but it lies within this one. Otherworldliness usually evokes images of planes of existence removed from the mundane, sublunary world and of people with refined sensibilities who have escaped entanglement in the trivial problems of daily life. Like White, I feel that there are other worlds to be explored and that these lie within the realm of the ordinary, so that exploration can only take place through paying attention to the aspects of existence which are so commonplace that we no longer recognize them. Time is a crucial feature of everyday life, at once mundane and mysterious.

The central notion I have been trying to develop in this book is that of temporal structure or style. Different forms of life are differentiated by their creation of time, which itself derives from the nature of recursiveness, how the past is used to give shape to present and future action. All practice creates time and the varying combinations of time within a social formation create a temporal structure or style. However, I believe that we should not merely say that social formations have their own temporal styles, but go a step further and characterize social formations primarily in terms of their temporal styles of life. In order to make this point more fully I will summarize here the argument that time is central to human life, as presented in the previous chapters, and from that go on to draw out the notion of temporal form.

A Summary of the Argument

Why is time central to human life? All life operates through recursiveness, which is to say that we make use of the past to create present and future action. The use that is made of the past changes all the time, but also has a certain consistency to it, due to the nature of habitual, unthought action. Habitual action derives from the ways in which the human body is used and skills inculcated in our bodies during our life. But the human body and its actions cannot be considered in isolation and skilled action is only learnt and maintained through interaction with the world. The properties of wood, clay and metal and the behaviour of other plants and animals provide a series of sequences of action which unfold without our noticing or thinking about them. Habit derives from the human body's involvement with the world and habitual action carries forward the bulk of our lives. The complexity of human life arises not from the sophistication of our cognition, but rather because we can operate so well in the world, and towards others, without thought.

Many sequences of action, which create the times of our lives, are carried through without deliberate thought. However, past experience does not allow us to anticipate all future occurrences and our involvement with the social or the physical world will always have unexpected consequences. Unexpected outcomes may be either positive or negative. New strands of involvement in the world are constantly being opened up: pottery-making and metal technologies created new dimensions to social being in the early and mid-Holocene in many parts of the world. Equally, as we are all well aware, hoped-for outcomes do not always eventuate, either due to the qualities of materials with which we are dealing, or to deficiencies in our skills. Habit can take us far in the world, but always needs to be complemented by conscious thought, which is brought to bear on unexpected outcomes. Our lives are thus a mixture of the habitual and the conscious, each of which draws on the past in its own way. Our consciousness is honed by problems and potentials in the material and the social world. Such problems and potentials are not just experienced singly by individuals, but are encountered by the social group as a whole. Many important elements of group life arise so as to cope with problems and make use of potentials. Consciousness has a joint, social aspect rather than arising from the life of isolated minds. Both habitual and consciously directed action have their own time-scales. I have been inclined to argue that habit represents a long-term basis for human life, changing slowly due to its unconscious nature, and that the public time of the group changes more quickly; but although there is some truth to this formulation, it is far too simple a distinction. Habitual and thought action are not polar opposites in human life, but more a useful heuristic distinction. Public time and action has a constant tendency to shade off into habit, through the process of repetition. Bradley, Hodder and others have recently started to probe the long-term persistence of forms of symbolism and deposition, which are both consciously manipulated and the basis of habit. Public time arises from the problems of habit, and public time also gains its legitimation from its congruence with the unthought patterns of life. Public time arises as a coping mechanism for the problems of habit, and over time shades off into habitual action, forming a temporal cycle of thought and unthought patterns of life.

Public time is initially a means of coping with habit, but as it rises into consciousness public actions are also open to manipulation. Consequently, there are questions of power connected with the relationship between the thought and the unthought. Public time must resonate with habit in order that it be accepted, so that habitual action sets limits to the manipulation of public time. Resonances between habit and public time are partly achieved through making public time long-term and habitual, so that it becomes part of people's social being. If the strands of time deriving from habit and those from public time are not in phase, then public time will encounter resistance from within the realm of habit – the manipulation of public time must seem natural, deriving from feelings about the rightness of particular actions within any cultural form. We can thus say that the continuation of forms of deposition from the Neolithic to the medieval period, as identified by Bradley, were a response to a certain constancy in the problems faced by these small-scale social groups, and that these problems changed fundamentally with the construction of the modern world. But such constancy also arose from the very continuity of public times over the long term which became part of people's social being over millennia. Public and habitual time are both cause and effect, locked into a complex temporal cycle.

We are dealing with a whole different series, or levels, of time-scales here. In the very long term is the creation of a depth of mutual involvement of people with each other and with the world, developing throughout the Palaeolithic, that is found in no other species. Human and material involvements are inextricably linked: we only have such a depth of social relations because we can bring material things into the creation of social relations in fundamental ways; we only have such a depth of material involvements because we can combine socially to change the world. It is the two-way penetration of material and social involvements which differentiates us from other species and forms our species being. From the Neolithic onwards, in Europe at least, this species being is given particular shape by the confrontation of public time, expressed in a whole new range of media from pots to monuments, and habit, which was taken in new directions so as to create novel material forms. In all social forms the real cutting edge of the social process is the meeting of habitual and public times. This meeting was destabilized in the Neolithic through new material involvements, creating new forms of social being centred around sharper conflicts between habit and public forms of life. The Neolithic to the Iron Age, in my view, saw a shift in the balance from mutuality to materiality, and the changing nature of public time is both a means of dealing with these changes and an added pressure on the nature of the social process. The Neolithic is not either an economic or a symbolic revolution, but both and neither of these things. By refusing to make an obvious division between the practical and the meaningful, between being and knowing, we can see that human life involves a complex interweaving of both these terms and it is from this interweaving that its dynamism derives.

Power and time are crucially connected. Both are generated by every human act, and power derives in part from the forms of recursiveness in operation in a social formation. The main bulk of time and power derives from habit, but public time can hem in and disrupt habitual time. I have defined three forms of time, each with a different pattern, in which actions unfold. Harmonious times exist when different forms of practice and recursiveness flow into each other without major conflict. Disjoint times exist when practices are refractory, so that the rhythms set up in one area of life cut across those generated in others. Concatenating times exist when different forms of practice are mutually reinforcing so as to produce instability. With concatenating times a series of dynamics exists which leads to ever faster motion, which in the end is unsustainable. The times of modern capitalism provide a fine example of concatenating times. As an initial hypothesis I put forward the idea that harmonious times are most likely to exist in the absence of well-developed public times. Public time is a response to problems encountered at the level of habit, but also public time sets up a dynamic of its own which may cut across other times or bind them securely into concatenating times.

To make these points more concrete we can refer again to the prehistoric British examples used throughout the book. In my view, the Neolithic saw forms of society in which connections between people were all-important: a system of mutuality. Mutuality created a world which ramified spatially as ever new connections were set up and which was inherently unstable as the pattern of interconnection changed. The very obvious public times set up to deal with the problems of space helped create precise spaces in which human action could be minutely ordered. Different practices were obviously carried out on different parts of the landscape in any one area and, taking Britain as a whole, quite different forms of public time were set up, as we saw in chapter 6. The difference in the nature of public time within and between regions increased from the Neolithic into the early Bronze Age and set up a whole series of social clocks working at different paces. The weight of disjoint times meant that the system as a whole over southern and central England collapsed and new forms of life arose in the middle Bronze Age. The ordered landscape of field systems and settlements derived from the long-term move towards more precise spaces found through the Neolithic, but also from a greater emphasis on materiality rather than human connections. Production, both agricultural and craft, becomes more apparent in the archaeological record from the middle Bronze Age onwards, and the long-term system of deposition investigated by Bradley moves from spatially differentiated actions involving materials with little inherent worth to the deposition of bronze at single points on the landscape. Public time shifts from creating space to regulating materials. The new emphasis on production brought with it a tendency to concatenating times, in which material production was involved in an inflationary spiral, so that from the Bronze Age many forms of public time were to do with regulating the amount of material moving within and between social groups.

The account of changes from the Neolithic to the Iron Age as I have given it here is incomplete in that it focuses on public time rather than habit. This reflects the emphasis within archaeological field research and interpretation. In order to understand the full complexity of social time and power were need to look at both habitual and public action. The landscape is the locus of both social forces and the archaeological evidence they leave. Here the Cranborne Chase project is a model in trying to tie together the landscape, the artefactual evidence and the monuments, although it is lacking somewhat in a theoretical basis for integrating these different forms of evidence. It is this theoretical basis that I have tried to develop in this book. However, the ideas put forward here are just a beginning and need much further development, which leads us to a brief final discussion of problems and further possibilities arising from this approach.

Further Potential of the Argument

An approach that starts from the idea of temporal structure centralizes a crucial archaeological problem: that of time. Instead of seeing acts as taking place in time, we can see action as creating time. Rather than time providing the medium for action, time and action become synonymous. Many of the forms of thought that we have borrowed from other disciplines have not been inherently temporal. Concepts concerning social formations provide a good case in point. Other disciplines, such as sociology and anthropology, have generated static images of society which then have to be set in motion in order to understand change. For example, in recent years social archaeology has become increasingly dubious about the notion of social structure, borrowed from anthropology or sociology. Many of the authors cited in this book who are writing on the Neolithic to the Iron Age avoid the topic of social structure and at most talk vaguely of clan or lineage. A notion of temporal structure is a means of categorizing patterns of social action and of comparing and contrasting varying types of life. For a view based around temporality, change is endemic in human action and the point of interest is how change itself changes. The changeability of change is brought about by the different ways in which the past is used to construct the present and the future. Change can thus also only be understood through the elements of constancy within it.

Doing away with the usual notion of social structure means that we have to discard static pictures of the group or the individual. Society should rather be seen as a flux of forces which are both human and material, and such a view helps do away with any stable notions of subjects and objects. We should be looking for streams of action and the materials which sustained them in the past and provide evidence for them in the present. I have made a somewhat crude distinction between habitual and conscious action, which needs to be further refined, but have tried to indicate some of the subtleties involved in the interaction of habit and thought.

In terms of archaeological practice, the place to start in understanding these activity streams and the times they generated is the landscape. Human activities show up as different densities and types of artefacts across the landscape. Differential artefact densities cannot be read in a straightforward manner, but depend upon rates of sedimentation on various parts of the landscape and subsequent human activities. The landscape has a dual importance as the locus of original activities and of the sedimentary processes which shape the evidence of these activities. Furthermore, the sedimentary processes are themselves often evidence of human action, as human activities have in many instances dramatically affected the shape of the landscape. A social interpretation of sedimentation is just as necessary as a social view of the artefacts contained in the soil. The temporal forms of past societies cannot be understood in terms of artefacts and structures alone; erosion and deposition themselves have temporal forms and which need to be understood. A full view of temporality derives from the rhythms of the landscape itself under human influence. Individual areas of the landscape, such as Cranborne Chase, can be understood in detail as a combination of a changing social ontology and local geomorphological circumstances. A number of different landscapes, such as those in southern Britain during the late Neolithic, combine to form a social geography which we can only understand in a more generalized and abstracted manner as a social geography. Landscapes and regions thus present different problems of scale and abstraction, but can be compared and contrasted in terms of patterns of habit, public time and the types of sedimentation shaping the archaeological evidence.

My aim here is to rethink categories of human action so that they can be picked up archaeologically and also be of interest philosophically. I do not want to produce a typology of temporal forms, but to use the history of temporality to reflect both on what makes us human and how we conceive of humanity. The Neolithic and Bronze Age societies focused on in the course of the book represent a particular conjuncture of habitual and public time, with its own dynamism and instabilities. This can be differentiated from the creation of time in the Pacific from the mid-Holocene onwards, with its setting-up of enormous spatial structures and connections between different regions, which we looked at briefly in chapter 2. Comparisons have usually been made between the Pacific and Europe in terms taken from neo-evolutionary anthropology, focusing on the concepts of big man and chief. However, the nature of involvement with the world in the two areas is so different as to form quite distinct social ontologies, and comparison in terms of the direct details of their social forms must be misleading.

I have used the ideas of reference and recursiveness as the means by which people create time and space in my attempt to construct a framework that can facilitate broader comparisons between social ontologies. However, these comparisons highlight the variability of human involvements rather than their sameness. Furthermore, time is not a single stream but a series of creations, with longer and shorter spans, and it is the really long-term effects of time which form the province of archaeology. Long-term involvements in different parts of the world are only just becoming apparent and provide strands of continuity to life in any one area against which change can be judged.

One of my main interests in constructing the schemes presented in this book is to rethink the terms in which we conceive of humanness. One of the central threads of the discussion has been the problems set up by the subject/object distinction perpetuated in different ways by both economic and symbolic archaeologies, the former emphasizing the power of the object world, the latter concentrating on the human creation of meaning. A breaking down of the subject/object distinction leads directly to an attack on the concept of mind and consciousness. We need to rethink the problem of consciousness from within the body, rather than focusing on mind as a separate container for our thought. Most of our skills, perceptions and forms of communication with others are bodily, as is our general awareness of the world. I have tried to emphasize the link between awareness and skill, in that most of our perceptions of the world arise in the course of action and help shape that action. Both action and perception are temporal, arising from our place within the world, which derives in turn from the social twists given to our biological being. A different biology would render up a different world, but the bodily form we have does not just create one world for us, but can be shaped socially in myriad ways. Until we can understand what the body can do and the basis that it forms for our lives we will have only a very partial notion of the creation of history.

A concentration on the human forms of involvement with the world necessitates not just a study of the human body or material culture, but rather how people and the world meet and combine. The long-term history of the Pacific arises partly from how people have shaped the world over millennia, plus the effects that these physical circumstances have had on them. The end of a movement away from the subject/object distinction should take us towards a joint notion of people and the world in which both are active, both created and creating. Time is again central to the process of mutual creation, particular structures of time deriving from the sequential and recurrent interplay of people and the world. The blending of habitual and conscious forms of action also takes place in temporal cycles and creates divisions in human practice, each with its own time-scales. The divisions that we currently call gender or class arise from a blend of habitual action, socially inculcated, and a conscious working-out of difference. It is the meeting of habit and public time which gives social differences anything like the form that we would recognize today. Gender and social divisions can only be understood against this changing background of social forces, and we can start to think about the circumstances under which particular differences may be created. Thought and unthought difference itself creates complex time-scales of action, and the fabric of social time is made up of many contradictory elements, each with their own power to pull and push the social process.

The present, like any period in the past, is a construct of contradictory social forces and times. One of the themes of this book has been that knowledge derives from forms of involvement between people and things. It follows that archaeology, as a form of knowledge in the present, derives in part from a whole series of taken-for-granted notions about space, time and material things that exist now. At different points in the book I have provided a thumbnail sketch of some of the modern elements of time and space. Over the last few hundred years, time and space have been recreated through a set of global forces which have been given a particular warp and weft through local circumstances. We are obviously aware of some elements of global space and time, but much critical thought is needed to tease out our particular forms of immersion in the world both in terms of habit and public time. Archaeology forms part of a growing realm of material culture studies stretching from past to present. An understanding of the past and the present is directly linked; the peculiar position we hold within the world provides particular views of other times and places.

Recent trends in social theory have sought to understand our own forms of thought and life through looking at different social forms. The Other has been used to undermine the dogmatism and spurious certainty in much of western thought by showing that ours is just one way of seeing and telling. The use of other social forms as a means of self-therapy has helped to make disciplines such as anthropology and archaeology more aware of their own fraility. But we do need to go further and to develop a sense of ourselves which will allow us to connect with the rest of the world. I am under no illusions about how difficult it is to set up forms of communication which allow the creation of some common ground without undermining the nature of difference. A joint sense of our present western being and knowing and the power relations stemming from each of these will make such connections easier, as will archaeology's attempts to understand the difference and similarity between long-term trajectories in different parts of the world. The recognition that different time-scales are at work in the social process provides a bridge between universalism and relativism. The fastest-moving strands of a social process will be those areas in which difference is most manifest, the longer strands of recursiveness may demonstrate a greater commonality between one region and another. At the heart of all historical processes is the human ability to involve material things in social relationships and to use combinations of people to shape the world.

Archaeology can become a philosophical discipline, providing food for thought about the things that make us human. Knowledge is not produced through detachment from the world, nor are we creating a system of truths. Rather we must try to find elements of self-understanding within a form of life with global dimensions. Understanding will come through seeing the manner in which we have placed ourselves in the world and how this differs from the placement of others. However, to phrase the problem in this way is to pose it wrongly: the problem of the modern world is that all areas of the globe, with their inequalities and differences in access to resources, are linked in some manner. These differences have deep historical roots and enormous present consequences. Archaeology is one of the few disciplines that can understand the breadth and depth of difference. Our task in the present is not to dissolve difference, to make it go away, but to find unparalleled forms of mutuality so that the divisions of the world move from the abstract measures of global time-zones and start to approach human time. If archaeology does become a philosophical discipline, this should not just change the way we think, but the manner in which we act.

Further Reading

The literature on social theory is vast. What follows is a selection of reading ordered around some of the major topics covered in this book. I have tried to choose works which are important for their content, clear in their expression and generally available in libraries and bookshops.

Space

Agnew, J.A. and J.S. Duncan (eds) 1989. *The Power of Place*. Unwin Hyman, Boston.

Appadurai, A. 1988a. Introduction: place and voice in anthropological theory. *Cultural Anthropology* 3: 16–20.

Cosgrove, D. and S. Daniels (eds) 1988. *The Iconography of Landscape*. Cambridge University Press, Cambridge.

Giddens, A. 1984. *The Constitution of Society*. Polity Press, Cambridge.

Gregory, D. and J. Urry (eds) 1985. *Social Relations and Spatial Structures*. Macmillan, London.

— and R. Walford (eds) 1989. *Horizons in Human Geography*. Macmillan, London.

Hägerstrand, T. 1975. Survival and arena: on the life history of individuals in relation to their geographical environment. In T. Carlstein, D. Parkes and N. Thrift (eds) *Human Activity and Time Geography*. Unwin Hyman, London.

— 1976. *Innovation as a Spatial Process*. University of Chicago Press, Chicago.

Munn, N. 1990. Constructing regional worlds in experience: kula exchange, witchcraft and Gawan local events. *Man* 25: 1–17.

Peet, R. and N. Thrift 1989. *New Models in Geography*, vols 1 and 2. Unwin Hyman, London.

Time

Bailey, G. 1983. Concepts of time in Quaternary prehistory. *Annual Review of Anthropology* 12: 165–92.

— 1987. Breaking the time barrier. *Archaeological Review from Cambridge* 6: 5–20.

Bender, J. and D.E. Wellbery 1991. *Chronotypes. The Construction of Time.* Stanford University Press, Stanford.

Bradley, R. 1991. Ritual, time and history. *World Archaeology* 23: 209–19.

Fabian, J. 1983. *Time and the Other: How Anthropology Makes its Object.* Columbia University Press, New York.

Giddens, A. 1984. *The Constitution of Society.* Polity Press, Cambridge.

Heidegger, M. 1962. *Being and Time.* Trans. J. Macquarrie and E. Robinson. Blackwell, Oxford.

Kern, S. 1983. *The Culture of Time and Space 1880–1918.* Weidenfeld and Nicholson, London.

Knapp, A.B. 1992. *Archaeology,* Annales, *and Ethnohistory.* Cambridge University Press, Cambridge.

Landes, D.S. 1983. *Revolution in Time.* Harvard University Press, Cambridge, MA.

Ricoeur, P. 1984. *Time and Narrative,* vol. 1. University of Chicago Press, Chicago.

— 1985. *Time and Narrative,* vol. 2. University of Chicago Press, Chicago.

— 1988. *Time and Narrative,* vol. 3. University of Chicago Press, Chicago.

Rifkin, J. 1989. *Time Wars.* Simon and Schuster, New York.

Thomas, N. 1989. *Out of Time.* Cambridge University Press, Cambridge.

Thompson, E.P. 1967. Time, work discipline and industrial capitalism. *Past and Present* 38: 56–97.

Young, M. 1988. *Metronomic Society.* Harvard University Press, Cambridge, MA.

Hermeneutics, phenomenology and ontology

Bapty, I. and T. Yates (eds) 1990. *Archaeology after Structuralism.* Routledge, London.

Bourdieu, P. 1990a. *In Other Words.* Polity Press, Cambridge.

— 1990b. *The Logic of Practice.* Trans. R. Nice. Polity Press, Cambridge.

Carr, D. 1987. *Interpreting Husserl.* Martinus Nijhoff, Dordrecht.

Dreyfus, H.L. 1990. *Being-in-the-World.* MIT Press, Cambridge, MA.

Gadamer, H-G. 1975. *Truth and Method.* Trans. G. Barden and J. Cumming. Seabury Press, New York.

Heidegger, M. 1971. *Poetry, Language and Thought.* Trans. A. Hofstadter. Harper and Row, New York.

Husserl, E. 1970. *The Crisis of European Sciences*. Trans. D. Carr. Northwestern University Press, Evanston, IL.

Lukács, G. 1971. *History and Class Consciousness*. Trans. R. Livingstone. Merlin Press, London.

Nehamas, A. 1985. *Nietzsche: Life as Literature*. Harvard University Press, Cambridge, MA.

Nietzsche, F. 1968a. *The Will to Power*. Trans. W. Kaufmann and R.J. Hollingdale. Vintage Press, New York.

— 1968b. On the Genealogy of Morals. In W. Kaufmann (ed.) *Basic Writings of Nietzsche*: 449–599. Trans. W. Kaufmann. Random House, New York.

Rorty, R. 1989. *Contingency, Irony and Solidarity*. Cambridge University Press, Cambridge.

Shanks, M. and C. Tilley 1987. *Social Theory and Archaeology*. Polity Press, Cambridge.

Warnke, G. 1987. *Gadamer*. Blackwell, Oxford.

References

Agnew, J.A. and J.S. Duncan (eds) 1989. *The Power of Place*. Unwin Hyman, Boston.

Allen, J. 1984. Pots and poor princes: a multidimensional approach to the role of pottery trading in coastal Papua. In S.E. van der Leeuw and A.C. Pritchard (eds) *The Many Dimensions of Pottery*: 409–73. University of Amsterdam, Amsterdam.

— 1991. Introduction. In J. Allen and C. Gosden (eds) *The Results of the Lapita Homeland Project*. Occasional Papers 20, Department of Prehistory, Research School of Pacific Studies, Australian National University, Canberra.

—, C. Gosden and J.P. White 1989. Human Pleistocene adaptations in the tropical island Pacific: recent evidence from New Ireland, a Greater Australian outlier. *Antiquity* 63: 548–61.

Appadurai, A. 1988a. Introduction: place and voice in anthropological theory. *Cultural Anthropology* 3: 16–20.

— 1988b. Putting hierarchy in its place. *Cultural Anthropology* 3: 36–49.

Arthur, C.J. 1982. Objectification and alienation in Marx and Hegel. *Radical Philosophy* 30: 14–24.

Bailey, G. 1983. Concepts of time in Quaternary prehistory. *Annual Review of Anthropology* 12: 165–92.

— 1987. Breaking the time barrier. *Archaeological Review from Cambridge* 6: 5–20.

Bapty, I. 1990. Nietzsche, Derrida and Foucault: re-excavating the meaning of archaeology. In I. Bapty and T. Yates (eds) *Archaeology after Structuralism*: 240–76. Routledge, London.

— and T. Yates (eds) 1990. *Archaeology after Structuralism*. Routledge, London.

Barrett, J. 1987. Fields of Discourse: reconstituting a social archaeology. *Critique of Anthropology* 7: 5–16.

—, R. Bradley and M. Green 1991. *Landscape, Monuments and Society*. Cambridge University Press, Cambridge.

Baudrillard, J. 1981. *For a Critique of the Political Economy of the Sign*. Telos Press, St. Louis, MO.

Beaglehole, J.C. 1974. *The Life of Captain James Cook*. A. and C. Black, London.

Bell, D. 1978. *The Cultural Contradictions of Capitalism*. Basic Books, New York.

Bender, J. and D.E. Wellbery 1991. *Chronotypes. The Construction of Time*. Stanford University Press, Stanford.

Berger, P. and S. Pullberg 1966. Reification and the social critique of consciousness. *New Left Review* 35: 56–71.

Berlin, I. 1963. *Karl Marx*. Oxford University Press, London.

Berman, M. 1988. *All That is Solid Melts into Air*. Penguin, Harmondsworth.

Bernstein, R.J. 1983. *Beyond Objectivism and Relativism*. University of Philadelphia Press, Philadelphia.

— 1986. *Philosophical Profiles*. Polity Press, Cambridge.

Bhaskar, R. 1989a. *The Possibility of Naturalism*. Harvester Press, Hemel Hempstead.

— 1989b. *Reclaiming Reality*. Verso, London.

Bintliff, J. 1991. *The Annales School and Archaeology*. Leicester University Press, Leicester.

Bourdieu, P. 1977. *Outline of a Theory of Practice*. Trans. R. Nice. Cambridge University Press, Cambridge.

— 1988. *Homo Academicus*. Trans. P. Collier. Polity Press, Cambridge.

— 1989. *Distinction*. Trans. R. Nice. Routledge, London.

— 1990a. *In Other Words*. Polity Press, Cambridge.

— 1990b. *The Logic of Practice*. Trans. R. Nice. Polity Press, Cambridge.

Bradley, R. 1990. *The Passage of Arms*. Cambridge University Press, Cambridge.

— 1991. Ritual, time and history. *World Archaeology* 23: 209–19.

Braudel, F. 1975. *The Mediterranean and the Mediterranean World in the Age of Philip II*, vols. I and II. Fontana/Collins Press, London.

— 1985. *The Perspective of the World*. Trans. S. Reynolds. Fontana Press, London.

Byrne, R. and A. Whiten 1988. *Machiavellian Intelligence*. Clarendon Press, Oxford.

Carr, D. 1987. *Interpreting Husserl*. Martinus Nijhoff, Dordrecht.

Carter, P. 1987. *The Road to Botany Bay*. Faber and Faber, London.

Cheney, D.L. and R.M. Seyfarth 1990. *How Monkeys See the World*. University of Chicago Press, Chicago.

Conkey, M. 1982. Boundedness in art and society. In I. Hodder (ed.) *Symbolic and Structural Archaeology*: 115–28. Cambridge University Press, Cambridge.

— 1991. Contexts of action, contexts of power: material culture and gender in the Magdalenian. In J.M. Gero and M.W. Conkey (eds) *Engendering Archaeology*: 57–92. Blackwell, Oxford.

Cosgrove, D. 1989. Geography is everywhere: culture and symbolism in human landscapes. In D. Gregory and R. Walford (eds) *Horizons in human Geography*: 118–35. Macmillan, London.

— and S. Daniels (eds) 1988 *The Iconography of Landscape*. Cambridge University Press, Cambridge.

Deetz, J. 1977. *In Small Things Forgotten*. Anchor Books, New York.

Dennell, R. 1983. *European Economic Prehistory*. Academic Press, New York.

Derrida, J. 1978. *Writing and Difference*. Trans. A. Bass. Routledge and Kegan Paul, London.

— 1981. *Dissemination*. Trans. B. Johnson. University of Chicago Press, Chicago.

— 1998. *The Post Card*. Trans. A. Bass. University of Chicago Press, Chicago.

DeVore, I. 1965. Mating dominance and mating behavior in baboons. In F.A. Beach (ed.) *Sex and Behavior*: 266–89. Krieger Press, New York.

Dewey, J. 1960. From Absolutism to experimentalism. In R.J. Bernstein (ed.) *John Dewey on Experience, Nature and Freedom*. Liberal Arts Press, New York.

Dreyfus, H.L. 1991. *Being-in-the-World*. MIT Press, Cambridge, MA.

Durkheim, E. 1965. *The Elementary Forms of the Religious Life*. Trans. J.W. Swain. The Free Press, New York.

Eagleton, T. 1990. *The Ideology of the Aesthetic*. Blackwell, Oxford.

Elster, J. 1983. *Explaining Technical Change*. Cambridge University Press, Cambridge.

— 1985. *Making Sense of Marx*. Cambridge University Press, Cambridge.

Ermath, M. 1978. *Wilhelm Dilthey: The Critique of Historical Reason*. University of Chicago Press, Chicago.

Fabian, J. 1983. *Time and the Other: How anthropology makes its object*. Columbia University Press, New York.

Farias, V. 1989. *Heidegger and Nazism*. Trans. P. Burrell and G.R. Ricci. Temple University Press, Philadelphia.

Flannery, T. and J.P. White 1991. Animal translocations. *National Geographical Research and Exploration* 7: 96–113.

Fleming, A. 1988. *The Dartmoor Reaves*. Batsford, London.

Fodor, J. 1982. Methodological solipsism considered as research strategy in cognitive psychology. In H.L. Dreyfus (ed.) *Husserl, Intentionality and*

Cognitive Science: 277–303. MIT Press, Cambridge, MA.

Foucault, M. 1981. *The History of Sexuality*. Trans. R. Hurley. Penguin, Harmondsworth.

— 1987a. *The Use of Pleasure*. Trans. R. Hurley. Penguin, Harmondsworth.

— 1987b. *The Care of the Self*. Trans. R. Hurley. Viking Books, London.

Gadamer, H-G. 1975. *Truth and Method*. Trans. G. Barden and J. Cumming. Seabury Press, New York.

Gamble, C. 1982. Interaction and alliance in Palaeolithic society. *Man* 17: 92–107.

— 1986. *The Palaeolithic Settlement of Europe*. Cambridge University Press, Cambridge.

Geertz, C. 1975. *The Interpretation of Culture*. Basic Books, New York.

Giddens, A. 1984. *The Constitution of Society*. Polity Press, Cambridge.

Glassie, H. 1975. *Folk Housing in Middle Virginia: A structural analysis of historical artefacts*. University of Tennessee Press, Knoxville.

Goldmann, L. 1977. *Lukács and Heidegger*. Trans. W. Q. Boelhower. Routledge and Kegan Paul, London.

Gosden, C. 1989a. Prehistoric social landscapes of the Arawe islands, West New Britain Province, Papua New Guinea. *Archaeology in Oceania* 24: 45–58.

— 1989b. Production, power and prehistory. *Journal of Anthropological Archaeology* 8: 355–87.

— 1991. Towards an understanding of the regional archaeological record from the Arawe Islands, West New Britain Province, Papua New Guinea. In J. Allen and C. Gosden (eds). *The Report of the Lapita Homeland Project*: 205–16. Occasional Papers 20, Department of Prehistory, Research School of Pacific Studies, Australian National University, Canberra.

— 1992. Production systems and the colonisation of the western Pacific. *World Archaeology* 24: 55–69.

— J. Allen, W. Ambrose, D. Anson, J. Golson, R. Green, P. Kirch, I. Lilley, J. Specht and M. Spriggs 1989. The Lapita sites of the Bismarck Archipelago. *Antiquity* 63: 561–86.

— and J. Webb In press. The making of a Papua New Guinea Landscape: geomorphological and archaeological evidence from the Arawe Islands, West New Britain, Papua New Guinea. *Journal of Field Archaeology*.

Green, R.C. 1979 Lapita. In J. Jennings (ed.) *The Prehistory of Polynesia*: 27–60. Harvard University Press, Cambridge, MA.

Gregory, C. 1980. Gifts to men and gifts to god: gift exchange and capital accumulation in contemporary Papua. *Man* 15: 626–52.

Gregory, D. 1985. Areal differentiation and post-modern human geography. In D. Gregory and J. Urry (eds) *Social Relations and Spatial Structures*: 67–96. Macmillan, London.

— and J. Urry (eds) 1985. *Social Relations and Spatial Structures*. Macmillan, London.

— and R. Walford (eds) 1989. *Horizons in Human Geography*. Macmillan, London.

Habermas, J. 1972 *Knowledge and Human Interests*. Heinemann, London.

Hägerstrand, T. 1975. Survival and arena: on the life history of individuals in relation to their geographical environment. In T. Carlstein, D. Parkes and N. Thrift (eds) *Human Activity and Time Geography*. Unwin Hyman, London.

— 1976. *Innovation as a Spatial Process*. University of Chicago Press, Chicago.

Haraway, D. 1992. *Primate Visions*. Verso, London.

Harding, T.G. 1967. *Voyagers of the Vitiaz Strait*. University of Washington Press, Seattle.

Harré, R. 1993. *Social Being*. Blackwell, Oxford.

Harvey, D. 1982. *The Limits of Capital*. Blackwell, Oxford.

— 1989. *The Condition of Postmodernity*. Blackwell, Oxford.

Heidegger, M. 1962. *Being and Time*. Trans. J. Macquarrie and E. Robinson. Blackwell, Oxford.

— 1971. *Poetry, Language and Thought*. Trans. A. Hofstadter. Harper and Row, New York.

— 1977. *The Question Concerning Technology and Other Essays*. Trans. W. Lovitt. Harper and Row, New York.

— 1979. *Nietzsche. Vol. 1: The Will to Power as Art*. Harper and Row, San Francisco.

Hodder, I. (ed.) 1982. *Symbolic and Structural Archaeology*. Cambridge University Press, Cambridge.

— 1986. *Reading the Past*. Cambridge University Press, Cambridge.

— 1987. The contribution of the long term. In I. Hodder (ed.) *Archaeology as Long-term History*: 1–8. Cambridge University Press, Cambridge.

— 1990. *The Domestication of Europe*. Blackwell, Oxford.

Humphrey, N.K. 1976. The social function of the intellect. In P.G. Bateson and R. Hinde (eds) *Growing Points in Ethology*: 303–17. Cambridge University Press, Cambridge.

Husserl, E. 1970. *The Crisis of European Sciences*. Trans. D. Carr. Northwestern University Press, Evanston, IL.

— 1977. *Cartesian Meditations*. Trans. D. Cairns. Martinus Nijhoff, The Hague.

Irwin, G.J. 1983. Chieftainship, kula and trade in Massim prehistory. In J. Leach and E. Leach (eds) *The Kula: New Perspectives on Massim Exchange*: 29–72. Cambridge University Press, Cambridge.

— 1985. *The Emergence of Mailu as a Central place in Coastal Papuan Prehistory*. Terra Australis 10. Department of Prehistory, Australian National University, Canberra.

Isaac, G. 1978. The food-sharing behavior of protohuman hominids. *Scientific American* 238(4): 90–108.

Jay, M. 1984. *Marxism and Totality*. Polity Press, Cambridge.

Johnson, B. 1981. Translator's introduction. In J. Derrida *Dissemination*: pp. vii–xxxiii. University of Chicago Press, Chicago.

Jolly, A. 1966. Lemur social behavior and primate intelligence. *Science* 153: 501–6.

Kaufmann, W. 1974. *Nietzsche: Philosopher, psychologist, anti-Christ*. Princeton University Press, Princeton.

— (ed.) 1982. *The Portable Nietzsche*. Penguin, Harmondsworth.

Kern, S. 1983. *The Culture of Time and Space 1880–1918*. Weidenfeld and Nicolson, London.

Kirch, P.V. 1984. *The Evolution of Polynesian Chiefdoms*. Cambridge University Press, Cambridge.

— 1988. Long-distance exchange and island colonisation: the Lapita case. *Norwegian Archaeological Review* 21: 103–17.

— 1989. Second millennium B.C. arboriculture in Melanesia: archaeological evidence from the Mussau islands. *Economic Botany* 43: 225–40.

— 1990. Specialization and exchange in the Lapita complex of Oceania (1600–500 B.C.). *Asian Perspectives* 29: 117–33.

— and T.L. Hunt (eds) 1988. *Archaeology of the Lapita Cultural Complex: A critical review*. Thomas Burke Memorial Washington State Museum Research Report No. 5. Seattle, Washington.

— and D.E. Yen 1982. *Tikopia: The prehistory and ecology of a Polynesian outlier*. Bishop Museum Bulletin 238. Bishop Museum Press, Honolulu.

Knapp, A.B. 1992. *Archaeology, Annales, and Ethnohistory*. Cambridge University Press, Cambridge.

Kockelmans, J.J. 1967. *Phenomenology*. Doubleday, New York.

Kolakowski, L. 1978. *Main Currents of Marxism*. Clarendon Press, Oxford.

Krell, D.F. (ed.) 1977. *Martin Heidegger Basic Writings*. Harper and Row, New York.

Landes, D.S. 1983. *Revolution in Time*. Harvard University Press, Cambridge, MA.

Leach, J.W. and E. Leach (eds) 1983. *The Kula: New perspectives on Massim exchange*. Cambridge University Press, Cambridge.

Lee, R. and I. DeVore (eds) 1968. *Man the Hunter*. Aldine Press, Chicago.

Lemonnier, P. 1990. Topsy turvey techniques: remarks on the social representations of techniques. *Archaeological Reviews from Cambridge* 9: 27–37.

Le Roy Ladurie, E. 1979. *The Territory of the Historian*. University of Chicago Press, Chicago.

Leroi-Gourhan, A. 1965. *Préhistoire de l'Art Occidental*. Mazenod, Paris.

Lilley, I. 1986. Prehistoric exchange in the Vitiaz Strait, Papua New Guinea. Unpublished Ph. D. Thesis, Australian National University, Canberra.

— 1988. Prehistoric exchange across the Vitiaz Strait, Papua New Guinea. *Current Anthropology* 29: 513–16.

Lukács, G. 1971. *History and Class Consciousness*. Trans. R. Livingstone. Merlin Press, London.

McLellan, D. 1969. *The Young Hegelians and Karl Marx*. Macmillan, London.

— 1977. *Karl Marx – Selected Writings*. Oxford University Press, Oxford.

— 1979. *Marxism after Marx*. Macmillan, London.

Makkrel, R.A. 1975. *Dilthey*. Princeton University Press, NJ.

Marcuse, H. 1973. *Reason and Revolution*. Routledge and Kegan Paul, London.

Marx, K. 1954. *Capital. A Critique of Political Economy*, vol. I. Trans. S. Moore and E. Aveling. Lawrence and Wishart, London.

— 1963. *Economic and Philosophical Manuscripts*. Trans. T. Bottomore. F. Ungar, New York.

Miller, D. 1987. *Material Culture and Mass-Consumption*. Blackwell, Oxford.

— and C. Tilley 1984. Ideology, power and prehistory: an introduction. In D. Miller and C. Tilley (eds) *Ideology, Power and Prehistory*: 1–15. Cambridge University Press, Cambridge.

Mithen, S.J. 1990. *Thoughtful Foragers*. Cambridge University Press, Cambridge.

Morgan, L.H. 1985. *Ancient Society*. University of Arizona Press, Tucson.

Munn, N. 1977. The spatiotemporal transformation of Gawa canoes. *Journal de la Société des Océanistes* 54–55: 39–53.

— 1983. Gawan kula: spatiotemporal control and the symbolism of influence. In J. Leach and E. Leach (eds) *The Kula: New Perspectives on Massim Exchange*: 277–308. Cambridge University Press, Cambridge.

— 1986. *The Fame of Gawa*. Cambridge University Press, Cambridge.

— 1990. Constructing regional worlds in experience: kula exchange, witchcraft and Gawan local events. *Man* 25: 1–17.

Natanson, M. 1973. *Edmund Husserl*. Northwestern University Press, Evanston, IL.

Nehamas, A. 1985. *Nietzsche: Life as Literature*. Harvard University Press, Cambridge, MA.

Nietzsche, F. 1968a. *The Will to Power*. Trans. W. Kaufmann and R.J. Hollingdale. Vintage Press, New York.

— 1968b. On the Genealogy of Morals. In W. Kaufmann (ed.) *Basic Writings of Nietzsche*: 449–599. Trans. W. Kaufmann. Random House, New York.

— 1971. *Thus Spake Zarathustra*. Trans. R.J. Hollingdale. Penguin, Harmondsworth.

Parkinson, G.H.R. 1977. *Georg Lukács*. Routledge and Kegan Paul, London.

Pawson, E. 1992. Local times and standard time in New Zealand. *Journal of Historical Geography* 18: 278–87.

Peet, R. and N. Thrift 1989. *New Models in Geography*, vols. 1 and 2. Unwin Hyman, London.

Potts, R. 1984. Home bases and early hominids. *American Scientist* 72: 338–47.

— 1988. *Early Hominid Activities at Olduvai*. Aldine de Gruyter, New York.

Proust, M. 1966. *Swann's Way*. Trans. C.K. Scott Moncrieff. Chatto and Windus, London.

Rabinow, P. (ed.) 1984. *The Foucault Reader*. Pantheon Books, New York.

Rapaport, H. 1989. *Heidegger and Derrida*. University of Nebraska Press, Lincoln, NB.

Renfrew, C. 1973. Monuments, mobilisation and social organisation in Neolithic Wessex. In C. Renfrew (ed.) *The Explanation of Culture Change*: 539–58. Duckworth, London.

— 1975. Trade as action at a distance: questions of integration and communication. In J.A. Sabloff and C.C. Karlovsky (eds) *Ancient Civilisation and Trade*: 3–60. University of New Mexico Press, Albuquerque.

Ricoeur, P. 1984. *Time and Narrative, vol. 1*. University of Chicago Press, Chicago.

— 1985. *Time and Narrative, vol. 2*. University of Chicago Press, Chicago.

— 1988. *Time and Narrative, vol. 3*. University of Chicago Press, Chicago.

Rifkin, J. 1989. *Time Wars*. Simon and Schuster, New York.

Robbins, D. 1991. *The Work of Pierre Bourdieu*. Open University Press, Milton Keynes.

Rorty, R. 1980. *Philosophy and the Mirror of Nature*. Blackwell, Oxford.

— 1989. *Contingency, Irony and Solidarity*. Cambridge University Press, Cambridge.

— 1991. *Objectivism, Relativism and Truth*. Cambridge University Press, Cambridge.

Sahlins, M.D. 1958. *Social Stratification in Polynesia*. University of Washington Press, Seattle.

— 1985. *Islands of History*. University of Chicago Press, Chicago.

Saussure, F. de 1959. *A Course in General Linguistics*. Philosophical Society, New York.

Seamon, D. and R. Mugerauer (eds) 1989. *Dwelling, Place and Environment*. Columbia University Press, New York.

Shanks, M. 1992. *Experiencing the Past: On the character of archaeology*. Routledge, London.

— and C. Tilley 1987. *Social Theory and Archaeology*. Polity Press, Cambridge.

Simpson, G.G. 1958. Behavior and evolution. In A. Roe and G.G. Simpson (eds) *Behavior and Evolution*: 507–36. Yale University Press, New Haven.

Singer, P. 1983. *Hegel*. Oxford University Press, Oxford.

Soja, E.W. 1985. The spatiality of social life: towards a transformative retheorisation. In D. Gregory and J. Urry (eds) *Social Relations and Spatial Structures*: 90–127. Macmillan, London.

Sperber, D. 1979. Claude Lévi-Strauss. In. J. Sturrock (ed.) *Structuralism and Since*. Oxford University Press, Oxford.

Spiegelberg, H. 1960. *The Phenomenological Movement*. Martinus Nijhoff, The Hague.

Spriggs, M. 1984a. The Lapita Cultural Complex: origins, distributions, contemporaries and successors. *Journal of Pacific History* 19: 202–23.

— (ed.) 1984b. *Perspectives in Marxist Archaeology*. Cambridge University Press, Cambridge.

— 1989. The dating of the southeast Asian Neolithic: an attempt at chronometric hygiene and linguistic correlation. *Antiquity* 63: 587–613.

Sturrock, J. 1979. Introduction. In J. Sturrock (ed.) *Structuralism and Since*. Oxford University Press, Oxford.

Thomas, J. 1991. *Rethinking the Neolithic*. Cambridge University Press, Cambridge.

Thomas, N. 1989. *Out of Time*. Cambridge University Press, Cambridge.

Thompson, E.P. 1967. Time, work discipline and industrial capitalism. *Past and Present* 38: 56–97.

Tilley, C. 1990. Michel Foucault: towards an archaeology of archaeology. In C. Tilley (ed.) *Reading Material Culture*: 281–347. Blackwell, Oxford.

— 1991. *Material Culture and Text: The art of ambiguity*. Routledge, London.

de Waal, F. 1989. *Chimpanzee Politics*. Johns Hopkins University Press, Baltimore, MD.

Warnke, G. 1987. *Gadamer*. Blackwell, Oxford.

Washburn, S.L. 1960. Tools and human evolution. *Scientific American* 203: 62–75.

White, R. 1982. Rethinking the middle/upper Palaeolithic transition. *Current Anthropology* 23: 169–92.

Wynn, T. 1990. *The Evolution of Spatial Competence*. Illinois Studies in Anthropology No. 17. University of Illinois Press, Urbana.

Yates, T. 1990. Archaeology through the looking-glass. In I. Bapty and T. Yates (eds) *Archaeology after Structuralism*: 154–202. Routledge, London.

Young, M. 1988. *Metronomic Society*. Harvard University Press, Cambridge, MA.

Zihlman, A. 1984. Pygmy chimps, people and the pundits. *New Scientist* 104: 364–77.

Zimmerman, M.E. 1990. *Heidegger's Confrontation with Modernity*. Indiana University Press, Bloomington.

Index